AFTER FIFTY YEARS, THE JOHNSON FAMILY BREAKS THEIR SILENCE TO EXPOSE, EXCLUSIVELY TO BARBARA GOLDSMITH, THEIR STORIES AND . . . THEIR DARKEST SECRETS . . .

1. BASIA PIASECKA JOHNSON, 1937–
Seward Johnson's impoverished Polish chambermaid who became his third wife. He was 76. She was 34. He left her over half a billion dollars.

2. ELAINE JOHNSON WOLD, 1928–
Second daughter from Johnson's first marriage. Net worth $82 million. She was astonished by her father's will and suspected skullduggery.

3. JAMES LORING JOHNSON, 1945–
Johnson's youngest child, gentleman farmer, and painter. Net worth $103 million. He felt his dying father was too ill to read his last will and testament.

4. MARY LEA JOHNSON RICHARDS, 1926–
Net worth $65 million. Seward's eldest daughter was sexually molested by him at age nine. The incest continued until she was sixteen.

5. J. SEWARD JOHNSON, Jr., 1930–
He tried to kill himself when he became convinced that his own father had seduced his wife. He gave his "stamp of approval" to Basia. Net worth $38 million.

6. DIANA JOHNSON FIRESTONE, 1932–
Her $63 million, her jet, her stud farms in Virginia and Ireland, her Kentucky Derby winner, could not insulate her from the pain of this court battle.

7. JENNIFER JOHNSON DUKE, 1941–
Amateur photographer and co-owner of the Gallery of Applied Arts. When Seward left her mother for Basia, Jennifer said, "It changed everything. . . . My mother was devastated." Net worth $106.2 million.

These people, as well as a crowded cast of corrupt lawyers, ex-wives, servants, and sycophants, open up in shocking, graphic detail a world of immense wealth, privilege, and decadence.

BARBARA GOLDSMITH HAS RECEIVED OVERWHELMING CRITICAL ACCLAIM FOR
JOHNSON v. *JOHNSON*

Please turn the page.

Johnson
v.
Johnson

ALSO BY BARBARA GOLDSMITH

The Straw Man
Little Gloria . . . Happy at Last

Johnson v. Johnson

BARBARA GOLDSMITH

A DELL BOOK

Published by
Dell Publishing
a division of
The Bantam Doubleday Dell Publishing Group, Inc.
1 Dag Hammarskjold Plaza
New York, New York 10017

Portions of this book were originally published in *Vanity Fair*.

Much of this book is based on in-depth interviews and on thousands of pages of trial transcripts, depositions, affidavits, and other legal papers. Often they are excerpted and abridged, and quotes are rearranged to create a logical progression, but in no way has the original meaning of the material been altered.

For information address: Alfred A. Knopf, Inc.,
New York, New York.

Dell ® TM 681510, Dell Publishing Co., Inc.

ISBN: 0-440-20041-5

Reprinted by arrangement with Alfred A. Knopf, Inc.

Printed in the United States of America

February 1988

10 9 8 7 6 5 4 3 2 1

KRI

For

Andrew
David
John

The number of those who undergo the fatigue of judging for themselves is very small indeed.

—RICHARD BRINSLEY SHERIDAN,
The Critic, 1779

Acknowledgments

*T*his book could never have come about without the encouragement and support of Frank Perry and Robert Gottlieb. They made it possible for me to write to the exclusion of all else.

I wish to extend my thanks to Katherine Hourigan and Martha Kaplan. And there are many others who made this project a reality: Ian Shearn and Linda Amster who supplied skilled research, Karen Sturges and Arlene Zigman, my indefatigable assistants, and two very special people at *Vanity Fair,* Tina Brown and Wayne Lawson.

I would also like to acknowledge members of the Johnson family, most particularly Mary Lea Johnson for her strength and courage, and J. Seward Johnson, Jr., as well as Basia Johnson, Martin Richards, Joyce Johnson, Ruth Dill Crockett, Keith and Elaine Wold, Diana and Bertram Firestone, Jennifer Johnson Duke and Joseph Duke, Eric Ryan, Christopher Johnson, Betty Johnson Bushnell, Nicholas Gouverneur Rutgers IV, and many others whose voices weave the fabric of this book. I wish to thank the judge, lawyers, and other legal personnel for contributing vast amounts of time and effort to this work; Dr. Henry Giarretto, of Parents United, and Dr. Elizabeth Mintz for their insights and knowledge; and Valerie J. R. Sonnenthal for picture research. Also my thanks to James Bracciale, Ellis Levine, Jane Friedman, Nancy Clements, and Virginia Tan.

Sylvester and Louisa Wood Johnson

11 children

Robert Wood Johnson 1845–1910
may have m. Ellen Gifford
or perhaps m. Etta G. Hayden

Roberta 1884–1965
m. Robert (Roy) Carter Nicholas 1875–1941

Robert Carter Jr. (Carter) 1909–1975

m. Evangeline Armstrong

Robert Wood Johnson, Jr. 1893–1968
(After father's death in 1910 drops Jr.
After World War II retained the title of General)

John Seward Johnson 1895–1983
m. Ruth Dill
(Now Mrs. Philip Crockett)

m. Elizabeth Dixon Ross

Robert Wood Jr. 1920–1970

m. Betty Wold (sister of Keith Wold,
now Mrs. Douglas Bushnell)

Robert (Woody) Wood IV 1947
Keith Wold 1948–1975
Elizabeth (Libbet) Ross 1950
Willard (Billy) Trotter Case 1952–1975
Christopher (Chris) Wold 1959

m. Margaret Shea adopted Sheila

m. Evelyne Vernon

THE
JOHNSON FAMILY TREE
(ABRIDGED)

m. Esther Underwood

m. Barbara "Basia" Piasecka

Edward Mead Johnson 1853–1934 · James Wood Johnson 1856–1932

m. Martha Law

　Louise 1884–1964
　Helen 1892–1961

　m. Nicholas Gouverneur Rutgers III

　　　Nicholas Gouverneur IV 1925

m. Carolyn MacBain

Evangeline Brewster Johnson 1897

Mary Lea 1926

m. William Ryan

m. Victor D'Arc

m. Martin Richards

m. Leopold Stokowski

　Gloria Lyuba 1927
　Andrea Sadja 1930

m. Prince Alexis Zalstem-Zalessky

m. Charles Merrill

Eric 1951
Seward 1952
Roderick 1953
Hillary 1954
Alice 1956
Quentin 1958

Elaine 1928

m. Keith Wold
　2 children

J. Seward Jr. 1930

m. Barbara Maxwell

m. Joyce Horton

　J. Seward III 1966
　Clelia 1969

Diana 1932

m. Richard Stokes
　3 children

m. Bertram Firestone
　1 child

Jennifer 1941

m. Peter Gregg
　2 children

m. Joseph Duke

James (Jimmy) Loring 1945

m. Gretchen Wittenborn
　2 children and adopted
　her 4 children

Part
ONE

"For him there were no rules."

J. Seward Johnson, the eighty-seven-year-old heir to the Johnson & Johnson pharmaceutical fortune, signed his last will on April 14, 1983, leaned back in his wheelchair, and remarked, "This solves a lot of problems." He died thirty-nine days later, leaving virtually his entire $500 million estate to his third wife, Barbara (called Basia, and pronounced Basha) Piasecka Johnson, a woman whom he had met fifteen years previously, when she was employed as a cook/chambermaid by his second wife. Basia had arrived from Poland in 1968, with $100 to her name, a degree in art history, and a smattering of English. Within fifteen months she was living in a luxurious Sutton Place apartment paid for by Johnson and serving her benefactor as a $12,000-a-year "art curator" and occasional scuba-diving companion. They were married November 11, 1971, eight days after his divorce. She was thirty-four, he was seventy-six.

According to Alexander Forger of Milbank, Tweed, Hadley & McCloy, who represented the six Johnson children (ranging in age from forty-one to sixty) as objectants to Seward Johnson's will, Basia "relied on her ability to enchant and captivate" Seward and "shattered" his second marriage of thirty-two years. Forger alleged, "One is drawn unmistakenly to the conclusion that the real attraction for Basia was the money." In the course of her twelve-year marriage to Johnson, Basia "came to dominate Seward's life in every way," cutting him off from trusted advisers and employees. Forger charged that Basia and the Johnsons' lawyer, Nina Zagat of Shearman & Sterling, "whose allegiance was to Basia" and who stood to gain approximately $8 million as an executor and $900,000 annually for the remainder of Basia's life as a trusteeship fee, had, through a series of twenty-two will changes, gradually given Basia more and more of the estate, "the last vestige having been erased as he lay in extremis the month before death arrived." Johnson had disinherited his children and in a final will even cut out a $72 million bequest to his beloved charity, Harbor Branch, an oceanographic institute devoted to marine exploration and research. The children charged that Johnson was senile when he executed his last will and testament. They also brought charges of undue influence, fraud, and duress against Basia Johnson and Nina Zagat.

Basia's lawyers, Donald Christ and Robert Osgood of Sullivan & Cromwell, told a different story: her husband had left her the bulk of his estate because he was madly in love with her, because he wanted to avoid paying unnecessary taxes, and because he had become increasingly disillusioned with the profligate and wasted lives of his children. In an affidavit Osgood pointed out that Johnson had given Harbor Branch $130 million during his lifetime and that, far from disinheriting his children, he had in 1944 established trusts for them of Johnson & Johnson stock which, if left untouched, not counting income and dividends, would now be worth an aggregate of $660 million. Johnson, he contended, had believed his children had enough money and had not used it wisely. The exhibits accompanying Osgood's affidavit highlighted seamy tales of aberrant sexual practices, messy divorces, drug addiction, mental instability, and suicide attempts:

The 1977 divorce of Mary Lea Johnson, the eldest daughter, from Dr. Victor D'Arc brought to light her accusation that he had commissioned his homosexual lover to murder her for her money and that he had demanded that she have sexual relations with other men while he watched. D'Arc charged that one of Mary Lea's sons had injected their dog with heroin and another had plotted to blow up the Far Hills, New Jersey, police station.

When Jennifer Johnson, the youngest daughter, and her first husband, race-car driver Peter Gregg, divorced, he received from her $800,000, for which he signed a loan note. He was remarried for ten days when he shot himself and left the money to his new wife. Jennifer considered contesting the will to get the money back, but his estate finally repaid her.

In Seward Johnson, Jr.'s 1962 divorce petition, the sordid details of his disastrous first marriage were graphically described. He claimed to have been reduced to servitude as "babysitter, chauffeur, and errand boy" while his wife's alleged lover kissed "her lips, legs, thighs, and other parts of her body." Another alleged lover took his place in the bedroom while he slept on a couch in his dressing room. Basia asserted that Seward Johnson had removed Harbor Branch from his final will because Junior controlled that organization and her husband feared his son's incompetence.

The trial was the longest (seventeen weeks), the most sensational (there were charges against Sullivan & Cromwell of bribing and intimidating potential witnesses, a riot in the courtroom, death threats against the judge), and the most expensive (legal fees are said to exceed $24 million) will contest in United States history.

Thirty-three witnesses for the Johnson children painted a picture of a senile Johnson suffering from twenty-three ailments, including cancer of the prostate which had metastasized to his bones, congestive heart failure, arteriosclerosis, anemia, and hyponatremia. His life with Basia was characterized as a nightmare existence of isolation, coercion, physical violence, and mental torture.

Basia Johnson's forty-one witnesses testified that her husband was competent, kind, sentient to the end, aware of current events, skillful as an art collector, and grateful for the love of his wife, who cared for him with utmost devotion.

After almost four months—eight hours a day, five days a week—on the day before it was to go to the jury, the case was settled. The Johnson children and Harbor Branch received $169 million. But if they were the true winners, no one was the loser. Basia's marital trusts are to be collapsed so that she will receive approximately $350 million outright. Nina Zagat walked away with the booby prize, $1.8 million. The television cameras photographed both sides claiming victory, the final newspaper stories were written, everybody went home.

Still, the case has left a wake of divergent opinions based on personal emotions about fathers, children, and stepmothers. People ask me, "What did you think? Who was right?" I can't give an easy answer. I'm not sure I can give an answer at all. While most of the press perceived this case as an exercise in greed by individuals who already had millions and millions and millions, to me it was a pathetic affair, sad for everyone concerned. I've come to view it as a contest rooted in emotional issues: feelings of unrequited love, unfinished business, denial, and loss of honor. J. Seward Johnson's behavior toward his children— his patterns of rejection and divisiveness—ultimately led them into a courtroom seeking to find what they had never had from him: recognition, a sense of worthiness, and a measure of a father's love. Perhaps restitution for this loss came to be equated with money. But money was all that was left.

By the time the matter of J. Seward Johnson's will reached the New York Surrogate's Court, I'd been researching the case for the better part of a year. I was prejudiced. I'd decided that there was only one real villain, and he wasn't in the courtroom, not in any actual sense. The deceased, J. Seward Johnson, represented during the trial by the testimony of doctors, nurses, domestic servants, and other witnesses, was a carefully fabricated legal image. Johnson's vast wealth had surrounded him with a veil of secrecy and evoked a reverential attitude in those who knew and served him. Sister Mary Louise Flowers epitomized this when she testified that "J. Seward Johnson *himself* carried flowers and mineral water" into the hospital room of his wife's mother. Her awe that a man so wealthy (he gave $850,000 to her home for the elderly) should carry anything at all was evident. Nurse Bonnie Weisser, when asked about Johnson's mental status, replied, "You've got to understand the Johnson household. There was an almost devout respect for Mr. Johnson. We would never ask him a probing question to determine what his definitive status was." Michael Loyack, administrator and fund-raiser for the Medical Center at Princeton, testified that he visited Johnson's hospital room three times a day and personally chauffeured him when he was constipated and thought a visit to his home would alleviate the problem. (Subsequently the hospital received Johnson's $1.8 million donation for a CAT-scan facility.)

Who was this billionaire with a passion for privacy who left behind him such a volatile brew of unresolved emotional and financial issues? The real J. Seward Johnson exists now only in the memories of those who knew him—relatives, wives, children, friends, acquaintances. It is the disparity between the image of this man projected in court and the remembered reality that intrigues.

"He liked women, sailing, farming, and the breeding of cows, in that order."   —F. SPAULDING DUNBAR, *yacht designer and friend.*

"He was born under Cancer, the sign of the crab. That was the right sign for him; he was impossible to read. Whenever you thought he was going in one direction, he would go in another. You never knew what he was thinking."   —J. SEWARD JOHNSON, JR., *son.*

"I never heard him talk very much about anything but the sea, and they were never lengthy conversations. He spoke more to the dogs than he spoke to human beings. When I came into his life he was just a frail little old man, but he still appeared in the memory of his children as this powerful destructive force. They loved him and wanted his love and approval right to the end. I'll never know why. They wanted something he was incapable of giving. He was as selfish and self-occupied as King Henry VIII."   —MARTIN RICHARDS, *son-in-law.*

"He was small, trim, well coordinated, with good manners, a childish charm, and an irresistible smile. Of course, the most irresistible thing about him was his money."

—LUCINDA BALLARD,
costume designer and former fiancée.

"I think part of him was a naughty little boy, way inside. He would kind of giggle and say, 'Ah, they're not going to get me.'"

—JENNIFER JOHNSON DUKE, *daughter.*

"He took a long time to read anything. He couldn't scan material. We know now that he had dyslexia, but no one recognized it. He did the best he could with what he had. He was okay at sea, but he couldn't function at a party. He was constantly on the defensive, which made him seem dictatorial. He was a functional illiterate."

—KEITH WOLD, *son-in-law.*

"He was spoiled. The money did it. I don't know how I stayed married to him as long as I did."

—RUTH DILL JOHNSON CROCKETT, *first wife.*

"He was the man of my life, my very most favorite man. We loved each other very much."

—BASIA PIASECKA JOHNSON, *third wife.*

Gradually a portrait of sharp contradictions emerges. Seward Johnson was taciturn, almost phlegmatic, but he demanded constant stimulation. He was domineering but childish, hidden but affable, abstracted yet shrewd. He was a powerful, rich autocrat and also an inchoate, insecure child. He could be angelically sweet or cutting in his coldness. He could spend months at sea, and often said that he might have liked the disciplined life of a monk, yet he was also an uncontrolled libertine. He could be a businessman, but most of his life he accepted token titles with no responsibilities. He was a simple man with few material wants who spent the last years of his life surrounded by splendor. He satisfied his every whim, need, and fantasy. He took what he wanted.

Seward Johnson was a second-generation inheritor. In order to accumulate his vast fortune, all he had to do was hold on to the stock in Johnson & Johnson bequeathed to him by his father and let his brother run the show. It was this domineering older brother, Robert Wood Johnson, Jr., an equal inheritor (upon his father's death he dropped the "Jr." and after World War II he retained the title of General), who guided the company in its meteoric rise.

One share of Johnson & Johnson stock in 1944, when the General took the company public, would today equal 223 shares, an appreciation of 22,000 percent. In 1944 Seward Johnson's stockholdings were worth approximately $9 million. Today those same holdings would be worth almost $2 billion.

During this expansion Seward took a back seat, passively going along with his older brother's leadership. He told his daughter Mary Lea, "You can't have two captains of a ship. My brother's the captain of Johnson & Johnson." In any case, he had little interest in business. It's a well-known story that at a company sales conference in London, Seward was asked which division had the best sales. Startled from a reverie, he replied, "Ratsey," the name of the famous sailmaker.

(John) Seward Johnson was born in 1895, the second son of Robert Wood Johnson and Evangeline Armstrong. The burly Robert Wood was not a family man. The only family conversation his son Seward was to recall concerned the devastating effects of the unseen germs that surround us. This atmosphere spawned a lifelong hypochondria in Seward, who was plagued with allergies and asthma. His sister, Evangeline, says, "Seward got all the children's diseases. I never got any." As an adult, he became a physical-fitness buff and followed one food faddist after another. At eighty-five he mailed copies of a low-fat diet book, *Jack Sprat's Legacy,* to his children.

Married to a work-obsessed husband, Seward's mother virtually ignored her rough-and-tumble older son, Bob, and turned her attention to her younger son. She often dressed Seward in velvet suits and made him wear long blond curls until he was fourteen. The boy suffered from severe dyslexia. In those days there was little awareness of how to deal with this perceptual problem, and so it was ignored, covered up by the kind of wealth that provides a curtain of secrecy and allows one to function in a controlled environment.

Seward was tutored at home. When he began to write, his spelling errors clearly illustrated the problem. "I would be pleased to attend your weeding," he wrote his daughter Mary Lea in 1978. He spelled *boat* "bod," *word* "wd," *Bob* "Dob." In the courtroom a four-line handwritten letter with six spelling errors was introduced as evidence of his senility, as was his last will, in which he spelled *April* "Aprul." But even members of the Johnson family who produced convincing arguments that their father was senile tended to discount such evidence. A daughter recalls that her father took an inordinate amount of time to finish reading a book. His first wife remembers how he would beg her to read to him for hours on end. Seward Jr. observes, "My father would dictate everything and have it typed. He also had a problem with composition. He couldn't easily express his thoughts. He had to work them over and over again." The legacy of dyslexia has passed from one generation to another. Dr. Keith Wold says of his wife, Seward's second daughter, "Oh, Elaine has that streak all right. She reverses numbers. We write them out big for her, and then there's no problem." Mary Lea says, "I can read a book upside down as easily as right side up." Several grandchildren are affected as well.

When Seward was fourteen, his father died, leaving the bulk of his stock in the company in equal shares to his two sons. Seward's mother moved with the three children from New Brunswick, New Jersey, to New York City, where, soon after, Seward met with a most peculiar sexual initiation. He was "kidnapped" by a close friend and contemporary of his mother's and kept in her Park Avenue apartment for sexual purposes for a period of ten days. Although his mother knew of his whereabouts, she did nothing about it; it was his older brother, Bob, who rescued him. Shortly after this bizarre episode, Seward's mother left her children and departed for England, eventually marrying John W. Dennis, a member of Parliament. Undoubtedly this incident both influenced Johnson's sexuality and instilled in him a lifelong fear of kidnapping. All his adult life he kept a gun beside his bed, a fact that would become an issue in the will contest.

Given an extroverted, forceful older brother, a mother who stifled him with attention and then deserted him, a perceptual difficulty that undoubtedly damaged his self-image, Seward Johnson seemed to retreat from reality into fantasy. As an adult he could go for days at a time without uttering more than a few sentences. He matured into a small man with a polite, somewhat stiff façade. He swam, played tennis, and rode to hounds.

Keith Wold observed of Johnson's personality, "Because he couldn't derive his knowledge from traditional sources, he led his entire life based on empirical experience. It was a hard way to live, and it made him extremely idiosyncratic." During the Depression, Seward Johnson's notion of dispensing charity was to slaughter a herd of sheep, grind them up, and distribute lamb patties to the poor, thereby assuring himself that no man got a better cut of meat than the next. During World War II he devised a bomb shelter to house his entire herd of Holstein cows so that in the event of a holocaust he could feed the survivors. (Today at Jasna Polana, his mansion in Princeton, New Jersey, a fully equipped nuclear-bomb shelter stands ready for occupancy.) He wanted a provision for his cows written into his will. During his scuba-diving days he proposed a time-sharing plan for an underwater habitat.

In 1917 Seward enlisted in the Navy and became second-in-command of a subchaser, a job he performed with proficiency. He served for a time as a vice-president and treasurer of Johnson & Johnson, and when World War II began, he founded the Atlantic Diesel Corporation. After the war he turned his interests toward farming and the breeding of cows. It was not until 1971, at the age of seventy-six, that he became fully involved with the affairs of the Harbor Branch Oceanographic Institute.

Johnson's wealth allowed him to deal with his fears and his desires in unique ways. He astounded Dutch customs officials by sending bottled water to Holland to stock his yacht. When he went to Bermuda in 1933, he took with him his favorite horse, his German shepherds, and also a cow and a goat so that he and his children could have homebred milk. He purchased a Gulfstream jet so that he could fly his dogs to Italy non-stop. When he learned that the heated towel racks in his home in Florida used up the entire electric-power supply, instead of removing them, he installed a second heating system, at a cost of over

$200,000 a year. One day he bought his wife Basia a dark-gray Mercedes. She said she liked the light-gray color better. The following day he bought one of those as well.

In the courtroom, certain of his later ideas would be presented as additional evidence of his senility. He suggested, for instance, that the assets of the Harbor Branch Oceanographic Institute be converted into gold bars and buried in a vault under his Princeton mansion. After reading about an ancient culture that had been destroyed in a conflagration, he proposed that the records of Harbor Branch be transferred to clay tablets so that eventual visitors from outer space could know what our civilization had been like. He said that he was considering a plan whereby, upon his death, he would be lashed to the table in the main salon of his yacht, the *Ocean Pearl,* and sunk with the ship. Was this a symptom of senility or an appropriate end for a man who demanded for himself the privileges of an emperor?

Seward Johnson's vast wealth masked a flaw deeply embedded in his psyche, an aberrant sexual appetite. Perhaps as a result of his adolescent sexual kidnapping, he often treated women as objects to be purchased for his pleasure and later discarded at whim. The stories of his sexual escapades proliferate, and he would pursue a secretary and the daughter of a head of state with equal ardor. He boasted of visiting brothels the world over with his brother, and would relate how they often availed themselves of the same woman. When he was sixty-seven, he asked his son, Junior, about a young woman, "What do you think of her?" Junior replied, "Dad, you know I'm in love with Joyce." To which the father retorted, "Not for you. For me." Even in his eighties Seward Johnson used binoculars to scan the naked-breasted females sunbathing on Riviera beaches.

Over the years his brother, General Johnson, had extricated him from many difficult situations. Seward Jr. asserts that the General's death in 1968 created a void which led directly to his father's entanglement with Basia Piasecka.

But Seward Johnson's sexual nature exceeded the bounds of even the most avid philanderer. Because of his money and power, he was able to transform his sexual fantasies into reality. Betty Johnson Bushnell, his nephew's wife, says, "Seward didn't know right from wrong. For him there were no rules." Eventually his destructive sexual nature expressed itself through a compulsion to obliterate the structure of his own family by violating the most sacred taboo.

"It's one hell of a story, more fantastic and scandalous than any episode of *Dynasty,*" says Nicholas Gouverneur Rutgers, the grandson of James Wood Johnson, co-founder of Johnson & Johnson. "It's a story that should never be told," cautions Betty Johnson Bushnell, "it's bad enough that it happened."

". . . Johnny was crazy."

*T*he portrait on the wall of the tiny chauffeur's cottage at Merriewold, the spacious estate Ruth Dill Johnson Crockett occupied half a century ago, is of a titian-haired young matron in a white satin evening gown, a diamond bracelet on her right wrist. Only the intense blue eyes remain the same.

At eighty-three, Mrs. Crockett is a soft-spoken, amiable woman with fluffy-cotton white hair, a tooth missing on the right side of her mouth, and liver-spotted hands. She walks with difficulty. On a bright spring day she sits in a faded velvet chair in the modest living room of the cottage. On the floor is a threadbare red-and-blue Oriental carpet, over the mantel a muddy painting of several saints. In a small L-shaped area a queen-size bed is set up under the bookshelves. A few feet from us, Ruth's husband, Philip Crockett, sits leaning forward, his face three inches from the television screen. The volume is turned high. A baseball game is in progress. He ignores our presence.

RUTH: What can I tell you? He followed his impulses. Whatever he felt like doing, he did. But he could be very

kind. I met him for the first time in 1921. I'm from
Bermuda, but my mother was born in Perth Amboy,
and my parents sent me to a boarding school, St. Mary's
Hall, in Burlington, New Jersey. Since they couldn't afford to bring me home for the holidays, I visited my
elderly cousin James Neilson in New Brunswick. We
were at a garden party, playing croquet, and Seward
came up to me. He seemed stiff and he affected this
veddy, veddy British accent and asked, "Do you know
Mrs. Trimingham? She's from Bermuda too." I was not
at all impressed with him. Then in the summer of 1923
Father let me be his secretary. The yacht race from
Newport came in, and I was busy typing when a man
walked in and introduced himself. It was Seward's
brother, Bob, and he said to Pa, "Sydney Carpender and
James Neilson said I should look you up." They were
chatting away, so I said, "Why don't you come down
tomorrow for tennis, a swim, and supper?" Bob Johnson
had no idea who I was, he thought I was the secretary
and acting very strange. But my father said, "No, no,
this is my daughter, Ruth." They arrived at the house
the next day, Bob and Seward and another friend, and
Seward asked me to call him when I got to the States in
September and I said I would, but I still wasn't very
impressed with him, and I didn't.

In September, Cousin James told him where I was, he
called me up, and I met him at the St. Regis. We had
lunch and afterwards he asked me if I'd mind coming
along while he did some errands. We walked into Cartier
—I'd never been to Cartier—and he bought a gold ciga-
rette case with diamond initials on it. Then he said
something very strange to me: "If someone saw us coming out of there, they might think that I was buying you
an engagement ring." That astonished me. The way he

pursued me, I couldn't believe it. He gave me all these gifts. But then he and his brother, Bob, and Carter Nicholas decided to sail around the world. They were looking for locations for J&J plants, they were gone about a year. First I got a cable that read "Miss you," and then several short letters. They were really short, but they came from exotic places. Now, this part is weird: you know what a lot of those letters said? A lot of them were boasting about the women that he and Bob had found. He'd always write as if it was Bob who'd found them, but it sort of sounded like he did too. My mother saw me getting all these letters, but she didn't know what was in them and she said, "Seward Johnson has serious intentions." I told her, "I don't care, I'm not at all interested in him." And I wasn't, I had a lot of other beaux. Mother said, "Well, you better stop, look, and listen."

In June of '24 our family was due to sail to England on the *Changuinola*. I wrote that to Seward, who was back in New Jersey, and got a wire from him saying that he was planning to come to Bermuda and go over with us on the ship. The captain told us he'd delayed the ship a day so that Seward could catch it. The first night out, Seward and I walked around the deck and finally stopped under the captain's bridge. Looking bow-ward, he asked me to marry him. I wasn't altogether surprised, but he sounded so upset that I quickly said, "Yes." The next morning at eight he went to Father's cabin. "May I marry your daughter?" he asked, and got the reply, "Wait till I finish shaving or I might cut myself."

It was fun having a fiancé in London to take you places, but wouldn't you know I would have an acute attack of appendicitis. My poor parents, who had just enough put aside for the trip, told him he would have to "take over." He arranged for a Harley Street specialist to operate. We were married at St. James's Church on July 14 and then left London by limousine to Dover, to a chartered plane waiting to fly us to Paris. How amazing and fantastic it all seemed.

From the first, Seward Johnson's wealth was the dominant factor in the relationship. There began an era of luxury for Ruth that she still remembers with relish. In Paris she enjoyed lunches in the Bois de Boulogne, dinner at the Tour d'Argent, nightclubbing, and her first sight of the nude *Folies* girls. Then they went on to Switzerland, Lake Como, Milan, Bologna, and Florence.

Ruth felt Seward had few interests of his own other than sailing and sports and seemed to take his direction from her. When she began to paint, he took up painting. When they returned home to New Jersey, as a wedding present Bob Johnson gave them eight acres of land in Highland Park adjoining his own property. The broad back lawn sloped down to the Raritan River and provided a view of the Johnson & Johnson headquarters across the way in New Brunswick. In the two-year construction of Merriewold, Johnson gave free rein to his whims—the house became known as "the Castle" to local residents. Johnson had admired the roofs at Oxford University and he imported five hundred tons of slate from the Cotswolds for his own roof. The exterior was stone from Germantown, Pennsylvania, the interior was English oak and Italian marble. A circular staircase was copied from one he had seen in the old Philadelphia City Hall. There was a secret room adjoining the library—the door was opened by removing a volume of the *Encyclopaedia Britannica*. Under the skylight, as in a royal house, the initials R and S and the year 1926 were inscribed.

Ruth's first child was born dead after she'd accompanied her husband on a sailing trip on the *Zodiac* in rough seas. Mary Lea was born in 1926, Elaine in 1928, J. Seward Johnson, Jr., in 1930, and Diana in 1932.

RUTH: After we got back from our honeymoon, I decided to call Seward "Johnny." It was his name also and I liked it better. I think of him by that name. Shortly after I returned from the hospital with baby Diana, I woke to find a figure beside me with something white on his face. I thought of Dr. Kilmer of J&J, who had a white beard, and then I thought of Filie [nurse Albertine Filiatrault] coming to tell me the baby wasn't well. I said, "Who's that?" He said, "Keep quiet and nothing will happen to you," and covered me with a gun. I froze. Johnny woke up and said, "What do you want?" "Where's your money?" the burglar answered. "In the other room," said Johnny, and he climbed out of bed and got it. My husband had quite a lot of cash in the house to pay the hospital bill. The burglar snatched the bills from him, and the handkerchief fell down so his face could be seen, even though he turned his flashlight in Johnny's eyes to blind him. He took about $3,000.

A month later, at the time of the full moon, everyone was full of the Lindbergh kidnapping, which had just taken place. We returned home and had turned in when we heard the sound of shots and running feet and someone yelling, "Get out of here, you SOB." We ran to the window. There was a ladder at the baby's window. Johnny grabbed his gun and ran down the hall, the gun going off into the ceiling. Filie was in tears, saying she had heard scratching and a screen being cut. She telephoned the gardener, who ran around the house and saw a man on the ladder and fired at him. The police were very quick in coming and the chief made the rounds of eating places and came upon a chap in a shabby brown coat who, when the chief said, "I'm a police officer," reached into his pocket, in which they found a gun. They took him in and later Johnny identified him in a lineup as the same man who'd robbed us. He got fourteen years. We were only about sixteen miles from the Lindberghs. Johnny was frightened, I was too. Those were bad times. Right away we shipped Mary Lea down to Bermuda. As soon as we could get the family together, we followed.

MARY LEA: After they tried to take Diana, I went off to Bermuda to live with my grandparents. Grandpa was a martinet right out of the movie *The Ruling Class.* He was Attorney General of Bermuda and he had a long, white, horsehair wig and a monocle because he'd been gassed in World War I and lost the use of a muscle in his eye, so he had this to prop it open. He was very distinguished-looking. His name was Thomas Melville Dill.

Grandfather was one of the "Forty Thieves" of Bermuda that sort of ran the island and kept things under control. He was really quite a character. Every morning he'd come along the hall with a stick and hit my door and say, "Show a leg, show a leg," which meant "get up." You had to get up and take off your pajamas and put on a jockstrap. You'd go outside and dive overboard from the little dock, it didn't matter if it was February. After that you'd dry off and march up the steps of a tower we had. My aunt Diana and I would stand ready with guns and Grandfather would raise the Union Jack, then off would go this little cannon. We'd do a goose step and sort of give the Nazi salute and we'd march downstairs for breakfast.

Dad told me the first time he saw my mother in Bermuda she was pushing my aunt Diana in a baby carriage and my mother had on a frilly white organdy dress and he thought, "That is the girl I would like to marry." Aunt Diana is only three and a half years older than I am and like a sister to me. Diana became an actress and then she married Kirk Douglas; Michael and Joel are her children. Now she's married to Bill Darrid, who's a very good writer.

SEWARD JR.: After the kidnapping attempt they put bars on all the windows and there was a barbed-wire entanglement encircling the lawn about seven feet wide. It was like a POW camp. We moved down to Bermuda in '33. We used to go down on the *Queen of Bermuda* and when it passed my grandfather's house on the north shore, he fired off his cannon. I was only three years old, but I ran away from home. My grandfather was about six-foot-two and he held court with all the solemnity and severity of a judge while my parents watched. He made me stand up to him and confess and then he administered the razor strop to my hand. We lived at Pembroke Hall and Dad bought an island named Morgan's Island. During the Second World War the government there confiscated it. They gave my father $30,000 for it and sold it for $4 million to the U.S. government for an air base.

Bermuda in those days was very much like the Deep South, from a racial point of view. There were two big landholders in Bermuda, the Dills and the Watlingtons, and they intermarried. I remember my grandfather chasing black boys off the dock with a bullwhip; he never hit anybody, but he snapped it over their heads. But when he died, the funeral procession was mostly

black and it went on for over a mile. I had my fourth
birthday while we were still down there and we had built
a tree house. We decided we wanted to cook or something up in the tree house, so we pulled this iron pot up
there. My father was walking underneath, and I don't
know what came over me, but anyway this iron pot
came out of the tree house and onto my father's head. It
cut his head open a bit. My mother said he was never
the same since. In fact, she told me later that she blamed
the divorce on that iron pot.

RUTH: Johnny didn't want any more children. He said it
weakened the blood line. After five births I began to
have abortions. He was always after me, but I didn't like
the consequences. Perhaps he treated women the way he
did to pay them back for his mother's desertion. It was
as if he wanted to get back at them. I don't know. Actually, we got on fine together until he told me he'd fallen
in love with my fourteen-year-old sister, Fannie. He was
twenty-six years older than she was. Johnny told me he
wanted a divorce so he could marry Fan. I was dumbfounded. Of course Fan was flirtatious, but she had
never been serious about him. All three of us had a
meeting and Fan told him so, she swore it. Why would a
girl of fourteen be interested in a man of forty?

Johnny wouldn't believe her, but when she refused
him he left the house and sailed for England. I got some
letters from him and I held out some hope for a reconciliation, but not much. When he came back, he still
wanted a divorce. That's all he said—he wasn't the kind
to explain. Fannie was out of the picture, but I expect he
just got tired of domesticity. He ran out of steam, I
guess. It's weird. There's nothing you can explain about
a man like that. I told him, "We have four children, let's

try it for a year. If it doesn't work out, then I'll go to Reno." We moved to England, to Hurley. I thought maybe he'd change, but he didn't. I'm old enough now to tell the truth—Johnny was crazy.

"Where I come from, they'd hang you for what he did."

*T*oday, Mary Lea Johnson, a quiet, generous, gentle blonde woman with intense blue-green eyes, is married to the silver-haired Martin (Marty) Richards. They founded the Producer Circle Company, which has produced such Broadway hits as *On the Twentieth Century, Sweeney Todd, La Cage aux Folles,* and the Pulitzer Prize-winning *Crimes of the Heart.* During the trial Mary Lea had several bouts of illness and was hospitalized. Her husband's concern for her was evident. She has led a difficult, trouble-filled life marked by physical illness and a sense of self-abnegation and unworthiness. There is about her a bruised quality and sometimes an unreachability, as if she existed inside a bell jar.

Those people who are close to Mary Lea know two things about her: that she was the first baby to appear on the Johnson & Johnson Baby Powder can, and that her father was the first man to seduce her. Not surprisingly, her earliest childhood memories center on her father.

MARY LEA: Daddy and Uncle Bob had one of the first autogiros. It looked like a giant mosquito up there. I ran through the fields to keep it in sight. I saw Daddy lean out and turn the crank on the side of the plane to bring the wheels down and then bang, splat, he flew right into a tree. But he was all right, they both just climbed out. During Prohibition, Dad and Uncle Bob had a speedboat called the *Bobbie Sue.* They'd go out beyond the three-mile limit and get as much stuff as they could and drink it out there. When they came back in, they'd be stopped by the Coast Guard, but the liquor was inside them. That was Dad's way of handling things. He loved the sea—that was one thing he loved. I remember his racing sailboats, six meters and then twelve meters, and he raced from Newport to Spain. We had a sailboat called the *Mary Lea,* then there was the *Elaine* for my sister, then *Jack* and *Jill*—very imaginative names.

My father was definitely a black-and-white person, there weren't any grays in his life at all. I would say that I've met very few people who didn't like Daddy. He was always very kind to people on the outside. He wouldn't let them take up any of his time, but he'd pay them off more or less, so people thought he was pretty wonderful. He'd get very enthusiastic about things, but it was only surface. I would say he was pretty cold. Dad was a strange combination—conservative, socialistic. He started a non-union dairy in Morristown, but the unions got very annoyed because he could offer the farmers a lot more than they could. When we'd go out on the boat, he'd often start dreaming about different ways the government could save money, like they ought to print an advertisement on the back of all American currency and that way they could decrease taxes because a lot of advertising income would be coming in.

Dad and Uncle Bob were very different. Bob was a typical business executive, charming but a shark underneath. Dad was more of a monkish type; in fact, he often said he'd love to be a monk, although he couldn't possibly have done it. Sexually, I don't think he could have done it.

SEWARD JR.: Did Mary Lea tell you that Ratsey "sails"-for-"sales" story? God, I hate that story, it makes Dad out to be a joke at Johnson & Johnson. It was his brother's way of putting him down and out. And that bears on my father's sexuality. A lot of Dad's secrecy and rebellion had to do with Uncle Bob.

My father's older brother was an egoist completely. I always resented that relationship. I resented it as a male because the lack of potency on my father's part was obvious. Probably he had to prove sexually to himself that he was a man, or it might have been a homosexual thing, or frustration, I don't know.

Seward Johnson followed periods of neglecting his children with sporadic intense attention that induced febrile excitement. He was obsessed with the young female form. His second wife, Esther, suggested that he see a psychiatrist because his interest in young women was not normal. Mary Lea recalls the bewilderment of having her father come into her bed and sexually excite her, eventually carrying on a full sexual relationship with her. This relationship continued intermittently from the time she was nine until she was fifteen.

Dr. Elizabeth Mintz, a psychoanalytic expert on incest and child molestation, provides a clinical explanation. "Nine or ten to fourteen or fifteen is a typical age span. After that it is not uncommon for the father to turn toward a younger sibling, if there is one. I'd speculate that in his own childhood this particular man was exposed to a

very contradictory range of environmental influences; that
he had an inconsistent childhood and might have been subjected to a type of incestuous relationship himself. On a
psychodynamic level, the father who molests his child
often is carrying on some form of what was done to him.
There were so many splits in this man's personality—this
is a man who never achieved personal integration."

Says Dr. Henry Giarretto, executive director of Parents
United, an amalgamation of 139 community groups devoted to the treatment of incest survivors, "An incestuous
relationship imposes severe stress on the structure of the
family. All family members usually suffer conflict and confusion." From the inception of Seward Johnson's incestuous relationship with Mary Lea the fabric of the family
was irreparably damaged as dark, uncontrollable un-
dercurrents swept the household. This child escaped the
experience she was undergoing by retreating into a fantasy
life where surrealistic images of monks and of her father
blended in her consciousness, and her guilt became physi-
calized in bizarre ways.

MARTY: Mary Lea has that Johnson trait of turning off
   and disappearing. Maybe it's helped her cope. I love
   Mary Lea very much, and I try to make up for all the
   pain she's experienced, for all the things she's never had.
   But I can't compensate for all the damage. And she
   loved her father till the day he died. I can't understand
   why. Where I come from, they'd hang you for what he
   did.

DR. MINTZ: These fathers are patriarchal and on a primitive level they regard their children as belonging to them
   —"This child is mine." He's possessive of his property.

The wife too is his property and has no right to object, and most often it's the father who's in economic control.

On another level, these men are weak, extremely unsure of their own sexuality, and have low self-esteem. They are anxious, frightened men and what better way to assert their masculine dominance than over a helpless child who cannot reject them? They're saying, "I'm really a helpless child myself, but I will prove I'm a big strong man."

MARY LEA: It seems so funny that it should have been Dad. I think I knew how babies came and things like that from the very beginning because living on a farm you learn that at about age four, so it seemed sort of natural until I started thinking about it. I think he sort of felt like we were a possession of his and so therefore he had a right to do what he wanted with us.

They took us to a place called Hurley-on-the-Thames. It had a twelfth-century monastery and its own church and secret tombs and a crypt with the bones of monks. Elaine and I were sleeping in the next room and we heard this terrible fight going on between Mommy and Daddy. This was after Dad fell in love with Mom's fourteen-year-old sister, Fannie, but I didn't know that then. I turned to Elaine and said, "I hope Mommy and Daddy aren't getting a divorce." I don't know what made me say it.

Mom just left, she went on a cruise. There I was with Dad. I remember waking up one night and seeing a hooded monk standing in the corner of my room. I was terrified. I called Elaine twice from my bed because I thought if I could awaken her, then maybe we could do something about it together. But she didn't respond at all. I pulled the covers up over my head and just lay

there. But then when I peeked out, he was still there. So
finally I got up the courage to dash out of bed. I ran into
Dad's room and I said, "I can't go back in that bed."
And he said, "All right," and he put a cover over me.

All of a sudden the room started to shake and the
pictures came right off the wall and smashed onto the
floor. In the morning a couple of the servants came up
and said they were leaving, that they were sure there
were ghosts in the house. Dad didn't say anything about
our experience at all. He just said, "All right, if that's
the way you feel, we'll get somebody else."

That wasn't all that happened at Hurley. Once I was
walking in the garden when all of a sudden I felt very
strange. My right arm started to ache and I felt as if I
were going to faint. The gardener's wife was with me
and she pulled at me and said, "Oh, look, you're on fire.
Your arm is being burned." Then suddenly the pain
went away. I looked over and saw a procession of monks
walk by, carrying a dead body on a stretcher—it was all
charred. They turned a corner and disappeared. The
gardener's wife didn't see them. Later I found out that
during the Reformation one of the monks had been
caught stealing jewels from the church altarpiece, his
right arm had been chopped off, and he'd been burnt at
the stake. It had been on just the spot where I had been
standing.

Then this other woman came in, the Countess Von
Something-or-Other. She did these sculptures of all of us
on horseback. Dad started having an affair with her. I
went back to Hurley about fourteen years ago. The place
had been changed into apartments. I went into the
church and stayed there for quite a while. I felt an urge
to cry when I went back, but it was probably just because of knowing what had happened there.

SEWARD JR.: They went away. Then it was a long time
that we stayed in England by ourselves. It seemed all
we'd eat forever when they were away was boiled mut-
ton and boiled potatoes and Brussels sprouts. It probably wasn't so, but that's all I remember. Then they came
back and we were deliriously happy when they were
both together, and we all went for walks in the fields.
But then I guess my father went away for good. Mary
Lea was sent away to school. Diana, Elaine, and I were
brought to Paris, where we lived a miserable, miserable
life. My mother was miserable and the apartment was
very dark and depressing. In the apartment across the
way there was a boy who used to scream at night and we
were told that he was mad.

Mom left, she went to Reno, and he went to South
America, chasing the daughter of a dictator. They were
both gone for months, maybe eleven. Our nurse, we
called her Mademoiselle, was a real bad number. She
would give us wine instead of orange juice at breakfast
because it made us easier to control. Later she was arrested for carrying dope in the heel of her shoe. She used
to take us around to things like the waxworks where
they guillotined a wax figure, but she didn't tell us it was
wax. She was real sick. One nice thing we did, though—
we used to go skating on the skating rink.

RUTH'S JOURNAL: I will never forget the spring in England with the gorgeous bluebells covering the hills, but
it was bringing nearer the time when the family would
be dissolved. I sailed in August and the Pratts were on
the same ship and they told me they knew a very good
lawyer in New York named Henry Johnson and that I
should meet him. I did and I liked him and engaged him
to look after my affairs. Brother Tommy came up and

joined me and we flew to Reno on October 17, 1937. We
had a bad flight, three forced landings. Evangeline
Stokowski, my sister-in-law, was in Las Vegas for the
same reason I was. I suggested since we were in the
same state she should come up to visit. She did, with
Prince Zalstem-Zalessky, whom she later married, in
tow. When I got to London, I was reunited with the
children and had to break the sad news to them.

MARY LEA: I was sent away to a school called the Upper
Chine on the Isle of Wight. Dad came down to see me in
December, he was supposed to tell me that they'd gotten
a divorce, but he didn't. He just took me out to lunch.
During Christmas vacation Mom came to London with
the other kids. She picked me up at the train station to
bring me to Claridge's for lunch. On the way she said,
"Oh, by the way, I hope you don't mind about the divorce." I knew my aunt Evangeline had gotten a divorce
from Leopold Stokowski, so I said, "I think it's going to
be hard on Lyuba and Sadja." She replied, "No. I meant
about mine. Your father's and my divorce." That's when
I realized she and Dad were divorced. I just burst into
tears. I couldn't stop crying. I waited in the car a long
time until I could pull myself together enough to go into
Claridge's. As soon as I saw my brother and sisters, I
started to cry again.

At the time of the divorce, in October 1937, Seward
arranged annual payments of $12,000 to his wife and
$6,000 to each of his four children. In these reduced cir-
cumstances Ruth moved back to Merriewold. In June of
1940, four months after Seward Johnson's marriage to Esther Underwood, Ruth married Philip Crockett, a Boston
businessman. To economize, the Crocketts vacated "the

Castle" and moved with baby Diana to the chauffeur's cottage they still occupy. Elaine, Seward Jr., and Mary Lea lived in a converted garage adjoining the chicken coop.

Ruth Johnson Crockett has lived for forty-six years in this modest cottage, in effect a woman fallen from grace. The mansion, a five-minute walk away, sold decades ago for $70,000, is now a warren of medical and other professional offices. The cottage in which she lives, the chicken coop, and the stucco garage that housed her children all bear mute evidence to the early blight on this life and the lives of the Johnson children.

RUTH: You must walk next door and look at Merriewold. Our initials are under the skylight. You can still see it, it says "R & S 1926." It hasn't faded.

SEWARD JR.: Merriewold has always been in my memory. Afterwards, to get to sleep at night, I'd picture myself flying over it—the roof, the tower, everything. It made me feel so secure, it was where I belonged, it was my identity source. I could draw you a map of it—every room. After Mom sold it, a Mr. Farmer bought it, and one day he shot and killed his wife there, right in Dad and Mom's dressing room. After that I didn't dream about Merriewold anymore.

"Incest is 100 percent selfish . . ."

SEWARD JR.: After the divorce, in May of 1938 my father came over to Paris. He'd been in Hawaii, and he was like a ray of sunshine. It was a glorious time. We returned on the *Normandie* and my father had a record player in his cabin and he played all these Bing Crosby records and taught me to hula. I mean, sort of life was beamed back into our life, you know. I sat at the captain's table and had my first taste of caviar. Then he rented a house on Cape Cod and we had a most glorious summer there. He really worked at being a father then.

LUCINDA BALLARD: We met at a dance, he cut in on me every five minutes and after that followed me everywhere like a little stubborn boy determined that his mother wouldn't go away. Seward always behaved more like a child than a man. He was terribly thoughtful and helpful. I was going to Reno, and he chartered a plane and put me up at his sister Evangeline's. We had a great deal of fun. There was a lot of divorcing going on at that time—me, Evangeline, and I think Seward's first wife was in Reno. Evangeline visited her, but of course she didn't tell her we were there. When he was with Evangeline, he was a different person. He would sparkle and be funny, he wasn't so reticent. She had a lot to do with promoting the romance. But Seward was very cool. Verbally he'd want to be with me all the time, he pursued me ardently, but he didn't overwhelm me with passion.

My memory works not in a continuous stream but in pictures: I remember a picnic with him on a sloop. From Paris a friend had sent me a modified sailor suit in light blue. With my red hair, I thought I looked dazzling. And Seward was crazy about sailing. He'd hire planes to fly you wherever you wanted—the luxury of it enchanted me. He'd court me ardently one minute and then he'd disappear with his brother, Bob, and I wouldn't hear from him for ages. Then he'd call from Honolulu or Paris or wherever he was. He gave me fabulous gifts of jewelry. At the end I returned them all.

I was engaged to him for a while in the summer of 1938. My house in Truro wasn't ready and I was really upset and he helped me rent another house. He had a place nearby. He kept proposing to me all the time. One day he came with some papers, they were Johnson & Johnson lists of figures. I wasn't interested in figures, but I remember that one of the figures was $92,000, which he told me was his quarterly allowance from his stockholdings. Seward said, "Lucinda, you know I do nothing constructive with my money. You have friends, you have causes, you could do something with my money." I thought about that, and the next time he proposed, I accepted.

Seward's children visited that summer. Mary Lea must have been twelve, she was such a dear child and thrilled that I was a theatrical designer. She was interested in all these books on design and fascinated with the theater. I was very close to my own children, so I couldn't understand why Seward wasn't close to his. He'd compare Seward Jr. unfavorably to my son, Bob. I scolded him about how much his children craved and needed his attention and affection, but he didn't relate to them. There was an almost malignant indifference about him that seemed unnatural. I encouraged him to include his children in his activities and for a while he did, but perhaps to please me. Those children were appealing—if you said a kind word to them, they'd be so loving. Especially Seward Jr., he seemed so needy. He'd get seasick; that didn't please his father much, I'll tell you. They looked totally neglected. Mary Lea and Elaine's clothes were so raggedy that they were ashamed. It was a disgrace. I told Seward, "You're always telling me how much money you have. Well, I'm going to spend some, I'm going to take your children shopping."

Maybe that soured me a bit. There were other things too. He rented a place in Peapack-Gladstone, New Jersey, it was huge and grand in a boring way. He started seeing a lot of the horsy set. He'd ask me to invite my friends down for weekends because he had so few friends. General Johnson, his brother, would come by. His wife at that time I felt was a pathetic creature whose only interest in the world seemed to be in the clothes of the designer Charles James. Bob Johnson was so manly it was disgusting, he practically pawed the ground. They were very different types; Seward was like the All-American boy, very sunburned, his eyes very blue, and General Johnson looked more Scandinavian and dressed more like an Englishman. He liked chorus girls and very submissive women, so he didn't like me much. I felt very sorry for his wife, who seemed the unhappiest of women.

We went riding and they'd been burning poison ivy and I got this rash around my neck. When Seward saw the rash, he was absolutely terrified by it, he was pathetic. His reaction was so abnormal that I decided that I didn't want to have much to do with him. I think what attracted me was the lavishness, the idea of leading a fairy-tale existence, but I'd begun to realize it wasn't a fairy tale, there was something creepy about him. But what really ended it was most peculiar. I walked into a bank to cash a check and the teller began flirting with me. I was terribly annoyed. I came out and I began walking away, and then suddenly I stopped still, because I realized something. That bank teller looked like Seward, and if it weren't for his money, I would have reacted the same way to him.

MARY LEA: After the divorce when we went back to New Jersey, my mother filled Merriewold with guests and relatives. We never had our own rooms after that. We never knew where we'd be sleeping. I'd carry a sleeping bag with me, and I'd look in a room to see if it was occupied. I'd sleep just anywhere. Mom didn't want children around after the divorce. At times when you were there she'd treat you like another adult rather than as a child. There was very little physical contact with Mom, I mean she isn't the kind that would throw her arms around you, though she isn't a cold person either; she just seemed to be closer to her family in Bermuda than to us. It's strange.

You feel absolutely abandoned by both parents, as if nobody wanted you. And I think this was the second time in my life that I felt that way because when I was a very young child I had very straight hair, but my sister Elaine had lovely long golden ringlets, and I guess Mom had read somewhere that if you shaved a child's head, it would grow in curly. I don't know what got into Mom, she shaved my head and my aunt Diana's too. Well, both of us looked like we just got out of a concentration camp and everybody would look and say, oh, how beautiful Elaine was and then they'd look at me and sort of make a face as if they wondered. I think from a very young age I decided that I was not the same as other people. As far as Mom is concerned, I'd do anything for her, but I feel definitely, even today, that she uses me.

DR. MINTZ: Usually they are as angry at the mother as they are at the father. The daughter feels the mother is inept at protecting them and cannot fulfill their father's sexual needs. The incest survivor longs to lead a normal life, but there's so much confusion to be overcome. Is this my father or my lover? Is this my mother or my rival?

DR. GIARRETTO: Parental incest in the family can be likened to terminal cancer in the individual. The whole family is critically traumatized.

MARY LEA: My brother, Seward, was sort of the crown prince, so to speak. When the divorce came, there was a complete rebellion on his part. I think it was harder for him than any of us, although it's hard to say because none of us discussed it, we all had our own trauma. Seward took it out in sort of destructive behavior. Mom asked him to kiss her art teacher, Miss Goldthawaite, and Seward said, "I'm called Old Arsenic Lips, the last old lady I kissed died." That was funny, but I can remember him taking a BB gun and shooting out every window in the barn, and looking very sloppy. Maybe he thought someone would notice him. No one did.

Elaine and I are fairly close, we're a year and a week apart, except that we're so different. She has a set thing she does every hour, every day of her life. That would drive me absolutely stark staring bonkers. She knows what she's doing a year from now and I'm lucky if I know what I'm doing next week.

I don't mean Elaine had no scars from the divorce, but she seemed more insulated. She always had a group of friends her own age, girls she went to school with at Ethel Walker. She still sees them. Keith, her husband, thinks Elaine was terribly damaged by the divorce, he has absolutely no use for my mother at all. Diana has always been interested in breeding horses and her love is the animal itself. After she went to Bennett, she went back to Madeira to teach dressage and then began to raise horses. Whatever happened in our lives, I think that all of us have not been able to confide completely in one another. Why, I don't know.

DR. MINTZ: In these families often everyone has something to hide. The incestuous father develops a passion for privacy. He's an expert at getting his needs fulfilled. Incest is 100 percent selfish, the child is deprived of real love and is left yearning for the love they have never experienced.

SEWARD JR.: After they divorced, Mom was completely depressed. I don't think she really acknowledged the fact that they'd gotten a divorce. I can't tell you why she acted the way she did, whether she was hurt or cold or British—somewhere in that triangle. I've resented it all my life, I think more than anyone else has. I feel she doesn't have a moral backbone. She has these sayings,

"There's a little good in everybody," "Get a stiff upper lip," "You eat a peck of dirt before you die," but there was always a reason not to take a position. I think that's lack of moral character, myself.

RUTH: Seward Jr. was always angry about things. He still gets so angry at me. He didn't talk to me for two years because I attended his first wife's son's funeral. Mary Lea's a real Johnson. Her uncle Bob said that if she'd been a man, she'd be running the company. She's Johnson through and through. Diana, she was always fine. It was always the horses with her. She fell off and broke her arm, but she still kept riding. Elaine was very popular. Nothing bothers Elaine.

MARY LEA: The first summer after the divorce we visited Dad, he was going with Lucinda Ballard, who lived in Truro, and we just adored her. The second summer we were in Chatham, Mass., and we saw less and less of Lucinda. I remember saying to Dad, "What happened to Lucinda? I thought you were going to marry her." But he said no, he was a day person and she was a night person, so they couldn't get their hours together.

In the summer of 1939 Nina Underwood McAlpin, a recent divorcée, invited Seward to visit her in Chatham, Massachusetts. Local residents speculated that Nina would become the next Mrs. Johnson and were considerably surprised when Seward announced that he was marrying her sister, Essie.

MARY LEA: We thought the next candidate was Nina McAlpin. We were close to the McAlpin kids, so we thought, "This is great." When he told Elaine and me that he was going to marry Essie, I remember running to

Nina and bursting into tears and saying, "I love you. I thought *you* were going to be the one that married Dad" —not very smart of me.

SEWARD JR.: I knew he was going to marry Essie by the way he acted. Essie was tutoring me that summer, and when she left he would dance around his room.

Esther Underwood Johnson wore flat shoes, little makeup, and enjoyed walking her Weimaraners. She was small, thin, cool, restrained, and elegant. Seward and his second wife enjoyed many luxuries, but, presumably owing to Esther's restraint, they were New England discreet. They had two children: Jennifer Underwood Johnson, born in 1941, and James Loring Johnson, in 1945.

MARY LEA: Mom married within four months of Dad's marriage to Essie. I think it was more or less of a "I can do it too." She married Philip Crockett. He was a bond broker who'd worked in Boston, a sort of a hatchet man, but also a Rhodes Scholar. He wasn't kind to me. Unless he could control you completely, he didn't want anything to do with you.

RUTH: I married Phil. I thought the children needed a firm hand.

MARY LEA: Dad had made that arrangement whereby we got $6,000 a year and Mom got $12,000, which was supposed to keep her alive, that's really how it went. She left Merriewold and moved into the chauffeur's cottage on the place with my stepfather and baby Diana. Elaine, myself, and Seward lived in a garage next to the chicken coop. It was divided into three rooms and a bathroom. One room was very small, my brother had that. It had bunk beds in it, you could just about walk in beside the beds, and my sister and my room had two little cardboard armoires that you could hang your clothes in. There was a rug on the floor that was set right on top of the concrete. There were two windows in our room, one on either side.

There were rats in there, they'd come into the chicken coop to eat the feed. There must have been a hole somewhere because the rats would crawl into our part of the house and climb up the walls and up the curtains—one would follow the other and go up and around one window and down, and then up and around the other window, then up and around the top of the cardboard place where our clothes were kept, and then disappear somewhere down the other side. You would just lie there and look at this parade. We didn't think much about money in those days. I mean, we didn't even think how Dad lived so nicely. The idea of wanting his money never occurred to me, really. I never sort of compared him to the way I lived, I thought I had what I should have and that was it. Except for a time maybe in that terrible house—I would get mad a little bit because it was so disgusting.

MARTY: It wasn't lack of money, both parents had money. The Johnson children lived like that through neglect. They were brutalized by everyone. There's no self-respect, they didn't feel they were deserving of more. Ruth would like to be a mother now. Maybe now it's too late.

MARY LEA: I used to stay over at Dad and Essie's sometimes. When I told my mother about Daddy, she believed me, but what she said was, "I think it's a very good idea to tell your stepmother, Essie." And I think that was the worst possible thing she could have said. I think she could have said, "I'll go to Essie with you." I needed somebody to back me up. I went alone. I told my stepmother, "I don't think it's a very good idea . . . would you please not have Daddy come to my room." She thought I'd made the whole thing up. After that she didn't want to have me around—she thought I was a bad influence on her children. Years later, though, she realized that what I'd said was true, and her own daughter, Jennifer, told me that she'd said, "I really should get in contact with Mary Lea and ask her forgiveness, because I brushed her off as a child with too much imagination."

I've tried to figure it out, what motivated him. He was an oversexual man and I think he liked defiance more or less. Then I think that when he married the second time —Essie was rather like a Katharine Hepburn type, a New England cold fish—he still needed a warm person. It was as if anything he wanted was perfectly all right. It was a strange thing, because any time we had beaux or anything like that and we were at Dad's house we'd be sent out with a chaperon, but at Mom's house anything went.

DR. MINTZ: Unconsciously, the incestuous father doesn't want to compete with the young men his teenage daughter begins to date, and he's afraid she'll tell them. That's why so often he's very strict.

MARY LEA: Dad would tolerate much less in us than he would in his own behavior. When I was up at Chatham the summer I was fifteen, I had a boyfriend. One night I came in about 10:30 and I hadn't told anybody I wasn't coming back for supper. My bags were packed and there was a note on top of them that John, my mother's chauffeur, would be picking me up the next morning and tak-

ing me back to New Brunswick, since I didn't seem to be
able to live by the rules. Only I hadn't been told there
were any rules. I think he realized that things were getting a little out of hand, but instead of talking to me
about it, it was easier to send me home. I don't think it
was jealousy, I think it was just he didn't want to be
bothered to cope with the situation. He wouldn't listen
to you. I was scared to death to talk to him about sexual
things.

I was sent to the Masters School in Dobbs Ferry and
they had a strict code of silence: as soon as you went
into the school building, you weren't allowed to communicate with the other students by word, look, or manner.
Once a week they had roll call and you had to answer
whether you were perfect, nearly perfect, or imperfect,
and it would go down on your record as to what you
said. And once a week, whether I'd done everything
right or not, I'd always report that I was *imperfect.*

I'd try desperately to please everybody, to make my
family pay attention to me. I can remember going to my
father and saying to him, "Dad, I just had an affair with
someone." And he answered, "Oh, well, that's nice. I
think it's time you went down to Johnson & Johnson
and had a talk with the gynecologist down there." He
wasn't angry. He wasn't anything. He was just completely indifferent to the situation. So I waited a couple
of years and I went back to him and said, "Dad, you
know, I think I'm a lesbian. I've just had an affair with a
woman." And he said, "Practically everyone goes
through that stage. If that's the way you want to live,
that's fine with me." But there was no human contact,
no feeling of let's help, let's do something. So I thought,
"Well, it's just useless to try."

DR. MINTZ: The incidence of lesbianism among female incest survivors is high. Not because the father physically injured them—Daddy is usually quite gentle and the child is often bribed but rarely hurt—they become lesbians because the mother provided such a poor model of a heterosexual woman.

MARY LEA: After Essie married Dad, instead of eating in the dining room we were sent in the kitchen to eat. To tell you the truth, it got so uncomfortable there as we got older we decided to stay away. I remember, when I was eighteen, visiting him one day. He walked out of the door and I said, "Hi, Dad." He looked around and said, "What do you want now?" I got back in the car and drove away. I had to stop the car because I was crying so hard.

DR. GIARRETTO: The incestuous relationship is extremely damaging both during the sexual phase and after it ends. The child suffers emotional trauma which often leads to self-abusive behavior that may last a lifetime. This typical self-destructive behavior includes promiscuity, drug abuse, and the sabotage of intimate relationships, schooling, and career. The child feels betrayed by both parents.

MARY LEA: It makes you feel so guilty and dirty. But it was very important for the time being.

SEWARD JR.: That was terrible, that whole thing with Mary Lea. I remember once my father did something toward me that made me wonder. I didn't let it get beyond . . . I did a feint away out of reach, because I didn't want to acknowledge it. We're very emotionally alike, Mary Lea and I. Mary Lea was tremendously affected by Dad's death and by the rejection of his will.

The relationships among Seward Johnson, the four children from his first marriage, and the two from his second were complicated and painful. At various periods throughout their lives, several of the children were alienated from their father and from one another.

Seward Johnson's children were denied the guidance most children receive from a father. There were few family celebrations, no Christmas gifts to his first four children. In later life Seward could not recall the names of many of his grandchildren, nor did he recognize all of them.

All of Johnson's children were indifferently educated. Only one of the six finished college—James, the youngest son, graduated from Upsala College in East Orange, New Jersey. The strong streak of dyslexia that ran throughout the family went unaided. The legacy that Seward Johnson was to leave his children was one of abundant inherited wealth and nothing more—no work ethic, no stress on education, little religion.

MARY LEA: He felt religion was a challenge to him. He'd usually choose the worst Sunday of the year to go to church. He'd get us all dressed up in coonskin coats and boots and we'd march down the hill to Oldwick because no cars could make it down the hill just after a snow. He was brought up an Episcopalian, but we'd go to the Lutheran church down there and stay for the service and then trudge up the hill again. It was an all-morning thing and I think he liked the challenge of being up against the elements. That was about it for religion.

MARTY: He was able to cope with his children later on because they were peers, but to him the grandchildren were just a sign of being old and Seward hated to be old.

He didn't like the feeling of their representing another generation.

ELAINE: He wanted to just go on to the next life, like he did with each marriage.

NICHOLAS GOUVERNEUR RUTGERS: Slum kids were brought up with more love and attention than Bob and Seward Johnson's kids. It was the poor-little-rich-kid story in spades.

BETTY JOHNSON BUSHNELL: I can tell you why it happened the way it did. They were never a family. You have to understand—there was no family. Their father was no father, Seward was no father, my father-in-law, the General, was no father.

MARY LEA: Jennifer's my half-sister. She's just remarried to a Greenwich Village artist. Her first husband committed suicide, his name was Gregg—Peter Gregg, I think, I'm terrible on names. I think he realized he wasn't getting anywhere. He won Le Mans and several important races, but he was not . . . He blew his brains out. She was no longer married to him at the time.

Diana was having a tough time in her first marriage. I flew down to see her and I told her, "Look, Diana, this is terrible, you've got to do something about it." That gave her a chance to get out and talk to someone about the horses and the children and what she wanted out of life and to sort of regain a perspective on herself. She's very happy now with Bert Firestone, they have a terrific stable of horses. I don't think Elaine's ever had an affair. She's been married for thirty-six years.

MARTY: Even today Elaine can drive through the worst slum and only see beautiful things. She's made her childhood into something nonexistent—Mary Lea and Diana don't even know what she's talking about. Diana was the most vulnerable of all, she just didn't understand. She was such a little girl at the time of the divorce, it was all over for her before it began. Jimmy's attractive, and, I understand, a very talented artist. He's a sweet man but he has enormous problems.

SEWARD JR.: The thing is that Jimmy suffered so much that he's absurd.

DIANA: None of us saw a great deal of each other.

ELAINE: Every one of us have our own interests and I saw, over a period of years, that our interests and endeavors never brought us together, so I started a campaign to draw the Johnson family unit together. I saw this will contest as an opportunity to use to get us together, and I capitalized on this bad thing to make something good out of it.

MARY LEA: My brother Seward went through a bad time. I didn't know about it. I remember Dad saying, "Seward should pull himself together." In the last years of Dad's life, my brother got back in. He ran Harbor Branch. It's fair to say that without my brother's leadership we wouldn't have contested the will. And he had the most to lose.

SEWARD JR.: After that summer of '38 I guess the war broke out and we were going back and forth, living between our parents' houses. I went to school in Far Hills and I was miserable because I was only nine and they tried to make me board there, so I was crying all the time and finally they moved me to a school in New

Brunswick. Aunt Evangeline came to visit and found me hiding in the closet. I used to do that a lot.

My father took me on a trip, just me, out West. We flew in a light plane out to Salt Lake City. We took a train up to Sun Valley. It just opened up in '39. Sonja Henie, the ice-skating star, was there. I went around charging everything: dog sleds, reindeer sleds. The usual ride was a quarter of an hour. I'd take them out for hours. All these bills were piling up and my father tried to get rid of me for a while, he hired a student to go skiing with me. My father was sick there and I remember I got a box of Kleenex and put it in the mailbox for him. We got quite close on that trip, I think.

He was both soft and hard at the same time. He could be amazingly soft—there was something quite wonderful and philosophical about him. It was very complicated. I mean, just like he was driven with this sex thing, he was also, I don't know, I just experienced so many things where his tenderness, his sensibilities were so acute. Except he couldn't be depended on. When he was turned on, well, there are people who loved him, who worked for him, and related to him. Only a lot of people were very puzzled too. Sometimes we would spend the whole day on the boat, maybe say six words to each other, yet we communicated. I hated boats in the way he loved boats. I always got seasick, but we had some wonderful times.

I lived in that fixed-up chicken coop for a while and then I went to the Forman School. I was around twelve, I think. Again I cried for the first three months solid, through meals, through everything. All of a sudden my father turned up at the school. Apparently he'd been called by Mr. Forman. They had considered that I had gone into deep depression, and so my father left me money to go buy myself some new clothes—but I mean he came up there. I was living in my fantasy world completely, obviously as an escape mechanism. I remember I loved my room, it sort of was my retreat, and they moved me into another room and I went into hysterics. In my own room I had an old stuffed chair with a blanket over it. This other room, it seemed so sterile. It seems funny because I couldn't see what they saw. As far as I was concerned, they did a terrible thing. I sort of felt as though I was in a hospital room when they moved me to that other room.

When I was kicked out of the Forman School for coming back drunk when I was sixteen, my father called up Mary Lea and said, "Poor Seward, they've kicked him out of school, would you go up and make sure he gets home all right. I'm sure he's very upset and I want to make sure that he doesn't do anything silly." That showed his tenderness. But once he made up his mind— like he would say to me, "I finally had to get a divorce from your mother, she used to get so angry when I wanted to sleep with other women." He had a way of turning off, you know, that was it. It depended on whether he was turned on or off.

In 1951 I was due to be drafted and starting my third year in college, doing terribly at the University of Maine. I was taking poultry husbandry, it was the thing that required the least scholastic achievability. So I went into the Navy, was shipped out to Great Lakes Training Center, and had a really miserable time there. They shaved our heads, and I caught pneumonia.

When I was a child or teenager and I would be with him, he would never introduce me. I think that was partially honesty because he never remembered anyone's name, but I think also he was tremendously insecure. I think he was not sure of himself, he could too easily be insulted or wounded. He never was that deeply involved in Johnson & Johnson. He tried to make it look like he was involved, but he wasn't. He was never there. He had an office there, but he went there to sort of pay his bills and he had a secretary and an accountant there to do work that all the rest of us do at home. That was about it.

MARY LEA: Dad didn't want to come up against Uncle Bob. At the company they called Uncle Bob "Johnson Number 1." My father was "Johnson Number 2."

SEWARD JR.: He desperately didn't want me to go into Johnson & Johnson, and I think the reason was he knew how it was going to end up between my uncle Bob and me at some point or other, so when I got out of the Navy, he suggested that I go into farming. He bought me a farm in New Jersey with three hundred head of Jerseys on it and everything, and I spent a summer down there. I was so miserable, I couldn't stand it—farming wasn't for me. So he sold it, and I went into Johnson & Johnson.

"Yippee! We're rich . . ."

Johnson & Johnson, the pharmaceutical empire, encompasses 160 companies, marketing health-care products in 150 countries, with $6.4 billion annually in sales. This company is the source of the enormous unearned wealth of every one of the participants in the will contest. To understand the genesis of this battle, certain themes, evident in the history of Johnson & Johnson since its inception, become pertinent: the theme of one brother's domination, of sexism and secretiveness, of an image of purity and Christian piety concealing self-indulgent behavior. It is widely assumed, and repeated in various biographies, that the company was founded in 1886 by Robert Wood Johnson, the father of General Johnson and Seward Johnson. Yet, according to the family historian, Nicholas Gouverneur Rutgers, and documents he has supplied, the founders were in fact Robert's younger brothers, Edward Mead Johnson and James Wood Johnson. The Johnson brothers were three of the eleven children of Sylvester and Louisa Wood Johnson, farmers and cattle breeders in Crystal Lake, Pennsylvania. In 1874 Robert moved to East Orange, New Jersey, and with George Seabury founded the pharmaceutical partnership of Seabury and Johnson. Robert brought his two younger brothers to work for him, but in 1883 Edward Mead, then thirty, and James Wood, twenty-seven, left to found their own pharmaceutical company. It is James's handwriting of the company name that constitutes the Johnson & Johnson logo.

Two years later Robert, seeing how well his brothers were doing, sold his interest in Seabury and Johnson and invested the capital in his brothers' firm. Although Robert had signed a covenant that he would not enter the pharmaceutical business for a period of ten years, on September 23, 1886, he announced, "I now beg to state that I have joined the firm of Johnson & Johnson, who are engaged in the manufacturing of a full line of preparations similar to those sold by Seabury and Johnson. I trust that old friends and patrons will be good enough to carefully examine the products of the new house and if they are found satisfactory that they will give them a reasonable share of their favors. I think no one will deny that legitimate competition should be encouraged."

Johnson & Johnson began with fourteen workers on the fourth floor of a small New Brunswick, New Jersey, factory. Six weeks after it was incorporated in 1887, Robert, who controlled the company by virtue of the money he had invested in it, replaced his brother James as president. Robert, the more experienced elder brother, was a disciple of the principles of antisepsis of the noted English surgeon Joseph Lister, who had identified airborne germs as a source of infection and had called them "invisible assassins." In a time when the post-operative death rate in hospitals ran as high as 90 percent, when the cotton used in surgical dressings was made from sweepings from the floors of textile mills, the Johnson brothers began to utilize Lister's methods of sterilization on a large scale to produce "the most trusted name in surgical dressings." Using an India-rubber-based adhesive, the Johnsons manufactured prepackaged surgical dressings that were the forerunners of the Band-Aid. After a decade of serving under his brother's domination, Edward Mead, feeling himself in a subservient position, left the company, founded the Mead Johnson Company, and eventually moved to Evansville, Indiana.

In 1886 Robert purchased a house near the Johnson & Johnson factory and moved in with his two-year-old daughter, Roberta. While the Johnson family Bible indicates a marriage in May of 1880 to Etta G. Hayden, the *National Cyclopaedia of American Biography* states that Robert Wood Johnson married an Ellen Gifford, "daughter of William Cutler," in 1880 and both women are listed in these books as the mother of Roberta. Numerous family members state unequivocally that Robert never married his first so-called wife. On June 27, 1892, however, he married Evangeline Armstrong, the daughter of a prosperous physician from Holley, New York. Robert Wood Johnson, Jr., was born in 1893, (John) Seward Johnson in 1895, and Evangeline Armstrong Johnson in 1897.

Robert was said to pay almost no attention to his wife or children, but was devoted to business and every day, rain or shine, would walk to the factory so that the immigrant workers who might be afraid to approach him in his office could stop him along the way and tell him of their problems or of the birth of a new child. The Johnsons led a small-town, prosperous existence. James Wood Johnson bought a house on Union Street. Dr. Fred B. Kilmer, who served as the company's scientific director for forty-five years, also lived on Union Street. Chemist Earle Dickenson, who was instrumental in developing the Band-Aid, lived nearby. The Johnson brothers had brought a new era of manufacturing to New Brunswick and had created a company town.

Robert's wife, Evangeline, considered herself superior to those around her and refused to socialize with members of the community. She spent her days at home in the company of her frail young son Seward, who was dubbed "the little angel" because he was sick so much of his childhood that Evangeline insisted he would soon join the angels. Family summers were passed on the New Jersey shore and occasionally abroad, in Italy. Robert, who rarely left the factory, did not accompany his family. Seward's first sail-boat was a canoe with a sail attached; it was to inspire in him a lifelong love of sailing, an occupation that suited this isolated, introverted child.

In 1910 Robert died. During his lifetime he had built the business into a plant consisting of forty buildings. Evangeline Johnson moved her children to New York, where Seward was "kidnapped" and used sexually by his mother's friend. Then Evangeline went abroad, virtually abandoning her three children. Daughter Evangeline, thirteen, stayed in New York with a governess. Bob, seventeen, and Seward, fifteen, went to live with their uncle James, who had assumed the presidency of Johnson & Johnson. As soon as his father died, Bob dropped the "Junior" from his name and went to work as a millhand at Johnson & Johnson. He became a surrogate father to his younger brother, Seward. It was Bob who set up an operating room in James's house so that Seward could have his appendix removed under sterile conditions.

The relationship with Uncle James was most peculiar. He was president of the company, but he had living with him two teenage nephews who had inherited in equal shares 84 percent of the stock of Johnson & Johnson. Because of their father's strong sexist feelings, sister

Evangeline received only a small bequest of preferred stock, which her brother Bob was later to persuade her to sell. James often complained to his daughter Helen Rutgers of the untenable position of being president of a company that was controlled by his nephew Bob Johnson and the "kid brother." In the evenings the president of the company, James, and millhand Bob would hold business conferences.

Occasionally Bob and Seward would stay for extended periods of time with their elder half-sister, Roberta, who had married Robert Carter Nicholas, the treasurer of Johnson & Johnson. The Nicholases lived in a house that is now the Rutgers University president's house. Their son, Robert Carter Nicholas, Jr. (called Carter), was to become Seward's lifelong friend. A family member, and therefore an insider, he was Seward's trusted adviser and lawyer.

In 1932 James Wood died and Bob Johnson, then thirty-eight, assumed the presidency of the company. Bob Johnson, a man of great life force, was ready to seize power and cast the company in his own image. He became as obsessed with Johnson & Johnson as his father had been before him. A forward-thinking, almost visionary business-man, he was a pioneer for fair wages and better working conditions. He was also a munificent but quiet philanthro-pist, with a sense of community and social responsibility. Profits were plowed back into the company to build for the future. Johnson wrote a Credo, an ethical code by which the company functions even today. It mandates that John-son & Johnson's first obligation is to produce "the highest quality" product for the consumer; the employees come second, then management, the community, and at the end of the line the last obligation is to the stockholders. It was this firmly entrenched belief that was to keep the dividends on the stock low and, later, to create the odd circumstance of Bob Johnson's nieces and nephews having substantial trusts that for years yielded little income. The philosophy of the Credo is still taken seriously, as was evidenced in the handling of the two Tylenol scares in 1982 and 1986. Corporate executives behaved ethically rather than from a profit motive, and it was their behavior that enabled them to retain the confidence of the American public.

Bob Johnson established a close rapport with his personnel. In the early days of his tenure, a production superintendent whose department was being moved from an old plant to a new one found that his production equipment had been moved, but none of his office equipment. No one had told him if he would be retained or fired. The man became despondent and finally, after writing a letter bitterly attacking management, hanged himself. Johnson immediately decided that a personnel department must be set up to teach management to avoid such errors in the future. He encouraged courses in employee relations and executive development. He wrote, "We are not robots. Workers need recognition and appreciation. They need to be esteemed in terms of the human equation as well as the production chart."

Bob Johnson ran his company with tight, hands-on management. He would appear in the office of a clerk or a chemist, sit down, and ask him exactly how he performed his job and what he thought about it. Within days the employee might find his working conditions improved. On a visit to a J&J affiliate, Bob found the top executives practicing their putting on a green behind the plant. "Gentlemen," he said, "you are fired." When he noted that one of his products had hit a substandard level, he asked his secretary to summon all the executives involved with the product to his office. When seventeen men paraded in, Johnson immediately said, "All right, gentlemen, you may leave. I see now what the trouble is." Bob Johnson was feared and respected because he expected those about him to adhere to the highest standards. Frequently he was heard to say, "I want this taken care of or I want to see a pile of uniforms in the morning."

General Johnson's personal style was individualistic, idiosyncratic, secretive. He trusted no outsiders. In 1965 the Johnson & Johnson treasurer, Wayne Holman, told a national financial reporter, "We have a policy of not appearing before security analysts. We have no reason to appear. We run a manufacturing and sales operation and don't pay any attention to our stock. We don't really have any public relations. At Johnson & Johnson, why bother? First of all, the major portion of the stock of this company is still in the hands of the family, secondly the company has not borrowed any money since the early fifties, when they borrowed to retire some preferred stock. And the company has no long-term debt. The value of Johnson & Johnson stock has been well recognized in the market place, our stockholders are satisfied."

The major factor that enabled General Johnson to build this company singlehandedly was that he and his brother, Seward, controlled 84 percent of the stock. To maintain his autonomy, Bob Johnson needed his brother's cooperation—and he got it. Spaulding Dunbar, a friend of both men, says, "I think General Johnson used his brother, Seward, as a sounding board. He knew he had Seward's complete loyalty and he could be open with him and discuss things with him he would never discuss with other people. Seward was the one person he trusted totally." Seward Johnson himself stated, "I think the most important decision was one my brother and I made jointly—it was to develop confidence in each other. We felt the possibilities of this company were unlimited so long as we maintained this confidence in each other."

Seward Johnson was to prove a perfect second man. In 1917 he enlisted in the Navy with a second-class seaman's rating. He specialized in naval communications and was based at Bensonhurst, Brooklyn, as a signal-code instructor. He requested sea duty and at twenty-one became second-in-command aboard subchaser 255. The subchaser had three propellers, and when the middle one was damaged, Seward discovered that removing it altogether enabled the ship to travel faster. It became one of the fastest subchasers in the fleet, and he, a respected commander, earning himself a promotion to lieutenant. He was later to tell his friend Spaulding Dunbar that this period of his life was one of his proudest, one in which he felt his accomplishments were his own. It was these days about which he hallucinated as he lay dying in Fort Pierce, Florida, in the spring of 1983.

As Armistice Day neared, Seward was transferred to an eagle boat based at Perth Amboy, New Jersey, where once again he was second-in-command. When the war ended, he went into the purchasing and planning department of Johnson & Johnson. Although official company literature credits Seward with the birth of the production planning department, General Johnson wrote, "I first heard of production planning in the early days of industrial engineering when experts like Gilbreth, Gantt, Emerson, and Taylor were blueprinting new concepts of how to make big enterprises efficient. It was immensely appealing. I cabled my brother, who was then in Spain studying old wines and young señoritas, and suggested he come back to take charge of the new planning department. He cabled back, 'Sure. What the hell is that?' "

In 1923 Seward Johnson interrupted his courtship of

Ruth Dill to sail to Great Britain, France, Egypt, India, Australia, China, and Japan with his brother, Bob, and Carter Nicholas, in search of possible sites for overseas expansion. It was the first move toward the diversification that was to be General Johnson's most significant contribution to the company. An official history of Johnson & Johnson states, "International growth began in earnest in 1923 with an around-the-world trip by the two sons of Robert Wood Johnson. These young men returned from their world-wide tour with the conviction that the company must establish a strong international position. The following year, in 1924, Johnson & Johnson created its first overseas affiliate."

During World War II, Bob Johnson lent his brother the money to establish the Atlantic Diesel Corporation, a company with five hundred employees that made rotors, propellers, and other strategic parts for the war effort. Seward too was an advocate of good working conditions and was well liked by his employees, who at the conclusion of the war presented him with a Civil War bayonet inscribed, "We collectively have worked in a great many plants and ships; not one of us has ever worked for so considerate a boss or so generous an owner. Our working conditions have been the best that we have ever known."

In 1942 Bob Johnson joined the Army Ordinance Department and was commissioned a colonel. The next year he became a brigadier general and vice-chairman of the War Production Board, a job he performed for only a year before returning to Johnson & Johnson. From that time on he retained the title of General. In 1944, to facilitate further expansion of the company, General Johnson decided it was necessary to make a public stock offering.

NICHOLAS RUTGERS: The General was closer to my
mother than almost anyone in the world. She was his
first cousin, but he regarded her as a sister. He was my
God-father and at my christening he gave me a gold
spoon. It was my first and last present from him. He
totally rejected me when it came to the company. Once
Uncle Bob took over, he rewrote the history of Johnson
& Johnson so everyone would think that it was founded
solely by his own father. My grandfather James's portrait languished in a closet at Johnson & Johnson for
about twenty years until finally one day, on a whim, my
mother went to Uncle Bob's office and asked him where
the portrait was. She embarrassed him into hanging her
father's portrait. You don't see the histories praising
James Wood Johnson, although he was president of the
company for twenty-two years. Uncle Bob took the
company public in 1944, but you could never really
think of it as a public company.

Central to the will contest were the 1944 trusts that are
the basis of the children's present wealth. These trusts,
described by Basia Johnson's lawyers as an example of a
father's "royal munificence," were to set off a chain of
powerful and complex emotions and reactions.

At the time Johnson & Johnson became a public company, General Johnson persuaded Seward to set up trusts
for his children. Each trust consisted of 15,000 shares of
Johnson & Johnson stock, then valued at approximately
$500,000. The trustees were General Johnson and two as-
sociates who would rubber-stamp his decisions.

The 1944 trusts were patterned after the classic Rockefeller generation-skipping trusts, in which the principal
was to remain largely intact until the second generation.
However, because of the distrust of outsiders, these instru-

ments were drawn by the house counsel and trusted retainer Kenneth Perry, rather than by trusts and estates experts. The trusts reflected views deeply entrenched in the Johnson family. The daughters were to have no power; the sons were to inherit the power through the vote of the stock. In 1951, at twenty-one, Seward Jr. was to become a trustee of his sisters' trusts and his own. In 1963, at thirty-three, he was to assume the voting power of the trusts. But the inexpert Kenneth Perry drafted into these instruments certain fundamental errors, not anticipating the enormous growth of Johnson & Johnson stock or the concomitant skyrocketing value that would accrue to the Johnson children's trusts. Eventually there would be no way around the fact that the trusts, ranging in value up to $110 million each, would provide the trustees with extensive powers and the beneficiaries with no access to the principal.

The principal of the trusts could not be invaded without trustee approval. The children's only right was to assign direct payment of the principal, upon their death, to their spouse or children. At the Johnson will contest, perhaps the most frequently asked question was, "Why would the children who have so much money be fighting for more?" One answer is that some of them do not feel the vast wealth in their trusts is their own. Both emotionally and in actuality they are correct.

JAMES PITNEY AFFIDAVIT ON THE 1944 TRUSTS: The stock of Johnson & Johnson was first offered for public sale in July 1944, during the height of World War II.

Undoubtedly, one of the thoughts paramount in the minds of the brothers in deciding to make a public stock offering was how to maintain family control of the company for as long a period as possible. The brothers had previously owned all of the common stock. The stock was to be issued at $35 per share and the number of shares held by each brother was worth at that price approximately $7 million. The effect of the eventual impact of death taxes upon such a large holding of a vigorously growing company was certainly a major factor to be considered under the heading of how to maintain family control.

At the time he executed these six trusts, J. Seward Johnson was 49 years of age and living with his second wife at his farm residence in Oldwick, N.J. He had a total of five children with a sixth about to be born. . . . From the point of view of the grantor at the time he transferred approximately 45 percent of his common stock ownership to these six trusts, it will be seen that they would provide a means:

—To retain the voting rights over this large block of stock in company-oriented trustees until each of the grantor's sons would control the voting right.

—To enable each of his sons eventually to hold a source of power and responsibility in the company, and to be on equal terms of power with their cousin, R. W. Johnson, Jr.

—To enable the company-oriented trustees to have complete and unhampered control of the distribution and administration of the trust property.

MARTY: None of the women were given the vote, it was the male member of the family that could vote the stock. It was typical of Seward and typical of General Johnson.

ELAINE: When Dad set these trusts up, his motivation was to take care of his obligations morally and legally to his children and his wife. And it turns out that legal jargon that was used in the formation of these trusts has not been good in many ways, but in some instances it has

stopped some of the other children from spending what
maybe they shouldn't. They're very, very strict trusts,
not to be touched at all—I mean that's the way they
were made up originally. I don't think Dad's motivation
was that, I think he just wanted to move on. But he had
a good lawyer. They were—I mean, they're beautiful.

SEWARD JR.: These trusts were very poor instruments. I
think it was my uncle who talked my father into it because it gave him control of the company. My uncle not
only had his stock, but then he was voting trustee of part
of my father's stock too. That whole thing harkened
back to their father. It was an old-fashioned and chau-
vinistic family tradition and that's why Mary Lea resented it terribly and I don't blame her.

MARY LEA: I was about fifteen and my sister Elaine fourteen when one day Kenneth Perry, the Johnson & Johnson lawyer, said he wanted to see us. We got all dressed
up like it was Sunday, in straw hats and little wristlet
gloves and knee socks and our Mary Janes, and we went
down to the factory. We always loved going to the factory because when we drove into the yard, people would
doff their caps or bow and suddenly you felt like you
were someone special. We went into Ken's office and he
sat us down in these big leather chairs and said, "Well,
girls, I think it's about time you knew some plans your
father has. We've set up some trusts that by the time you
need them will probably buy you a great deal." We sort
of glanced at each other out of the corner of our eyes.
Then he brought out checkbooks and put one on each of
our laps and said, "I think it's about time you started to
learn something about finance, so we've set up an account for you at the People's Bank in New Brunswick.
Each month you'll have $100 and from that money

you'll learn to be able to cope with larger sums when they become available to you." Again we took a quick glance at each other. I thought, "Oh, larger sums, that's nice." Considering our allowance at the time was something like fifteen cents a week, the idea of $100 was mind-boggling.

As soon as he left the room, Elaine and I jumped up and practically threw our checkbooks up to the ceiling and danced around in a circle, shouting, "Yippee! We're rich, we're rich, we're rich, we're rich!"

They kept changing the trusts after that and three years later we got our J&J trusts. This is a real Horatio Alger story, it started out with a quarter of a million dollars in each trust and it's grown tremendously. My trust, I would say, is worth in the realm of $60 million. Every time we went for an accounting, we had the same judge and he couldn't believe what was happening to the Johnson & Johnson stock. Of course, for years the trustees only gave us the same $6,000 a year.

The trustees at that time were just acting for Uncle Bob, the other two were Frank Cosgrove and Kenneth Perry. Over the years Ken Perry would keep in touch with us and he'd ask, "Is there anything I can do for you?" but he never told us that we could have more than the $6,000 if there was an emergency. They were trying to let the corpus accumulate, but we never knew that if we needed something, there would be money to pay for it. I always thought Ken Perry was a good friend of ours, but now I don't believe it anymore. I'm sorry to have come to that conclusion, because he was a nice, comfortable man.

Those trusts weren't set up for love and caring, they were done because Uncle Bob wanted to control the vote on ninety thousand shares of stock without experiencing the tax consequences of ownership. Those trusts were never supposed to take care of us, we were supposed to be taken care of in other ways. I might sue my trustees. Every time I ask them for something, they throw it up in my face that they have to protect the remainderment for my heirs. I wrote them a letter and quoted the trust agreement; it said that this money was being put away for *my* welfare, *my* good, not for someone to get after I die.

"She was looking for an identity, but they took her."

Mary Lea's troubled childhood adumbrated the life that was to follow. At eighteen she went to work in the public-relations department of Johnson & Johnson. She collaborated with her uncle Bob, General Johnson, on a book called *Workers Speak Out;* her job was to get the workers' opinions on work practices. But Mary Lea says she knew Johnson & Johnson had no place for a woman on the executive level. Women were not even allowed in the executive dining room, and when she and her aunt Evangeline had lunch, they were served on trays in her father's office.

MARY LEA: I used my $6,000 a year to put myself through the American Academy of Dramatic Arts. I lived in this tiny walk-up on Ninth Avenue. There was a tub in the kitchen with a board over it. I was in a lot of little things, *Sweeney Todd,* the original one, and *Salome,* and I toured with Tallulah Bankhead in *Private Lives.* I played her maid—I played a lot of maids. When I first met Bill Ryan, I had gone over to Perth Amboy with a group of union stewards from the factory to try out for a

comic role in the theater there. He handled the publicity
for the theater and that was my introduction to him. Bill
was deeply religious, an arch-conservative who believed
in discipline. At first he reminded me a lot of the way
Bill Buckley is today, his command of the English language, but—I don't know how to explain it—it seems to
me he never grew. Dad didn't want me to marry a Catholic, he said I'd never be accepted back in.

In 1951, a year after we married, I received $20,000.
We bought a farm on fourteen acres and we paid $20,000
for it. We sold vegetables by the side of the road, we had
a farm with two cows, about two hundred chickens, four
pigs, and a lot of apple trees. My first piece of furniture
besides the bed was a candling machine. I'd go out and
gather eggs at 5:30 in the morning and run them
through the candling machine before packing them.
Then Bill decided broilers would be more lucrative. We
had about four thousand broilers, but then they con-
demned our land for a reservoir, so we moved to Flem-
ington and raised sheep. They were always jumping out
of the fences.

I found I was pregnant most of the time—six kids,
eight pregnancies in eight years. In 1951 Eric was born
and I decided I needed some help with the house, so I
imported this woman from the South. She'd had to leave
because she'd had a knife fight with her husband and
was on the lam. Gosh, she loved to watch boxing
matches and wrestling matches on television. And she'd
take Eric as a baby and put him upside down across her
knees and she'd have a great time sitting in front of the
television. That was great, because it freed me for doing
other things.

I had very bad back problems and I was in the hospital a lot. I had a spinal fusion and once they had to

administer the last rites. In the hospital I found that Demerol was the best thing as far as stopping pain was concerned. But when you start waiting for the next shot, you know that something has happened in your system where it's a little dangerous. Then you have to control yourself and slow it down.

Bill started a paper in Maryland. A Ku Klux Klan-type organization threatened us and we closed the paper and went back to New Jersey, which I thought was a great mistake. Bill became more and more of a recluse. As I said in my divorce papers, in the later years of our marriage he'd have periods of depression and withdrawal so severe that more than half his time was spent in his own self-imposed exile.

ERIC: I'm thirty-five now, I'm a lawyer, and I'm developing real estate in New Jersey. Because of my training and being the eldest, I'm a kind of spokesperson for my generation and I work with my mother's 1944 trust in that I often can see both points of view and try to prevent misunderstandings by encouraging the free flow of information.

During a period of four or five years starting in 1957 or thereabouts my mother had a series of operations on a slipped disk in her back, and because of that my dad kind of assumed both roles in the family, both a motherly role and a fatherly role. When my mother emerged from the hospital and regained her health, there was no place for her in the family, kind of. I felt my dad would sort of treat her in a demeaning way at times, as if she were one of the children, as if she didn't have good judgment in her own right. My mother was in a very hard position. She had ideas that she could have a lot more freedom, that she could accomplish a lot more than she had been permitted to do. When Mom would say, "Bill, I really want to do something with my life beyond being pregnant," my father's response was that she should buy a partnership interest in a local gift shop, that having an occasional Bloody Mary with the girls would satisfy her need for self-expression. She wanted desperately to become a full person. There was a Christmas party in 1970 and my mom missed a step. She didn't fall, but she missed a step and sort of stumbled. My father doesn't drink at all, he said she was too intoxicated to be entertaining her guests. My dad's got total tunnel vision about right and wrong.

MARTY: After seven pregnancies she decided to have a coil.

ERIC: A diaphragm, I think it was. What horrified him as much as the use of the diaphragm itself was that she got it at a local drugstore. He said, "How am I supposed to walk into Trader's Pharmacy now that they know that they've dispensed this diaphragm to you?" My father's acceptance of the church's position on birth control resulted in a severe strain on their relationship.

MARY LEA: He said that about Trader's, and after that I didn't use birth control and I had another pregnancy.

ERIC: The child died in childbirth.

MARTY: The child was deformed. They showed her that dead child, and she cries and screams in the night about it to this day.

MARY LEA: He called me a "disciple of the devil" for buying the diaphragm and I feel blamed me for what happened. He never went near me sexually again.

ERIC: Mom was surrounded by a series of very autocratic men.

MARTY: It's been a very painful existence. Mary Lea wanted to convert to Judaism for me. I said, "You've been one of everything. Forget it already. Don't convert for me because I don't know what the whole thing's all about." She's a very God-loving person and she wants to find God wherever it be. She's desperately searching for God and she wants to accept anyone who will lead her to God. She's very fragile and childlike and she's been so bruised and hurt that if you say something to her, she thinks it's a condemnation. She doesn't realize you can make mistakes and you won't get punished for them.

MARY LEA: When some of the boys first started on drugs, all four boys were in the Canterbury School in New Milford, Connecticut, and it was during the sixties. It wasn't just drugs, it was a whole atmosphere. I'd get a call from the headmaster saying, "We can't find your son Eric anywhere," and finally he'd end up in Washington marching. Then the boys decided to grow pot in the woods. Not that they used it very much, but they had friends that were over at the Kent School and they would sell it back and forth. When Bill found out about this, he went up to his room and said to me, "I want to die. I don't want to see the children. It's all your fault."

In January of 1971 I dreamt such a vivid dream that it scared the hell out of me. I dreamt I killed my husband with a pair of scissors. I stabbed him and stabbed him, there was blood all over me. I crawled out onto the roof of our house, we had peacocks on our place in Maryland, and I sat on top of a peacock's back and he flew with me down the Chesapeake. I could see the blood spreading out on the Chesapeake all around me.

Then I knew I had to go. The next morning I told Bill I was leaving.

After I'd left, I went up and stayed with my doctor, Dr. Hurley, in New York, and I was there in the spring of 1971 when I got this phone call that my sons Seward and Hillary had been in a car accident and there was doubt that they'd live. When I got to Johns Hopkins hospital, Hillary's back was broken and Seward was in a coma in another hospital in eastern Maryland. I bumped into Bill in the hall and he started shouting at me at the top of his voice, "Do you see what you've done to these boys? Chloroform conscience! You have a chloroform conscience!"

By 1971 Mary Lea's trust had swelled to approximately $65 million, but her home life was a shambles. Her son Seward Ryan became a patient of Dr. Victor D'Arc, a psychiatrist then on the staff of St. Luke's Hospital, and Mary Lea began to rely on him. In their divorce proceedings, William Ryan denied Mary Lea's characterization of him and counterclaimed that there had been no trouble in their marriage until "one Dr. V. D'Arc appeared on the scene." On July 15, 1972, two days after her divorce from Ryan, Mary Lea married Victor D'Arc. In the summer of 1971 Eric Ryan had been arrested, but subsequently all charges were summarily dismissed. In the fall of 1972 her sons Seward and Roderick also were arrested on drug-possession charges. In his divorce petition filed September 24, 1976, Dr. D'Arc alleged that after this arrest "Seward had devised a plan to blow up the Far Hills police station in an effort to obtain the evidence the police had seized. . . ." D'Arc stated that subsequently Seward Ryan was hospitalized. He also alleged that in 1973 Roderick "became so negativistic" that he administered "a large dose of heroin" to their dog. Also, that in 1974 Quentin Ryan "was apprehended selling LSD to several students" at the Lawrenceville School in New Jersey and subsequently he was institutionalized at the adolescent division of the Pennsylvania Hospital for an eight-month period.

ERIC: Mom left Dad. The family split up, half went north and half stayed down in Maryland. My brother Seward was seeing Victor D'Arc. Seward had a very bad drug problem, a dangerous drug problem. The others were at an age where they were beginning to run wild a bit, to drink too much beer, probably to smoke too much pot.

MARTY: You have to understand Mary Lea was trying to find herself and she was very vulnerable. Then she met Victor and he started to send her flowers and have friends invite her to cocktail parties, and with her going to bed with a man for the first time in so many years. . . . She's told me he was very amorous and very much a male in bed with her for all the time prior to their marriage. He knew exactly—

ERIC: What buttons to push. What kind of ethics is it for a doctor to take a patient and derive from that patient information about the family background, about the discontent in my mother and father's marriage and how my mother was kind of chafing under the restrictions that had taken place in her marriage? My brother Seward conveyed to Victor all sorts of private information and Victor managed to manipulate the situation to seduce my mother, and I don't mean in a purely sexual sense.

MARY LEA: For the first three or four months I thought, "Gee, this is something terrific. I've never seen anything like it before." I know now that he's one of those people that basically likes men better than women, but he could perform with a woman sexually for a while until the novelty wore off.

MARTY: She'd just left her first husband and then she became involved with this other wack.

ERIC: When the drug problems were developing with Seward in particular, my mother and father had been estranged. My mother wanted us all to go back down to Maryland to have Thanksgiving with my dad. It was largely so that my dad would come to understand that my mother hadn't created the problem, that we were his children as well as her children. Mom asked us if we would go down *en masse* to Dad's house. It was a really sad thing. We were driving down the driveway and I look in the back seat and Seward is passing out Valium to various of my brothers to prepare them for dealing with our father. And I said, "Where did you get those?" and he said, "Victor gave them to me."

VICTOR D'ARC: Her own father didn't do any more for her than she did for her kids, and it's one of those old situations that you read about or hear about in psychiatry all the time. Parents treat their children essentially the same way they've been treated, unless they acquire some insight and understanding into themselves and don't want to repeat that process.

ERIC: There was a small house on the estate we owned in New Jersey. Mom lived in her apartment in New York and would sometimes come out to the country for weekends. Seward, Rod, and eventually Hillary enrolled back in the local high school. All of us were pretty much undisciplined and unchaperoned during a large part of this period. We lived on a narrow dirt road and there was a lot of nighttime activity at the house. It became sort of a crash pad at times.

I remember one local kid in particular had an argument with his mother and she had her groom hold him while she horsewhipped him with a riding crop and then threw him out of the house. Mom said he could stay in our basement. We ended up with a lot of lost souls living at the house from time to time.

About this time I heard rumors that my dad was involved in a custody fight for Alice and Quentin. I think his feeling was that my mother's influence or lack of discipline was such that we were hopeless. He definitely felt that she was both drinking excessively and that Victor was a Svengali kind of character. My dad, in a very general way, asked the police to keep an eye on things.

My mother hired a friend of mine to work on the grounds and she planted some marijuana in the greenhouse and that led to the police arresting her. I mean, if you could have seen the size of the plants and stuff, you would really think it was silly. I got a call to drive down to the police station to pick her up. But it was a ruse. The chief of police asked me to roll up my sleeves, looked at my fingers, took my photograph. There was no probable cause for the arrest, and when the charges against me were dismissed, the judge admonished the police for arresting me with nothing to link me to the contraband. After that, they'd swear out search warrants for practically everybody in the house. Rod was arrested for possession of marijuana and I believe he had a bottle of pills, ten or twelve Quaaludes. After my brother was arrested on a drug charge, in fantasizing, my brothers Seward and Roderick said, "You know, if we could just get the evidence, there wouldn't be a

case." That's as far as it went. Later, in his divorce action, Victor inflated it into a plot to blow up the police
station, but it was conversation—on that level only.
There was no bomb ever made.

During my ex-stepfather Victor's divorce from my
mother, he was trying to establish we were all out of
control, that my mother was incapable of running her
affairs and that she was hallucinating the whole thing
about him being behind a murder plot. Victor said that
the dog had been shot up with heroin. That never happened. The dog was fed something, I think it was PCP.
There was no injection involved, something was put in
the dog's food.

It was a bad time for me and my brothers. There was
a period where we basically got involved in the horrors
of the late sixties and early seventies, but today they've
all put these problems behind them and they're all leading productive lives. I think that's important.

VICTOR: When we married in the summer of 1972, she had
almost $5 million free of the trust. Interestingly, her
husband, Bill Ryan, had apparently, out of her income,
built up that amount of money. The money went. I remember when we bought a house in Far Hills [Mer-
riewold West] we paid $600,000 for it and she paid for it
in cash. And the remodeling of the house was about
$700,000. And in the course of the years that we were
together, I guess over $1 million was spent on art and
antiques for the house. Then we went into the art business. One show we had, the first big show, I think cost
well over $100,000. In the last year of our marriage the
$5 million was gone and we were borrowing money. As
a matter of fact, I remember that we owed almost $1
million to the Fiduciary Trust Company.

ERIC: There were two gallery phases. Initially, she started in New Jersey, using the Far Hills place as an outdoor sculpture studio. Later she had the M. L. D'Arc Gallery on 57th Street and Fifth Avenue. She had some interesting artists, Les Levine, Dennis Oppenheim, George Segal, but most of them just took terrible advantage of her. The works of art were not accessible to the general public. There were performance pieces—tape recordings and light shows. I recall distinctly there were press receptions, and art critics would ask Mom questions and essentially she was way out of her depth and she would make nice noises—you know, she would struggle to say something without saying anything.

MARTY: But she does know about art, she's not a novice or an ignoramus about art. She knows more about plants and botany and other things and she's an astonishingly bright woman. The only thing is that she sometimes struggles with things because she's uncomfortable talking to people, but she's never pretentious; she'd never try to impress you if she didn't know something, she'd simply say, "I don't know it."

ERIC: Here she was managing a gallery that was in the forefront of minimalism, and the artists' worth was largely determined by how much nerve they had in terms of how they would price their work. People would pump her up with "You're a wonderful patron" and all that, they would praise her and set her up and then fail to deliver on the art they'd contracted for. One guy got in a situation where the gallery guaranteed to buy $15,000 worth a year of his stuff, and he did this performance piece. I was going through some old *Artforums* and I saw that he'd done the same thing a year and a half before. He'd recycled parts of a show he'd done on the West Coast, and I said, "Those God-damned rats are famous and he's foisted them off as new work, you know, he's really just collecting on his contract." She was just a patron, right? It was more the great sugar teat in a way.

MARTY: She was looking for an identity, but they took her.

ERIC: The kind of stuff they would do would be like two guys standing behind a lectern debating, and inside the lectern was a video camera that revealed that there was a woman on her knees giving one of the speakers fellatio. The audience could see on the monitor one guy getting a blow job. The point of the piece was to figure out which of the two debaters was the one involved.

MARTY: It's hard to take that seriously.

"Victor ordered up my death as if he were ordering a grocery list."

Under the pretext of hiring a chauffeur, in December of 1973, seventeen months after Victor and Mary Lea's marriage, D'Arc brought a twenty-nine-year-old ex-Marine, John Fino, to the Far Hills, New Jersey, estate. Shortly thereafter, according to Mary Lea, Victor suggested that she have sexual relations with John and also perform sexually with both John and himself. Major problems arose when John Fino became attached to Mary Lea. She says that Victor began to use her to attract other men whom he himself desired, and insisted that she have sexual relations with them while he watched. Mary Lea could not extricate herself from this relationship, she was incapable of saying no.

Even as one pursues this story, the parts played by Mary Lea's husband Dr. Victor D'Arc, their mutual lover, John Fino, her son Eric, her husband-to-be, Marty Richards, and a shadowy hit man named Frank grow increasingly elusive.

MARY LEA: Shortly after we were married, Victor told me that he was having a patient of his stay in his apartment when he was out in the country because he wanted to help this patient who was a very disturbed young man. Then he brought John Fino out to the country and John's ego trip was certainly fulfilled there because he had a Jaguar to drive and he thought this was super, and Victor had him do some work around the place and in the meantime he ate in the dining room with us. I would say it was well into our marriage before I realized what was going on. I mean, I hadn't seen this before.

You know, I had hired this cook and butler and I went out in the kitchen and nobody had any shoes on— not that that bothered me, but then I looked at Mary's feet and I said, "Victor, come out in the kitchen and just pretend you're getting something and look at Mary's feet. Because, Victor, I wouldn't be surprised if Mary had another name." I mean, there was hair growing out of his toes. Of course, you don't look at a person's toes when you hire them. I discovered that one was dressed in drag and the other was butchy, and they hired out as a couple.

ERIC: Johnny Fino certainly didn't look gay, he didn't look like a cruising gay kind of guy. He was sort of macho-looking, very tall, raw-boned, large features. I don't understand how he ever thought he'd make it as an actor. He was, I would say, more like a kind of YMCA guy—you know, those kind of guys who hang around gyms.

MARY LEA: When I discovered that John was living with Victor, I got so depressed that I painted this long wall and I took thirty Seconals and a whole bunch of aspirin and a whole bunch of—oh, let me see what else—about, you know, a dozen Demerols, and I pinned a note on me and got into bed. I just thought it was enough to kill an elephant, but nothing happened. I think I threw up. And then Victor came home, and when he found me, he said, "That was a very hostile act toward me."

MARTY: Victor was jealous of her because the lover was trying to prove to Victor that he was straight. Fino was having his own fight with his own thing. And I mean I wasn't there so I don't know, but I can imagine it was awfully ugly.

MARY LEA: John would get up and lock the door and not let Victor in. John feels that if Marty hadn't come up that I probably would have married him.

JOHN FINO: Mary Lea . . . she's a nice lady, you know. Like we were friends. And what I did, like I, you know, I did for her, I didn't do it for money.

We were pretty close, you know. It was a period of time when I could have said, "Oh, Mary Lea, I love you, let's go." We would have went, believe me. But that wasn't my shtick, you know, and I feel it would have been wrong for both of us. Money, you know, I wouldn't marry for money. I don't know if you would believe that or not. Then Marty came along.

Martin Richards was a casting director when he met the rugged John Fino, who wanted to become an actor. Richards referred him to the Herbert Berghof school of drama and was instrumental in casting Fino in bit parts. Richards' close friend, the acting coach Mervyn Nelson, remembers the first time he met Fino: "There was an instability in him, an anger barely masked. I told Marty, 'Get rid of him. He's dangerous.'" Subsequently Fino told Richards that he knew this "Doc" who might underwrite a project, and he took him to meet Victor and Mary Lea. (It

was Mary Lea's money that financed the development of
the film *Fort Apache, the Bronx.*) Richards and his partner
Gil Champion began several projects with the D'Arcs.

MARTY: My background? I was born and raised in the
Bronx to first-generation American parents. I went to
Music and Art and Taft High School and then New
York University. I did my first Broadway show when I
was eleven, it was called *Mexican Hayride,* with Bobby
Clark and June Havoc. I played a Spanish newsboy. I
was a nightclub performer and I recorded for Columbia
and I recorded for RCA Victor and I went on the God-
frey show and I did the Ed Sullivan show and I played
at the Sands and I played at the Copa and I played the
Living Room and the Bon Soir. Then I woke up one
morning, I was working at the Thunderbird Hotel in
Las Vegas, and I found myself singing Vic Damone
when Elvis Presley was in, and I just realized, "This is
ridiculous," and I was offered a job at Fox as a casting
director and I took it.

I had seen Mary Lea twice, once very chicly dressed
with her lawyer and after that at a party at her Far Hills
estate. I remember an orchestra was playing and there
she was greeting everyone in an evening gown and she
looked stunning. I said, "My God, I don't believe the
way they live in this place, in Far Hills. This is a fantasy." The third time I saw her, she ran into my office.
She had a bandana over her head and no makeup on,
and she was crying. I'd brought an actor from California
to the party and at first I couldn't understand what
Mary Lea was talking about. She said, "I'm so ashamed.
I don't know you well and you don't know me well, but
you've got to help me. You've got to keep this man
away, because Victor wants me to try to get him into

bed with me to get him involved because Victor has this tremendous desire for him." She kept begging me to get the actor to go back to California, because she didn't want to do that. When I understood, I told her that the actor was straight and that he was going back to California that day. "You don't have anything to worry about," I said. That was the first of our getting to know each other. I took her out to dinner for the first time that night, I just wanted to pet her and take care of her.

MARY LEA: We produced *Rockabye Hamlet*. It wasn't a success, but at the first preview the audience just went wild. We were having dinner afterwards at Sardi's, Victor, Marty, and I. Victor was sure it would be a smash and he kept telling me that he wanted my share of the show. He wanted to take everything away from me. I began to get angry at him.

MARTY: She was so upset, she got hysterical at that; she said, "He wants all my points." So I said, "So, you don't have to give them to him. Anyone can ask." Then she turned to me and said, "I'm not going home. I have no place to go, can I stay at your apartment?" And I said, "Certainly."

In my bedroom I had two queen-size beds and there were sort of Spanish screens and it looked as if you were lying in a confessional. It was a bachelor's apartment, dark brown and beige and a lot of heavy wood like the Spanish Inquisition. And I told Mary Lea, "I'll go into the bathroom while you're getting undressed and when you're ready you get into bed and you stay in that bed and I'll stay over there." I was thinking, "Here's this married lady and we were all going to work together."

When Mary Lea and I first started going together, I didn't know we were going together. I really didn't know what it was. Before I knew it, Mary Lea was staying there and absolutely nothing happened for about a week. And then one morning she started crying and I said, "Why are you crying?" and she said, "It's so dark and depressing in this apartment, I want to go someplace that has light."

MARY LEA: He lived in a mole hole.

MARTY: And I started to love this lady.

JOHN FINO: Well, when we started out on *Fort Apache,* I was hoping to get, like, the part that Ken Wahl played. It wasn't such a hot acting job, it's not a Shakespearean part, but I could have done all right. I'd have acted with Paul Newman. I was really bent out at the idea of making a film—you know, to be a star, it's every boy from the Bronx's dream.

But what hurt me was that Marty didn't include me in any of the, you know, the pre-production things. They'd always go behind my back. I started to get into arguments, telling him, "Come on, Marty, what are you doing, man? You're making all this money," you know. Then one thing led to another and I guess Mary Lea and Marty were in love. I just felt like he should have made the movie instead of falling in love. He took off with Mary Lea and then there was the scene with the doctor, and bingo, everything got screwed up.

MARTY: Victor came to Mary Lea and he said he was in love with John Fino and he wanted a separation, and he thought that Mary Lea would say, "No, no, no, I can't live without you," and instead of that she said, "When do you want it?"

About four months before all this happened, John was angry at my partner Gil and me. So John brought up a guy to Victor's apartment and said, "I'm going to have this guy break both their arms and legs because they've taken advantage of me, not having done *Fort Apache* yet. It's not done and they're fooling around with it and I think they could use a beating, the two of them." Victor said to John, "Are you crazy? No violence, no, I don't want Marty and Gil beaten up, I don't want anything like that; that's silly stuff with your dramatics and all the rest of it."

After Mary Lea's separation from Victor, he said to John Fino, "Remember the guy you sent up to beat up Marty and Gil? I would like to have them worked over a little bit now." The guy came up, and John Fino went to the bathroom, and when he came back to the living room, Victor was sitting with this guy and said to him, "It's not Marty and Gil I want beaten up; I want my wife killed and there's $50,000 in it for you and I'll give you $10,000 up front." John said, "No, no, you can't do this." But Victor said, "John, you've got to finger Mary Lea and Marty," because she was living at my apartment at the time. John started shaking, and then the guy, the hit man, turned and, according to John, said to him, "I would throw acid in my mother's face for $50,000."

JOHN FINO: I told them, I said, "Look, this lady, you know, was so nice to us, she's trying to help me make a movie, we ate at her table, I can't go for this. I'm sorry, it's not that way."

MARTY: John ran home and told his father, Ted Fino, about it. And his father, in order to get him off the hook and to get Victor onto the hook, called up Victor and said, "What are you allowing, are you allowing my son to get you some punk off the streets, some kid hit man that's going to get you all into jail for the rest of your lives? This is business. Let me get you a professional guy." And that's how they started planning it. And every time they planned it, John Fino's father taped the conversation.

John kept calling and calling and saying, "You've got to put Mary Lea on the phone with me." Mary Lea didn't want to talk to him. She didn't want to speak to him because he was a part of her life with Victor. Finally he said, "Well, she'd better talk to me because I've got something so important to tell her that she's got to know what's happening. I don't want to be anywhere where there are police or lawyers or any of those things because it's about your lives. It's a matter of both your lives, of life or death." So that's when we hired Tony Maffatone as a bodyguard. Already at that time we were very frightened about our lives.

John Fino came up to the office with his father, and they walked in and Mary Lea sat down in a chair and I sat down in a chair and they told us that Victor D'Arc was going to have us killed. Then they played tapes, it was four individual phone conversations between Victor and John's father that lasted a total of about forty minutes, all planning and plotting Mary Lea's death and mine if I happened to be in the same house. Victor said, "You can take care of him, but I only want to pay for one of them, I don't want to pay for both of them and it's her I want out of the way. After she's out of the way and the estate is settled, I will then take care of him."

MARY LEA: Victor ordered up my death as if he were ordering a grocery list. It was just so cold and calculating it was amazing.

JOHN FINO: I wouldn't lie to her. I told her, "Mary Lea, you're in danger, go home to your father, get away from the doctor, get away from New York, get away from Marty, go home to people who are financially as stable as you are, who are with you because they're your family, not because you have money."

MARTY: Mary Lea fainted in the middle of the room and I didn't know what to do, so I called up my own father and I said, "Dad, you've got to come down here right now," and my father got into the car and he came down and heard the whole thing. He said, "All right, how much money do you want for the tapes? They'll give you $50,000." And John said, "No, we just wanted you to hear the tapes and we can talk about them another time."

Now I think what happened was that when John and his father found out how much money Mary Lea would pay for the tapes, when my dad offered them the $50,000, I think that they were trying to use it as extortion against Victor, but then Victor made a turnaround, according to John Fino, and threatened John and his father's life and said, "I will kill the two of you because now I have nothing to lose any longer."

JOHN FINO: I guess Marty was kind of scared too. He said, "Well, now that he's not going to kill her, he might try to kill *me*." I couldn't see it at that time. All I kept thinking was about the movie, the movie, the movie.

MARTY: Till we heard the tapes, Mary Lea knew nothing about the plot. They had left very friendly, she had hugged Victor and he had kissed her on the cheek and said, "Let's be friends and just have a separation." All the time he was planning to kill her for $30 million in the will. He would've inherited that.

MARY LEA: More like $20 million, I'd say.

MARTY: $20 million. So he hugged her and kissed her and he plotted and planned her murder. It had nothing to do with anger, it had to do with greed.

MARY LEA: John's father talked to Victor on the phone and said, "I think I can arrange somebody. Now, exactly what would you have in mind?" And he taped it. And Victor said he wanted me eliminated and he thought the best time possibly to do it was when I was going to be in Italy for an art show. Well, when I got to Naples, I suddenly got the desire, I don't know why, I got this very itchy and ominous feeling that I wanted to get out of there. So I said, "Look, I've just got to go, I'm going back to London." I left my then partner at the time, Anna Canepa, in charge of the exhibit and got on an airplane and left. It was during that week that supposedly it had been set up for me to be hit. They were going to hire someone to make it look like a purse-snatching in the ladies' room. They would use a knife and take my purse. So I was very fortunate to have left. You never know whether they would have done this or whether they were just pulling Victor's leg as far as setting the whole thing up and then blackmailing both of us, more or less.

VICTOR: Those tapes were conversations that I had had with old man Fino which were subsequently doctored by Marty Richards and whomever else worked that whole thing with him.

MARTY: Mary Lea and I were hiding out in my New York
apartment and we'd hired Tony Maffatone. On a Tuesday at five o'clock in the morning Tony was sleeping at
the doorway of the kitchen. He thought he heard me at
the refrigerator and he called out, "Marty, Marty?"
When I didn't answer, he went into the kitchen and
there was a guy standing there. As Tony went for him,
someone came up behind him and slugged him over the
head with a crowbar. Tony didn't go out, he began to
fight with them and yelled for us to lock ourselves in the
bedroom.

Mary Lea said to me, "We can't stay here, we've got
to help Tony." There were the most terrible noises going
on. I had this gun, but it was in a leather holster and I
was so excited I couldn't pull it out of the holster, so I
asked Mary Lea, "You think I can shoot it through the
holster?" Mary Lea calmly reached over and grabbed
the gun and pulled it out and ran out of the bedroom. I
came right behind her, carrying a coat hanger. By that
time Tony had chased them down nineteen flights of
stairs. There was blood everywhere. The next day the
police found these two garrotes, piano wire with black
leather and black adhesive tape where you hold on to
whatever it is you hold on to. The police said it was
probably not a robbery but an attempt on our lives. Two
days later I got a call from John Fino. He said, "I understand you've had some problems at the house." No one
knew about the break-in, it hadn't been in the newspapers. We went to the District Attorney's office. We tried
to tell them what had happened, but no one would believe us. Everyone thought we'd made it up. I said to the
officers there, "What happens? I don't understand, how
long does this go on?" They said, "Well, the terrible part

is until we find a body we can't—" and I said, "I don't want to be the body."

JOHN FINO: If I would have listened to my dad, maybe things would have been okay, you know. He told me, "Play the tapes for the doctor and then tell him that there's a copy of it in a safety-deposit box," and that a friend of mine had another copy, and if I die my friend would give the copy to the District Attorney and that the safety-deposit box would be opened. But I didn't do that. I thought if I did that, Victor would get all sorts of mad and screw up *Fort Apache,* so I just told him I knew what he was doing. And then I handed this guy Frank the tape, I said, "Here, give this to Marty," and it was supposed to be put in a vault so the doctor wouldn't do anything. I gave it to this guy to give to Marty so it would just be used for protection and nothing would come of it. I think what happened was maybe this guy who gave it to him got money for it. He said he'd gotten it from me by force, which wasn't true. Then Marty just called up one day and said, "Oh, Gil Champion made a copy," and it was a different story. They just lied, you know, for whatever reason.

MARTY: My partner Gil Champion's wife was the sister of Steve Bauman, who worked for Channel Five News. We got a copy of the tape—if I told you exactly how, both Mary Lea and I would be dead. Bauman played it on television. Then we got lucky—Mary Lea got a death threat in the mail. They had it all wrong. They thought she was the Johnson Wax heiress. The threat came from some terrorist group from Texas.

MARY LEA: An ecology group. A militant ecology group.

MARTY: Right. There were these dead bugs in an envelope
and the note said, "We're going to kill you like you're
killing us. You can take your Johnson's Wax and shove
it up your ass. These bugs have the bubonic plague." So
we went back to the District Attorney and finally he
assigned a Sergeant Hardiman and a Detective Brenner
to the case.

JOHN FINO: Marty turned her against me, I'm sure of that.
He turned her children against me. That stuff Steve
Bauman said on TV and he said that I was a—you
know.

    Maybe Marty felt he was in jeopardy, but I just felt
like I was had. I had a grudge against Marty because I
felt he cost me this motion picture I was trying to put
together. It just happened so fast, you know. At that
time I was a little screwed up. I was mad at Marty, I was
mad at the doctor.

MARY LEA: It's a hard question to answer whether Marty
saved me or not. We saved each other, so to speak. You
never knew who was your friend or who was doing anything. If I hadn't had Marty at the time, I would have
been, well, probably in an institution by this time.

MARTY: Her sons did very bad things at that time. They
were upset and their father said, "Here she goes again,
she's going to bring notoriety on the family." And Bill
Ryan packed up his daughter, Alice, and himself and
moved to Paris, like it was going to besmirch him and
his daughter, that thing that went on with Mary Lea and
Victor. And he told the rest of his sons to leave so none
of the mud would be slung at them, and a few of them
went to the trustees and said, "Mom's really not altogether there, she's not capable of handling her own af-

fairs." They thought the whole murder plot was a figment of Mary Lea's imagination. And John Fino was very friendly with a couple of the kids and he kept going back and forth saying it was all a lie too. He said the murder plot was planned between Gil and myself to get Mary Lea away from Victor. They were afraid that somebody else was going to marry their mother and they were willing to believe anything. Out of the bunch, Eric's the brightest, but he's the one that tried to have his mother committed and have her money taken away from her. You don't know what this woman has gone through in her life.

VICTOR: When Mary Lea and I first separated in February of 1976 and Eric learned that she was running off with this Broadway hustler Martin Richards, all the boys were very concerned. But, you see, she has them in a bind because she can, if she elects to, disinherit them. They're not bound into her trust, she can leave it to her husband or her children, so they have to keep on her good side.

  Eric came to me and said he wanted to have her declared incompetent, which would take away her right to manage the income from her trust. I inadvertently discussed this with her attorney Phil Broughton, and then Broughton told her that Eric had said this to me. So Eric, in an attempt to repair his poor relationship with her, then agreed to collaborate actively for the Bronx District Attorney.

ERIC: That's been thrown back in my face a couple of times. When the whole murder plot first came to light, I went to the Bronx District Attorney's office with my mother and Marty to talk to Sergeant Hardiman in the Special Investigations Unit. Marty's a very emotional kind of person and a hardboiled New York City cop couldn't really relate to someone shouting hysterically, "You've got to do something. They're going to kill her." They didn't really understand the money involved, and I was in law school, so I was able to give them a calmer analysis.

I went to dinner with Victor. I was wearing a recording device taped to my chest and the police were monitoring it. There were two cops at the next table and a cop outside with an FM receiver. In the course of the meal Victor made some overtures to me to the effect that because he was a psychiatrist, if we could get our stories straight together, we could probably see that Mom was institutionalized and he would make sure it was worth my while. Victor and I talked about forming an alliance and then maybe if we could have my mother put away we could distribute her wealth together. He was still going on the theory that he could get out from under the whole accusation if Mother were seen to be unfit and mentally unbalanced. Up till then they only had Marty's wild accusations against Victor, and they didn't have any handle on who Victor was. They had their doubts as to whether to take these wild accusations seriously or not. I'm not trying to take undue credit for what happened, but a lot of the conversation that I drew out of Victor that night is what made the Bronx DA's office say, "Yeah, this guy is capable of this sort of thing." Here he is making overtures to this woman's son to get her committed. At dinner and at various times, to draw Victor out about the murder plot, we discussed what we needed to do to put Mom away. And that's what's been remembered out of the whole incident.

MARTY: Mary Lea met with John Fino. She was wired and they had a police stakeout to protect her, and Fino repeated the whole thing on police tapes. They had it red-handed, so both Finos agreed to turn state's evidence and testify before the grand jury to get an indictment on Victor.

JOHN FINO: She knew the deal. She knew the deal. I don't know if it was right for her to get wired up and come to me and ask me why I wouldn't testify, you know. And afterwards all that stuff about me in the *Times,* TV, radio, prison, the whole bit. I just felt like, wow, it's a hell of a way for people to act, you know.

I guess if they would have done what they first said they were going to do, maybe something might have worked. I told her oldest son, Eric, "I really don't want to be involved in this. I have parents that live in the Bronx, we don't have the money to take off to Paris to hide or hire bodyguards, and I have brothers, little brothers," and stuff, and Eric said, "Oh, we'll bug the apartment and we'll make it seem like we found out on our own." But it just didn't work like that. I guess Marty was, you know, in a fireball himself. He seemed to be very concerned about her, but she was really out of danger because it was for the money and not for vengeance that it was supposed to happen. I went and I told the man, "Victor's out of her will, so why kill her?" It was pretty well over.

New York *Daily News,* June 3, 1977:

SPOUSE, HITMAN HIT
IT OFF, HEIRESS SAYS

Socialite Mary Lea Johnson D'Arc, heiress to the Johnson & Johnson pharmaceutical fortune, accused her estranged husband, Dr. Victor D'Arc, of having a homosexual relationship with the man with whom he allegedly had made a contract to kill her, it was disclosed yesterday.

The charges were made by her attorneys during proceedings for a divorce action filed by D'Arc in Somerset County Court in Somerville, N.J. Her attorneys said that D'Arc made "arrangements to liquidate her through a paid assassin," and filed with the court a transcript of a telephone conversation that they said was between D'Arc and Ted Fino, whose son John, a part-time actor, was allegedly offered a substantial amount of money to have D'Arc's wife killed.

Court papers showed that Mrs. D'Arc charged that since Dec. 15, 1973, her husband pursued "an open, notorious, continuous course of deviant homosexual intercourse with one John Fino." Meanwhile, in Bronx Criminal Court, Fino is on trial for criminal contempt stemming from his alleged refusal to testify to a grand jury about the reputed murder plot.

JOHN FINO: I was a little hurt that, um, like the boys, her sons, you know, somebody told them I received $50,000 and I was going to kill their mother, and it was just not true.

MARTY: When the Finos went to the grand jury, they said they didn't know anything and they totally reneged on everything. The reason John Fino now says he went to jail is because they asked him, "Now, what is the name of the hit man?" and he said, "If I give you the name of the hit man, I might as well go to jail because I'll be killed in or out of jail."

JOHN FINO: As long as I was alive, she was never in danger. I would have died first before I let anything happen to her.

MARY LEA: He's got very much of a love-hate relationship with me, he feels that I've helped him out and yet he feels that I've put him in jail, which I didn't do. I mean, he put himself in jail by refusing to testify after making a statement that he would. He changed his mind, but the reason why he said he changed his mind was that he told me Victor would have him killed.

VICTOR: When John was testifying in the Bronx, when they were asking him to testify, Marty Richards was running around the courtroom with two armed bodyguards. He tricked John Fino into setting me up in that whole thing. I got lots of threats on the telephone during that whole period. I'm sure Marty Richards was behind it. He even sent me—what do you call those little dolls? —a voodoo doll with pins sticking in it. It's crazy. Nevertheless, that's what inhibited Fino from really telling the truth, because he was really afraid that either he would be hurt or his parents would be hurt.

MARY LEA: I don't know what the situation was. In fact, I still don't know today. Except that I do know that poor John, who brought me all this material, ended up in jail and Victor was scot-free. Except it did do one thing: we were allowed to use the tapes in a court of equity, so Victor got nothing from me.

JOHN FINO: When there's a group of people and they're all very close and they're all very friendly and then something goes wrong, and you take a producer, a millionairess, a doctor, a guy like me, and put them all together, you know, it's kind of hard to say what somebody is going to do. Mary Lea is a nice, gullible woman, and I did what I thought was right to help her. I mean, I took a helluva beating out of it, but it was worth it. She's alive.

"I'm the only one that knows it's her money."

*A*fter the highly publicized Fino-D'Arc incident, Seward Johnson cut off his daughter totally, but Richards effected a reconciliation at the time of their wedding reception at New York's Stork Club in October of 1978. Several guests remember Seward as a man who resembled an aging, diminutive Ernest Hemingway. Rather than returning to his Princeton estate after the reception, Seward slept in his private Winnebago camper in New York City's Central Park, guarded by his own private force of security men.

MARTY: I called him up and invited him to our reception and said, "Please, you don't know how important it is to your daughter, she adores you and apparently in your backgrounds you're both unable to talk to one another. But, being a Jew, we were never able to shut up. I'm going to tell you something, that she loves you very much and I would consider it a great honor if you came to the wedding." And he said to me, "Wait one minute, I'll put you on the phone with my wife." I repeated what I'd said to Basia and she said, "I'll get back to you." The following day she called me up and said, "We're coming." I never told Mary Lea because I didn't know whether they were really going to do it. When he walked into the reception, she started crying something terrible because she wanted him there so badly.

My stepson Hillary refused to sit at the table with me because his mother had committed another crime by marrying me. He went to her trustees and said she'd married a "Broadway Jew fag," that's how I was described to her trustees.

MARY LEA: I think Hillary did sit with us, but also I think he was one of the ones who went to the trustees. Our lawyer came to us and told us, "I don't know how to cope because three of your sons described Marty this way to the trustees." It's my personal opinion that the trustees did not like the whole idea that he was Jewish.

MARTY: Mary Lea's lawyer Phil Broughton said, in front of Mary Lea and me, that they told her trustees, "my mother married this Broadway Jew fag." How dare they call me that and I'd never even met her trustees. There's a lot of pain in a lot of places and it has come all the way down, her sons' pain, her pain, my pain, all came down from the beginnings, all to do with the trusts.

ERIC: I'm trying to be as frank as I can; we came from a very conservative background and Marty is not a conservative person, he's flamboyant and involved with the theater. The fact is that Mom had gone from one really bad relationship with my dad to a worse one with Victor, and then to a third man, Marty, that they were equally as uncomfortable with as with Victor. I can't emphasize enough the real difference in Marty, particularly with my dad being the primary other male figure in all our lives. I mean, they don't dress the same way, they don't carry themselves the same way. My dad looks like he dresses out of an L. L. Bean catalogue, he dresses WASPy and he might once have had a pair of those green corduroy golf pants but that would have been like the loudest thing that he would ever wear. And it's really a contrast between tweed jackets and white, oxford-cloth, button-down-collar shirts and Marty's shirts from Bijan and Gucci loafers. The only way I could picture my dad stepping out of a limousine would be at a wedding or a funeral. It's just a different lifestyle.

Dad is a private person. For instance, in the *New York Times* article there are references to my mother's homosexual ex-husband who tried to kill her. Dad was in a tizzy for a couple of days over that because it didn't specify Victor D'Arc, he was afraid that people would read the article and assume that he was a homosexual. In the course of my parents' divorce, my youngest brother, Quentin, had been the baby of the family all his life and he sort of was determined to carry on that role as long as he could. He was afraid to sleep by himself at night and when he would sleep by himself he would sleep with lights on in the room and stuff. At the time when my parents split up, it was quite traumatic for Quentin and he would sleep in my dad's bedroom. There were twin beds in my dad's room. During the course of the custody fight, one of Mom's attorneys alluded to that, and I think that the intention was probably to show that Quentin wasn't adjusting all that well to living with Dad, but the way my dad described it afterwards was that the question was asked with a smirk, "Do you continue to sleep with your son, Mr. Ryan?" or something like that . . . to suggest that there was something sexual going on between my father and his youngest son.

Basically, my father has never really forgiven my mother for that at all. Dad has an absolute abhorrence of anything that would smack of deviate sex . . . He has a very puritanical background and it's just ingrained into him.

I guess my point is basically to show that when my parents split up that it was a real rending. Both my father and my mother were left raw and bleeding, and that in some ways kind of created some behavior patterns in Mom. Sometimes she has difficulty in dealing with unpleasant situations. She retreats from them. She sometimes tries to allow time to resolve unpleasantness, as opposed to taking direct action. In this particular situation she kind of sat back and let her attorneys do the dirty work, and then disavowed much of the responsibility for what her attorneys had done.

MARTY: I thought I was going to walk into this family and I was going to be a good father. I took them out for all kinds of clothes and presents and things, and I kept saying to Mary Lea, "Why don't they like me? I never did anything to them, why don't they like me?" I've tried to be friendly with them no matter what, it's not my fault that I'm not their father. Then I stopped trying.

MARY LEA: I don't think they would have accepted him if he was the second coming. They felt threatened; their inheritance is according to my largess.

The structure of the 1944 trusts set up resentments within Mary Lea's family. Both she and her husband feel that in their endeavor to preserve the principal of the trust, Mary Lea's trustees are depriving her of money that is rightfully hers. On the other hand, Mary Lea's son Eric

Ryan points out that her children feel that if the trustees were to permit it, she might squander her money during her lifetime, or her husband might inherit it all upon her death and leave them with nothing. Certain of Mary Lea's children, although future recipients of sizable trusts, now have little money of their own and look with resentment upon their mother's opulent lifestyle. This situation has evolved over a period of years as Johnson & Johnson stock continued its astounding appreciation.

ERIC: Those trusts are what set up the jealousies between whomever Mom is married to and her children, because the terms of the trust turn them into adversaries. The other thing it's done to her kids is that I'm the only one of the six that has a graduate education. My sister and I are the only ones that have a college degree. Both the existence of the trust and my parents' divorce coming when it did took the desire to achieve goals away from a lot of my siblings. I struggle with it myself to some extent.

Then, on the other hand, when her trustees say "No" to Mom, "you can't have money, we have to look out for the remainder," by extension it becomes that there's an antipathy between her and her children, because her children are seen as what deprives her of the present enjoyment. That's the underlying reason for the friction; those trusts are a model for friction. There's also the effect that it creates a resentment of my mother's present lifestyle to an extent. One, there may be nothing left, and, two, using for example my brother Seward, he's married and he had certain expectations from my grandfather's will that caused him to buy a house and take a large mortgage on it. To be blunt about it, while his stay at the Hazelden clinic was able to help him get off drugs, there was a personality there that started off with a pro-clivity towards drugs and he still has the same passive personality, so he finds it hard to go out and beat on doors for a job. Mom just doesn't know what to do about this, she's caught between continuing to support him and at the same time trying to kick him out of the nest.

When Seward had the severe drug problem [in the early 1970s] and he was living in New York, she saw that he was incapable of working for himself, so she arranged that his hotel bill be paid every week, and I think that he got $100 a week for food. If you've ever had any contact with junkies, you know that $100 a week for food means that you have drugs on Monday and perhaps part of Tuesday. And that by continuing to subsidize him she was really continuing to subsidize his drug habit. I mean it's hard to know what would have been a better thing to do. Whether if somebody had taken a really firm stand with him much earlier on in his life and said, "Look, if you're going to do this, you're on your own." I would think my brother Seward would have the most difficulty with the situation because he's in much more dire financial straits than I'm in. I mean, I'm employable in any event.

MARTY: It's a shitty trust. There's an enormous amount of money, but the thing is, her father set it up in a way that's the most humiliating. Mary Lea, her sisters and brothers are all like beggars. If Mary Lea goes in and says, "I need $500,000 or $600,000," the trustees at first say nothing. They all have to meet and it goes on over a period of time, and by the time she gets sick or upset or demanding about it or whatever, they finally break down and have three more meetings and she gets

$300,000. If she asks for eight, she gets four. Everything she asks for, she'll get about half. And it's gone on for years and years and it will continue to go on. I said to her trustees, "Can't I give you a letter now and say I don't want money when Mary Lea dies? Give it to my wife now, while we're alive and we want to enjoy our life together." And then her children think if we use up the money there won't be anything left for them, so naturally we're at odds.

When Mary Lea was having problems with her trustees and she wanted something desperately and they said she couldn't have it, she got sick about it and she cried. It was no great thing, and she'd waited so many years having nothing. Here she is, a grown woman, and what's she going to do? She's going to die now and leave all her money to her children? And when she hasn't had it at all, only the last few years. Let them all go out and get a job! And, finally, what's so terrible? They all know they're going to be worth a minimum of $10 million later on, that ain't so bad, no one guaranteed that to me.

I'm the only one that knows it's her money. I don't say it's ours, I never have. I'm a romantic. I got married because I wanted to. I hated it when Victor used to say "our money" and "our this" and "our that." After I found out it was hers, I'd say, "That's Mary Lea's car, that's Mary Lea's money, that's Mary Lea's." The thing is with marriage it does become ours, but it will never be *our* trust.

Everybody wants something from her; they don't protect her and they don't care about her at all. The only time I confronted her trustees was when Mary Lea desperately wanted money to buy a house for her son Roderick. She got so upset that she woke up one morning with palpitations and we had to rush her into a coronary-care unit. I called up the lawyer of her trust and I said, "Look, Mr. Pitney, let me tell you one thing, I don't give a shit if you ever give me a nickel. I don't want your damn money, but if anything happens to my wife and if she dies because of you, you have fifteen minutes after she's dead for me to get there and blow your brains out. I hope you get the picture, because you make her life miserable, and now you've taken me on."

I only went to two meetings with her trustees and I'm not going to any more. I'll kill them if I go to any more. Once there was a meeting at the Downtown Athletic Club. Only men could use the elevator because it went through the men's gym, so they made her walk up five flights of stairs. It was so humiliating. When we got there, the three trustees in their pin-striped suits were standing against the window; they looked like they'd all been cloned—gray hair and glasses. I said, "Which one of you son-of-a-bitches made my wife walk up five flights? Look, this is her money, you're working for her!" I am not fond of her trustees.

Mary Lea told me, "You know, I never had a birthday party in my whole life," and that hit a nerve, it drove me crazy. Mary Lea's birthday is August 20, and I said, "Well, I'm going to make you a birthday party," and I took charge of it. It started at eleven o'clock in the morning with an orchestra playing at the pool, and we served lobster salad for two hundred people, and then we served dinner, a filet-mignon dinner, and it went on from eleven o'clock in the morning to five o'clock the following morning.

Her son brought a group to us and I didn't know who

they were, and I said, "Who are all these dirty people who keep running around and plugging things in in the house? They're just so filthy," and it was the Grateful Dead. They played on and on and then all of a sudden cars started to drive up on our lawn, we had this tremendous lawn, and then all the kids came and started throwing blankets down. There was a priest and another group smoking pot and Mary Lea handing out bottles of champagne to all these strange kids and as we sat there it became an outdoor concert.

Mary Lea's given me so much through the years, she's made it fantasy time for me and I didn't know what to do in return. I started buying her enormous amounts of jewelry, all of which she hates—I like jewelry, she hates jewelry—and then I bought her furs and she hated furs. I've never met a lady that didn't like furs. But you can only have one first birthday party, where do you go from there? If somebody gives you a tremendous life, you want to give it back in some way, but you can't always be nice, then you'd be awfully dull, and she's very, very vulnerable and I'm vulnerable to her vulnerability, which is worse. I've made it a chore to try to make up for all the miseries of all the men in her life, and you find yourself working so hard at it that you're exhausted; there's no place to go with it any more. But the scars remain—her scars remain, my own personal scars remain, they get in the way of a relationship. It's very hard to please somebody after a length of time and those special moments are all filled in.

She was down, so down, and she was looking out of the window today and saw the exact scene that two weeks ago made her say, "God, aren't we lucky, look at the beauty out there, aren't we lucky!" And today she was looking out the window and saying, "I could just jump right through that plate-glass window."

MARY LEA: It has very little to do with outside influences. I mean, it's something inside of me.

"... my life is hell."

When Junior returned from the Navy in 1955 at twenty-five, he entered the competitive environment of Johnson & Johnson, acquiring an entry level job at Ethicon, the suture-manufacturing plant in Somerville, New Jersey. Gradually, Junior had formed a dual resolve: to protect his sisters and to redeem what he felt to be his father's failures. In 1963, when he reached the age of thirty-three as specified in the trust instruments, he was to assume the vote of the 1944 trusts, thereby transferring the power from the General to himself.

To Seward Jr., success in the will contest represents his final restoration after a devastating fall from grace that began in 1956, when he met a brunette commercial-art agent, Barbara Maxwell, who exuded charm, warmth, and, for the unsophisticated Junior, exoticism. A suspicious General Johnson launched an investigation into Barbara's past. Detectives were sent to Germany, and her father, an attorney and minor official at a Frankfurt bank, was threatened with dismissal because of the inquiry.

Seward Jr., unaware of the detectives' findings, became more and more distraught. "My father had promised me many times that the investigators had stopped. Therefore, I was getting angrier and angrier with frustration as this proved not to be true." He says that at one point he was so upset he wrote Barbara a letter saying that he would shoot his father if he did not bring the investigation to a halt. He also wrote her a letter in which he referred to his father as a "stupid jerk." Subsequently, when he telephoned his father, Seward Sr. coldly reported that Barbara's full name was Barbara Eisenfuhr Kline Bailey Maxwell, informing Junior that she had been married three times and "probably had good reason to fear investigation." On September 16, 1956, Seward and Barbara eloped to Virginia City, Nevada.

SEWARD JR.: I had been living at home, working at Ethicon, and it was quite dead. I was trying to not involve myself with the secretaries—and there were some mighty nice-looking ones. I was starved for something different. It was a really small-town feeling. I met Barbara when I was twenty-six. I was still living at home and extremely undeveloped—very naïve and young for my age. I lived in sort of privacy, I just wasn't in real contact with the world. I had a sort of yearning to get out there and do something.

The first thing I did was really quite interesting. I built a new factory. I was the clerk of the works, I guess you would call it. I counted the welds, and looked at the specifications, and worked under an engineer, checking all the contractors to make sure that they were living up to specifications. And then they had me build a model of the new factory. I mean, I had the machine shop do it, but I directed them.

Actually, everything was interesting, except there was something missing. There was nothing spiritual going on in my life, it was a suburban, country existence with the lowest of standards of cultural contact. All of a sudden, I just seemed to be there in a suffocating environment. I felt very shy, very strange. I was always kidded a lot because I was a Johnson. It was very strange because I was always at the bottom level, but at the Christmas party I sat at the president's table.

Barbara was selling commercial art to Young and Rubicam, and Johnson & Johnson had an account there and she was trying to sell their account and she was also trying to write a television series on things to do with sailing ships. She was a hyper sort of person, dressed in fairly high style. She had energy. None of these people had any energy, and she knew New York, and to me New York was the open door. She knew New Hope, Pennsylvania, and that, compared to New Brunswick, was quite exotic. I didn't feel extremely comfortable there, but I liked not feeling comfortable.

So, anyway, I ended up moving in with her. She had a tiny house, but she'd managed to build a swimming pool. I think she had bought it for $18,000. Today it would probably be $75,000. It was in a little development part of Princeton. Everything was white—the living-room rugs were white, the sofa was white, the books had white covers over them, everything was hyper-style.

I found it was awfully strange to wake up and go to the refrigerator and find a fruit cup with Kirsch in it for breakfast. And so my father and uncle began to become alarmed about my moving in there. Around then the investigation on her started. That's when I found out that she had been married more than once. And, finding it out that way, I was embarrassed and it made me angry to be embarrassed, but I turned my anger in the wrong direction. The investigation messed up her father's job somewhat. She threw her engagement ring at me and I threw it at Ken Perry, and then he and I went down to the wine cellar and got drunk together. I thought it was all over. But then she called. Ken Perry went back and forth, you see; he was wildly anti-Semitic and he said Barbara was part Jewish, and this was the reason that I took such exception to his approach. They made it impossible for me to see her as the individual she was. I was so busy defending, defending, that I wasn't able to use my own perception of the situation, and I didn't realize where the hell I was. So then I was really into it, I was committed. I had cut off my family. I had cut off everybody and there I was.

BETTY JOHNSON BUSHNELL: She was a woman of immense charm, big and sexy. They had a great tortoise that wandered around the house, and a tailcoated butler who wore a monocle and was baldheaded like Erich von Stroheim.

Within a year of their marriage, Junior asserted, Barbara was pressuring him into asking for the principal of his trust. He adopted her son from a former marriage, thereby putting him in line as a trust beneficiary. Although Junior had qualified as a trustee at twenty-one, he would not receive the vote until age thirty-three. The trusts were controlled by General Johnson because Kenneth Perry, also a trustee, was his pawn. Repeatedly they refused Junior's requests for the corpus of his trust.

As Junior's fragile emotional condition began to deteriorate, his conduct became more erratic. He was plagued by feelings of mortal danger under what he deemed to be his uncle's recalcitrance and the subtle torture of his wife.

SEWARD JR.: Since the age of seven I'd felt disen-
franchised. I felt I didn't have a home, so it was important to me to have one. But she was incredible. As I said
in my divorce petition, Barbara kept demanding that I
fight with the trustees. When I told her how depressed
and anxious I was over the situation, she told me, "If
you can't be man enough to protect your family, you
should be dead." Once I said, "I don't think life is worth
living," and she answered, "I don't think your life is
worth living if you can't protect your family." When I
said, "I feel like jumping off a cliff," she coldly replied,
"Why don't you."

I was called into Uncle Bob's office to sign checks for
the trust, and when I got there I saw that the checkbooks were filled with checks already signed by me and
therefore I could not understand why I had been summoned. But on leaving Johnson & Johnson the guard
beckoned to me and pulled me aside and gave me two
pistols. I felt my uncle had arranged this and he was
trying to aggravate my relationship, which did not need
much aggravation, with my first wife, and it was part of
a total scheme, not necessarily completely defined at the
beginning, but to deprive me of the vote I was to receive.
I believe it was more than a generous act on my uncle's
part to give me a means of protecting myself from someone he felt was out to do me in—my wife. They snuck
me two revolvers, one of which I nearly killed myself
with.

In this tempest there was a brief respite. During Christmas vacation in 1957, Seward Sr. invited his son and Barbara to cruise the Bahamas with him. According to Junior,
the trip was tranquil, and his spirits began to rise. He felt
that perhaps once again there might be peace and that

family relations would begin to mend. When they returned to Fort Lauderdale, however, Junior remembers that his stepmother, Essie, was waiting on the dock. She began a fierce argument with her husband, accusing him of sleeping with his daughter-in-law, Barbara. Junior instantly felt certain that this was true.

The following week Seward Jr. returned to Princeton. He went out and bought ammunition for one of the two guns supplied by his uncle. The ammunition did not fit the gun. Junior then fastened a hose to the exhaust of his car and tried to asphyxiate himself. A young boy walking by called the police, who took Junior to a hospital. There was doubt that he would live.

Junior left a suicide note that read, "Dear Barbara, I am dying very happily. I love you very much. You are as beautiful inside as a saint. I know my father will see that nothing will harm you and no one will do you injustice, because he knows you are good and I love you."

SEWARD JR.: I was nearly dead when they got to me. Some fellow walking along found me. I had the trunk open because I had the hose from the exhaust in through the trunk and into the back seat. I was parked on a road in the woods. The gun that had been given to me was in the front seat, so he didn't dare do anything about me. He called the police and by the time the police got there I was unconscious. They pulled me out of the car. I sort of remember bumping my head, but that was about all. I was all pink. My lips were numb. The next thing I knew, I was in an oxygen tent in the hospital.

My cousin Bob showed his colors, he came and stayed by my bedside all night. Then Barbara came with a man and a wheelchair and said she was taking me out of there or my father would have me committed to an asylum. The chief of police said he would prefer charges unless I went to stay with my cousin Bob. He wouldn't allow me to leave in Barbara's custody, so I went and stayed with Betty and Bob, who'd stood up for me.

BETTY JOHNSON BUSHNELL: When Barbara came to our house, he was sleeping in this little twin bed and he was shaking, so Barbara got into bed with him and held him. She told me how he was shaking all night.

Seward Jr. says that when he began to recover, Barbara continued to pressure him about the trust, saying that the next time he tried suicide he should do a better job. He was beset with emotional problems and General Johnson arranged for him to take a leave of absence from J&J. After a few months, however, Junior says he received a letter firing him for absenteeism. He wanted his job back and said he would see an analyst if it was restored to him.

The Johnson family had long established another pattern, that of working out emotional problems through litigation. In July of 1958 Junior, age twenty-eight, was to plunge into the legal morass for the first time. He engaged his own attorney in an effort to effect a corpus distribution from his trust, the first in a series of legal actions that eventually would extend to the 1986 will contest. By that time litigation had become a way of life for Junior, who remarked, "I've spent half my life in a courtroom and I don't see why it should change now."

Seward Sr. was in close contact with his brother and Kenneth Perry. On August 19, 1958, he wrote to his son, ". . . I am also told that you are not undergoing analytical treatment and that you will not undergo analytical treatment until a number of things come to pass, some of which I am sure will not come to pass until some progress

is made with your analytical treatment. . . . I am sure
your Uncle Bob will not wish to subject any employees of
J&J to the contacts which you have requested until these
controversial problems are swept away. This appears to be
a complete impasse! I think you had better get advice from
your psychiatrists as to what to do, and if they are unable
to advise you perhaps we better start fresh and get a new
analyst. It seems to me that enough time has elapsed that
these tragic time-wasting situations should come to an
end."

Again, on August 22, Seward Sr. wrote pointing out to
Junior that his 1944 trust fund yielded between $55,000
and $65,000 a year and stating, "I urge you to settle down
and make the best of life with facts as they are. Start your
psychoanalysis and straighten out your environment such
as house problems, budget problems, debts . . . and demands on you for chauffeur service. When the necessary
time has elapsed to measure the success of your analytic
therapy, then I believe it would be time to consider resum-
ing your business activities at Johnson & Johnson. At this
time my recommendation to the trustees would be as
stated above." On August 23, 1958, a distraught Seward
Jr. wrote to his father, pleading for his support. "My marriage is under threat . . . my life is hell." He ended the
letter with, "Dad, show me your colors." When his father
was asked in a court deposition if he had responded to that
letter, he answered, "I'm sure I didn't."

SEWARD JR.: I was saying, "Show your colors. They're
    hiding behind you, and you're hiding behind the trust-
    ees. I don't know who's doing what, and I don't want to
    think that my father's doing this. I'm saying now you've
    got to take the position." He was really impotent more
    than awful. I mean, I think he was a selfish person, but it

was his impotency against his brother that really made
him incapable of helping me.

JOYCE JOHNSON: I blame his father, he just stood by and
let the General wipe my husband out.

In January 1962 Seward Jr. left Barbara and filed suit
for divorce. It was to be "a protracted and bitter affair."
Junior says a divorce lawyer persuaded him to put forth in
detail accusations about Barbara's conduct during their
troubled marriage. Seward Jr. stated that she had "completely dominated" him and that by September of 1958 he
was spending his "entire time at home engaged in domestic
duties such as making his wife breakfast and serving it to
her in bed." He accused Barbara of two adulterous affairs
and stated that in June of 1960 she had invited him to
engage in a *ménage-à-trois,* an invitation he refused. Of the
first alleged lover, David Proudlove, his divorce petition
stated, "She permitted herself to appear scantily clad in
nightgowns and in compromising positions with
Proudlove.

"She frequently permitted Proudlove, while in their
home, to embrace and fondle her amorously while she was
scantily clad, and kiss her lips, legs, thighs, and other parts
of her body."

Of the second alleged lover, Darby Bannard, his petition stated, "Defendant has on many occasions permitted
herself to appear nude or scantily clad in the presence of
Darby Bannard, and has permitted herself to be kissed and
fondled by Darby Bannard.

"Defendant has permitted Darby Bannard complete
access to her person. She requests him to dress and to
undress her. She permits him to watch her while she goes
to the toilet and while she takes baths and showers. She

permits him to watch her nurse her young daughter while she, defendant, is completely unclad to the waist." According to Junior, there was also doubt about the paternity of the daughter born January 11, 1961, Jenny Anne Josephine (inspired by J&J). As a provision of the divorce settlement, Seward Jr. was forced to acknowledge paternity of this child, but later he publicly repudiated it.

SEWARD JR.: I felt that Barbara was tough as nails, and I became terrified. I knew that I could not get rid of her without paying her off. I also knew the courts wouldn't be favoring me, being well off, and so that is why my complaint read in such a terrible way.

At that time, under New Jersey divorce law in a contested case, one could only claim two years' desertion, adultery, or extreme cruelty. Donald Jones had represented my ex-wife in the past; this created, as he put it, a conflict, so he brought in another lawyer, Nicholas Politan. But rather than turning the case over to him, Jones directed and controlled it behind the scenes.

Proudlove, the first claimed correspondent, an Englishman, was flamboyant besides whatever he was beyond my knowledge in relating to my ex-wife. He would always greet her by kissing her hand in a flurry of superficial intensity. There was one occasion when he arrived and she was lying on a deck chair. Instead of offering him her hand for the usual bussing, she extended her foot in the air theatrically and he theatrically responded by repeatedly kissing her foot, her ankle, and her leg (with comic Terry-Thomas overtones). The theatrics, I feel, were meant to disarm me, to make me believe everything was strictly superficial.

When I related this above occurrence to Donald Jones and Nicholas Politan in the lawyers' office, Politan asked me if Proudlove kissed her above the knee, I answered, "possibly." I didn't really remember. Politan then rephrased my statement to: "He kissed her thighs and legs in front of me." Jones, getting into the spirit, repeated thighs, legs, and other parts of her body. "The foot is other parts of the body, isn't it?" he said. There was much guffawing following, and I joined in, thinking they were exercising in banter by caricaturing the legal ability to twist a benign statement into consequence. When it became clear to me that they were serious, I became troubled. They reminded me how difficult it was to get a divorce in New Jersey, and the facts I had relayed to them to that point wouldn't get it. I remembered that until I got my divorce, if anything happened to me, accidental or otherwise, I could not prevent my ex-wife from getting all the assets of my trust, no matter what. I glumly acceded to their change of my statement.

On my complaint in my divorce I said that my ex-wife hit me with a hanger while her lover held me [May 29, 1960]. But this was when I admitted to her that I had met Joyce up in Nantucket, not realizing what I was doing. What happened was I'd gone up to see about a house up there and had met Joyce. We both were on the same airplane up there, and we went out to a bar and had a drink, and damned if the police didn't come into the bar looking for me. I'd landed maybe around two o'clock in the afternoon and this was seven o'clock in the evening. Barbara had called the police. So the damned police said I was up there with a blonde. Barbara managed to find out where Joyce was, up in Nantucket, and she called her and said that I was a little bit crazy.

In February of 1963, seeking further grounds for his divorce action, Junior hired private detectives to raid his former home at 75 Cleveland Lane in Princeton. The raid turned into a melee: Barbara Johnson shot one of the detectives, then jumped out of her bedroom window, dropped ten feet to the ground, ran to a neighbor's, and called the police. On the witness stand a sobbing Barbara told the story of a black stranger approaching her bed as she screamed, "Don't come closer or I'll shoot!" In all, a total of seventy-seven charges were filed by all parties concerned; they included assault with a deadly weapon, conspiracy, and a complaint of psychological damage to Ebenezer, their bulldog, who had been squirted in the eyes with an ammonia mixture from a water pistol to keep him from attacking. Barbara, in an affidavit, denied all of Junior's accusations and countered with some of her own.

BARBARA E. JOHNSON AFFIDAVIT, DECEMBER 10, 1963:
What is important is that plaintiff concedes he was a sick man, and I maintain that such sickness not only pertains at the present time but exists in an aggravated degree for the following reasons:

I attribute to him the constant threats against the lives of myself and my children—reported to the Princeton police prior to the February 1963 raid . . .

Plaintiff engineered and was personally present at the February 1963 raid directing the forced entry into my home of an armed band of seven or eight men, who brandished loaded weapons . . .

Plaintiff's condition today—more than ever—demands psychiatric, psychological, and psychoanalytical assistance. The depositions of his father show that both he and plaintiff's uncle begged him to undergo protracted treatment during the early years of his marriage, which he commenced and then promptly abandoned.

The advent of the tragic assassination of our late President in Dallas shows the lengths to which an afflicted mind can go. Plaintiff once attempted his own suicide. Must we wait until positive disastrous actions are taken against me and the children before a medical action is ordered!

Junior felt that his mental health depended upon his getting a divorce. Once again he asked that funds from his trust be distributed to him, this time for a divorce settlement. James Pitney, the lawyer who represented the General and Kenneth Perry as trustees, answered for them, telling Junior "they would make a distribution for the settlement of my divorce *only* on the condition that I resign as trustee." At first Seward refused, but, pressured from all sides, he recalls, "It became the loneliest time of my life. Finally I buckled and resigned in order to get the money to settle the case."

From General Johnson's point of view and that of his brother, Junior's bizarre behavior, requests for capital, and the publicity engendered by the raid on his home and his lurid divorce petition were an extreme embarrassment. On December 18, 1964, under his bold, illegible signature, General Johnson cut through like a knife. He wrote Pitney that "from time to time I have attempted to follow the thread of the massive peregrinations of this case over the past year. It is difficult for me to have more than certain general impressions:

"The two persons involved are abnormal . . . any reasonable price that will extricate Seward Jr. from these complex problems should be paid. He is wise to resign from various trusts at this time. I hope that he can be given a chance to lead a new life and will do so successfully."

On December 21, 1964, in James Pitney's office, Seward Jr. resigned.

SEWARD JR.: At the end I looked to Kenneth Perry as a friend when Uncle Bob forced me to retire. We spoke on the phone for forty-five minutes before I signed the resignation. He was very sympathetic. Perry died two days after I resigned. He was so upset, he had a heart attack. It might have been a complete coincidence, but I don't think so. He was a man of a different time. Of course, this left my uncle Bob as sole trustee. I was supposed to be the protector of the females and, as such, I was the trustee. When I lost that mantle, it was selling me short at thirty-four. What I never accepted was my uncle's using my mistake to take away from me part of my inheritance—my voting powers in the family company, plus millions of dollars of trustee's commissions.

MARY LEA: It was blackmail. Uncle Bob was a black-mailer.

Totally crushed, Seward Jr. left Princeton. But the episode was not entirely over. There were to be more lawyers, more legal maneuverings. At the time of Junior's resignation, both Mary Lea and Diana filed legal objections. They wanted their brother to remain and also felt their own trusts to be endangered because the IRS might rule that the replacement trustee, yet another person controlled by General Johnson, could void the trusts by violating their arm's-length restrictions. Furthermore, they wished to sell some of their J&J stock, which paid low dividends, and invest the money in high-income-producing instruments.

Seward Johnson, as ever, sided with his brother and the tenuous tie between father and daughters was broken. (Ironically, approximately eighteen months later General Johnson's own lawyers determined that Mary Lea and Diana had been correct in their misgivings about the replacement trustee and the General apologized to them.)

ERIC: At the time we lived in Bedminster and her father lived in Oldwick, a distance of about six miles. Prior to this fight, we would go over to my grandfather's for Sunday lunch. About once a month we'd be scrubbed and cleaned and we'd put on our Sunday best and we'd be guests for lunch. Suddenly that just ceased. My mother's relationship with her father deteriorated completely over this suit.

LETTER FROM SEWARD JOHNSON TO MARY LEA RYAN, April 19, 1965:

Dear Mary Lea:

You are turning out to be a troublemaker beyond my imagination. I have explained to you the disadvantages of attacking the trustees with a law suit, and twice you have agreed to withdraw the suit.

I am profoundly sorry that I made a substantial trust in your favor. I am putting my thoughts in this letter because I refuse to discuss the matter further and I wish to avoid further frustration.

You are giving a perfect example of why trustees should have large fees and are submitting yourself and others to the added expense and disgrace of court appearances, the only advantage of which can accrue to the lawyers over years of interminable litigation.

Under the circumstances, I will not include you or your family in any further estate planning.

LETTER FROM SEWARD JOHNSON TO GENERAL JOHNSON, April 26, 1965:

Dear Bob,

. . . These trusts are certainly turning out to be a headache. . . . the girls' lawyers spend time on "compromises"—this is all fine for the law business. I think it should well be brought to your attention. I could probably be put in jail for what I think!

"The General stopped at nothing . . ."

VICTOR D'ARC: What's the complaint? Uncle Bob made them all rich.

NICHOLAS RUTGERS: He was an egomaniac and he liked to be feared. When he assumed the presidency of Johnson & Johnson, he fired everyone who wasn't his person, he virtually decimated the town of New Brunswick. Guys died just from the disgrace. General Johnson's genius was for business. He had a vision of the future. At one point he cut the dividend to one percent so he could plow money back into the company. Everything was for the company and about the company. Even his son and relatives could be seen as enemies of his grand plan. The policies of the company were totally private, clannish, like the Mafia. That's why sometimes they used inferior people, because they were company men.

MARY LEA: "Damn it," he said, "I wish you were a man because you're the only one that isn't a nonentity in this whole family, and that includes my son." It wasn't a real compliment, it was a double-edged sword. Women didn't exist as far as he was concerned, they were ornaments, or a necessary part of life. I would say the highest job held by a woman in Johnson & Johnson was the head of personnel, but that was in baby products. Aunt Evangeline doesn't have anywhere near the money that anyone else has, I mean not much money at all, because Uncle Bob bought her preferred stock. I don't think he really did a nice thing to her as far as that was concerned.

I think it's very very hard to draw an accurate picture of Uncle Bob. I admired him a great deal, and yet I disliked him. He did little things that were cruel to people. I can remember when I was a child when he came to the house I asked him to see a trick I'd just learned to do. I took off my shoes and climbed up the sides of a door to the very top and then I climbed down again. I was so pleased I'd discovered I could do this, just like a monkey. And he gave me a swift kick in the behind, so much so that I really was hurting like anything, and he said, "Run along now, get out of here," laughing as he did it. Now, whether he didn't realize the force he was using or whether this was a torture of some kind I don't know, but I can remember just fighting back the tears.

Uncle Bob took speech lessons so he could speak fluently and publicly, and he spoke to his employees—he made tapes that were broadcast throughout the plant. It was almost as bad as IBM. In the morning he'd say, "Good morning, ladies and gentlemen," and they had to get up from their chairs and say, "Good morning."

Uncle Bob was the general in charge of small war plants in the Second World War. It's funny because Aunt Evangeline at the time was married to a Russian prince whose name was Alexis Zalstem-Zalessky and Uncle Bob would sit back and say, "Damned if I can understand why that woman insists on calling herself a princess, she's no more a princess than the man in the moon." I remember saying to him, "Well, I guess it's the same reason you call yourself a general."

His third wife was a ballroom dancer. She and her partner did the tango, you know. They lived on a very grand scale. I can remember he had one man on board his yacht to polish the silver. It was very *fawncy.*

KEITH: He was a very business-motivated individual. He liked to dance, and he liked to sail, and he liked to run his business, and that was about the extent of what he did. We were at a dinner party and were discussing the fact that truly brilliant, successful men never had brilliant, successful children. And I listened to this for about a half an hour or so, and I said to the General, "You know, this is an awful thing to say about your father," and he got really upset, but it was typical of him.

ELAINE: General Johnson didn't even recognize that his daughter, Sheila, that he adopted was there; she was totally left out of everything. I think Uncle Bob was a very selfish man, a self-indulgent egomaniac. And he was cruel. Dad didn't have any of that, he was a gentleman. They were very different people.

SEWARD JR.: It was control, power, to have power over everyone. He really loved that. He had sort of a cynical philosophical thing that everyone was going to fall into place, that all he had to do was set up a straight line and because people weren't straight they would bump up against it one day and he would have the advantage over them. He rejected his son, Bob, because he was obese. He was so disciplined himself and I think he saw it as a lack of discipline.

We're all complicated, but he was a funny man. In a certain way, I felt that he half wanted to adopt me when I first started at Johnson & Johnson. It was a push-pull relationship. He and I exchanged lots of letters, I remember, and I was very frank with him and he would always compliment me on my letters, but he might have been toying with me too. I don't know whether he was rejecting his son, Bob Jr., and was sort of promoting me, but I felt very competitive with my cousin at an early age. I knew with my own background that I couldn't really compete with my cousin. He had done his lower stint and was up—he'd spent two years in the machine shop. He finally became president of Johnson & Johnson national.

Like his brother, like their father before them, the powerful General Johnson seemed to have no sense of family continuity, as reflected in the parallel stories of his own son, Robert Wood Jr., and that of Seward Jr., the two Johnsons who were slated to take over the company.

In 1944, when the Johnson children's trusts had been created, one of the primary reasons as stated by James Pitney was: "To enable each of his [Seward's] sons eventually to hold a source of power and responsibility in the company, and to be on equal terms of power with their cousin, R. W. Johnson, Jr."

Although in the abstract the General and Seward wanted their sons to assume the mantle of power, in practice they did not. The General, from all accounts, wanted total power, even to the point of authorizing the brutal dismissal of his own son.

Robert Wood Johnson, Jr., had been a shy boy, eager to please—a boy who loved nature, fishing, and hunting. He married Betty Wold, a doctor's daughter from St. Paul,

Minnesota, and they had four sons and a daughter. (It was Betty's brother Keith whom Elaine Johnson was to marry.) Starting in 1941, Robert worked his way up in the company. He was a hard worker, as eager to please in his maturity as he had been as a child. In 1954 he was appointed to the executive committee of the Board of Directors, in 1955 Executive Vice-President for Marketing, in 1960 Executive Vice-President and General Manager, and in 1961 President of Domestic Operations.

In 1963 General Johnson retired from the company, but in name only. He kept a tight rein on company affairs, never believing in his son and openly criticizing him to family members and Johnson & Johnson executives.

In April of 1965, four months after Seward Jr. was forced by his uncle to relinquish his power over the trusts, Robert Wood Johnson, Jr., was voted out of his position at a Board of Directors meeting. The *Wall Street Journal* commented, "The company declined to give any reasons for Mr. Johnson's resignation. . . . Mr. Johnson's resignation apparently marks another step in the withdrawal of the Johnson family from active management of Johnson & Johnson." The personal fallout from this dismissal was devastating.

MARY LEA: Uncle Bob believed definitely in the theory that it was overalls to overalls in three generations and he was out to prove it. He resented and disliked his son and he really did his best to destroy him and Seward Jr. too. Young Bob was really a bright man. He was always overweight and Uncle Bob didn't help matters at all because he hated that. Uncle Bob's first wife was a stockily built woman, and so Cousin Bob inherited that tendency, but I think it was also from neglect that he put on weight. As a child he was always left with the chauffeur. When he went on fishing trips, the chauffeur went with him—he was his best friend, which to me is sort of a strange situation, in that you pay a salary to your best friend. It's not a good way to do things.

Anyway, he came into the company and he brought with him some good people, capable people, but there were one or two who were a little slick too. And eventually Uncle Bob and young Bob had a disagreement over managerial affairs. Cousin Bob was asked to leave. Our dad arranged it. I know it was done very abruptly and he wasn't given any notice. He came back to the company the next day and found all his files out in the hall and everything torn apart. He was just ousted so completely and so fast, it was a very cruel thing to do. With Uncle Bob it seemed definitely sort of the seal-fighting-the-young-seal type of thing, almost to the death to oust him from his rock. My cousin went to Florida and started a company using aloe as a base for all sorts of skin lotions and lipsticks, and it was getting to be fairly successful, but he was dying. I think he only survived his father by two years.

SEWARD JR.: The '44 trust plan was that there would be equal voting power between the descendants of Seward and Bob, and that's why I felt that my father was the one who fired Bob Jr.—it was a total *quid pro quo* balancing act for having my uncle get rid of me. Dad relished the experience. When he told me he'd taken a mistress and when he told me he'd called for the vote to have my cousin removed were the only two times I saw him strutting around the office with a brandy and a big cigar. They blamed Bob Jr. for the Micrin overrun, but the real reason was he was operating on his own, outside of his father's domination. He had his own division.

NICHOLAS RUTGERS: The General stopped at nothing to take control of the company, and, like many famous men, he thought his own son was worthless. He used to tell my mother, "Bobby is nothing, Bobby will amount to nothing." My mother always said Bobby should have gotten out of the company while he still had a chance. The pressure on almost all the executives at Johnson & Johnson was ungodly. Bobby Jr. developed diverticulitis. By the time he left to form his own company, he was almost too sick to function, but he kept hanging in there, hoping he could prove himself.

BETTY: After it happened, people we'd known all our lives would turn away. I guess I don't blame them—it was a company town, they were interested in keeping their jobs and their houses and their two-car garages. But it was hard. My husband died of cancer about five years after he left the company.

MARY LEA: I was very fond of Betty's children, who are very close to my own children in age. Unfortunately, I think they were, as my own children were, products of the sixties. Two of the children are dead—Billy and Keith died within two months of each other. When the boys died, their share went to the others. My gosh, they must practically be billionaires at this stage of the game. Betty's been through hell, but she survived very nicely. She's a lovely woman.

ERIC: It was a terrible thing for their mother, she lost a husband to cancer and then her two sons. Keith died of a cocaine overdose and Billy died in a motorcycle accident. The cocaine overdose died first.

SEWARD JR.: I really feel as though Uncle Bob was spending his last years solidifying, making sure that there would be no other personality in that company to take his place. There's a painting of the general at Ethicon, surrounded by his toys—his autogiro, his sailboat the *Stormy Weather,* and so forth. J&J was his kingdom, and at the end he definitely wanted the company to be his tombstone.

". . . an easy guy to have around."

Today Jennifer Johnson Duke, an attractive woman who wears a barrette in her blonde pageboy, is an owner of the Gallery of Applied Arts in New York, where her husband, Joseph Duke, a furniture designer, exhibits. At the trial Jennifer mused, "Some days I think of Dad looking down on us, and I wonder if he'd think we were doing the right thing. He was so reticent about discussing anything. I guess he might say things got so bad that someone else had to do something about it."

James (often called Jimmy), an artist and gentleman farmer, became estranged from his father and did not see him for several years. In a deposition he stated that his father had removed him as an executor of his will. "I've been racking my brain to try to remember what I said that changed his mind . . . and I just cannot remember it. I think it was perhaps for some political view I had." When Seward was hospitalized in 1981, a visitor found James sitting outside the room crying. "Why don't you go in?" he asked. "I don't think he wants me," James replied. During the testimony about his father's painful final day, James concentrated on the *Daily News.* "It's not that I don't talk to the press," he told a reporter, "it's that I don't talk." When asked what his style of painting was, he replied, "Bonnard." When asked what his father would think of this trial, he said, "He'd hate the publicity."

Essie and Seward Johnson's main residence during their thirty-two-year marriage was a farm in Oldwick, New Jersey. A drive lined with cedar trees led to a gem of a New England farmhouse. Johnson seemed comfortable in the role of a working farmer, living a somewhat secluded life. His was a model farm with barns made of a blue plastic compound that retained heat. In his own hand he proudly kept a log of the bloodlines of his two herds of cows, one called Milk and the other Honey. He was determined to improve the breeding of his prize-winning Holsteins in order to increase their milk production, and he grew his own crop of rye and alfalfa. Johnson responded favorably to the regular schedule imposed on his well-ordered household. Breakfast was at 7:00, lunch at 12:30, dinner at 7:30.

JENNIFER: We lived a nice life. It was the same kind of life that the people around us lived. I had breakfast, lunch, and dinner with Dad every day of my life until I went away to boarding school. He was just there. He was an easy guy to have around. At the trial there was testimony about how Basia had made us have a good relationship with Dad. Well, I didn't need Basia. I wish I'd spoken up and said that. I always had a good relationship with him, certainly until the time he left Mother, because after that I didn't see him for about four years.

Life at Oldwick seemed simple, but whatever Seward Johnson wanted in the way of material things, he had. A friend remembers visiting and observing the curious contrasts in Johnson's life. Seward sent his private airplane for his friend. A chauffeured Cadillac limousine took him from the airport to the farm, where he was greeted by a barefoot Seward wearing a torn Viyella shirt and Levi's. After lunch, which was served by a uniformed maid, they took a walking tour of the farm. At one point Seward thrust his hand into a compost heap and expounded on the virtues of nitrogen. At the end of the day Seward drove his guest back to the airport in his Jaguar roadster at a hundred miles an hour.

In the winter Essie and Seward Johnson went to a vacation residence that resembled a Swiss chalet on five hundred feet of waterfront on Jupiter Island, Hobe Sound, Florida. Since Esther refused to fly, she commuted to this home by private railroad car. Summers were spent in Chatham, on Cape Cod, in a comfortable, sprawling, shingled house covered with ivy, set on a broad lawn sloping down to a millpond.

Spaulding Dunbar, the designer of many of Johnson's sailboats, was his constant companion in Chatham for more than three decades. They had met the summer of 1939 when Seward asked Spaulding to design a boat for him. Dunbar recalls Seward Johnson's extreme shyness and passion for privacy. In 1941, when his sailboat won a race to New Providence in the Bahamas, Seward was too shy to accept the trophy and sent Dunbar in his place. The trophy was presented by the Duke of Windsor, who stammered so badly he was barely able to complete his speech, and it struck Dunbar that one person had been too shy to come for the cup and the other too shy to present it.

DUNBAR: Seward was what I'd call strictly a six-mile-an-hour man. He'd bike over here to my boatyard in the morning if he felt like going fishing. He had no car. He had a Crosby catboat and a skiff he'd use to get around in.

In 1949 Seward asked for a boat with an extremely shoal draft for cruising the shallow waters around the Bahamas and the Virgin Islands. He also wanted to try tandem centerboards to make the boat almost self-steering. Dunbar suggested they experiment with a forty-three-foot ketch of inexpensive construction, use it to gather data and experience, and then junk it and build a proper boat. Seward Johnson agreed, but when the boat was under construction he insisted on better materials, interior finishing, then proper sleeping and cooking facilities. What emerged was the *Sea Goose,* one of Johnson's favorite boats. It drew only 4.5 feet and for many years he used it to cruise from Maine to Cuba, in the Bahamas, and around St. Kitts, St. Barts, and St. Thomas.

The *pièce de résistance* of Dunbar's designs for Johnson was the *Ocean Pearl,* a classic sixty-four-foot sailing ketch constructed in Holland. The keel, twenty-six inches wide, ten inches thick, and forty feet long, was carved from a single teak log. The vessel was finished entirely in teak. The hand-sewn sails were the distinctive bark color favored by the Breton people. The *Ocean Pearl* took two years to construct. It was budgeted at $93,000, but Seward kept trying new ideas and adding extra luxuries, so that it ended up costing $220,000. It was completed in June of 1956.

KEITH: We had a pretty good shakedown cruise on the *Ocean Pearl.* Spaulding and Seward and I left Portugal and went down to the coast of Africa and on to the Canary Islands. In a way, we retraced one of Columbus's voyages, and we went from Las Palmas to Barbados in the Caribbean, and that was seventeen days and one hour across open ocean. It was a marvelous experience.

ELAINE: And they weren't allowed to take a bath, fresh water was too precious, so on a calm day they'd jump overboard into the Atlantic holding on to ropes and swim and use soap and then get up and out. They couldn't rinse off, so they had to wear their clothes on salty bodies, but at least they were washed by the ocean.

DUNBAR: Seward was the cook. It was my job to think up things to do. One day, to pass the time, I suggested we play a game. He was supposed to write down all the Johnson & Johnson products he could think of. He told me, "There's no way I'm going to do that. There's Baby Powder and Band-Aids and that's about it for me."

JENNIFER: I must have been about fifteen when the *Ocean Pearl* arrived in Chatham for the first time. They let me take the helm. There were brooms painted black for buoys and I was supposed to steer by them. It was so exciting and I was so frightened when I hit one of them, I thought I'd wreck it.

Spaulding Dunbar says that the cost of Johnson's sailing vessels was of little concern to him. "He wanted his comforts, he wanted what he wanted. He didn't get past that. I doubt Seward Johnson could have lived in the real world." A small act typifies Johnson's attitude. A trash can was purchased for the boat for $17.95, but later it was cleaned by a boatyard at a cost of $52. Dunbar was infuriated, but Seward said he wanted no fuss and paid the bill.

Almost every acquaintance has a "no fuss" story about Seward Johnson. Once he arrived at a boatyard to pick up the *Sea Goose* for a race, only to find that the ship's motor had been totally dismantled. Instead of reprimanding people, he simply asked for a box, gathered up the pieces of the motor, and took the boat out under sail.

According to Dunbar, Johnson did not particularly like to have his children Jennifer and Jimmy on the boat because "they squabbled and were fidgety." But Seward Jr. perceived Jennifer and Jimmy as "insiders," while he and his sisters were "outsiders." Junior never felt comfortable at Essie's house, and recalls a particularly painful time when at sixteen, after a summer of hiking, he visited his father at Chatham. Essie found him so dirty and disheveled that she would not let him sleep in the house—his father had a bed made up for him on the boat. Junior's sisters kept telling him how much trouble his father had gone to, to prepare the bed, but Junior felt that his father would not stand behind him in even so small a matter.

Whenever he wished, Seward Johnson took long boat trips without his wife. Esther Johnson did not share her husband's interest in sailing. Spaulding Dunbar recalls that once when Essie was due to arrive at Jupiter Island, he and Seward sailed for two days straight because Seward was so excited at the prospect of seeing her. However, when they arrived and he asked Essie to come out on the boat, she said she would on condition that they only go out between ten in the morning and two in the afternoon and never leave the inland waterway. After a time Johnson gave up on trying to have his wife accompany him.

Over the years the *Ocean Pearl* numbered many beautiful women among its guests. When Seward embarked on a

fishing trip on the St. Lawrence Seaway, he produced from
his pocket a picture of a handsome Norwegian stewardess
and told Dunbar, "That's my Norwegian salmon." Dunbar, who described his own wife, Doris, as "not the jealous
type," also pursued many women. On one occasion, according to Seward Jr., Essie's sister Lorna Sagendorf stood
with binoculars in her living room in Chatham, observing
Seward and Spaulding with a woman on the *Ocean Pearl.*
On another occasion Essie arrived at the Dunbars' house
and persuaded Doris to accompany her on a trip so that
when their husbands arrived home and did not find them
they would begin to appreciate them more. When the two
wives returned a week later, their husbands were in residence, but the subject was never discussed.

The end of Spaulding Dunbar and Seward Johnson's
close friendship came over a woman. In the late 1960s
Seward unremittingly pursued a young woman who sum-
mered in Chatham, but she preferred the company of
Spaulding. Seward never discussed this with his friend, but
a coldness grew between the two men. Dunbar says that in
retrospect he would have liked to have cleared the air, but
that once he asked Seward Johnson if anything was wrong
and Seward asserted that nothing had changed. During the
will contest Ray Gore, captain of the *Ocean Pearl,* testified
that four months before Seward Johnson's death he had
said, "When I'm gone, will you please go by and see Mrs.
Esther Johnson and Spaulding Dunbar. Say goodbye for
me and buy Spaulding a drink." Gore added that Johnson
then went on, "And watch out for Mrs. Zagat. I don't
trust her."

In 1971 Seward Johnson sent Dunbar to Poland to super-
vise the conversion of the *Mazurka,* a North Atlantic
trawler that he had purchased from a relative of the soon-

to-be third Mrs. Johnson, Barbara Piasecka. According to
Dunbar, this old steel boat, fine as a trawler, was a disaster
as a yacht. Eleven million dollars went into it, but the
conversion was never successful. Dunbar was convinced
that for the first time since he'd known Seward Johnson his
desire to please a woman had superseded his nautical
sense. The *Mazurka*, complete with red flocked walls and
gold-trimmed curtains, was a barely seaworthy hotel, and
it was finally donated to the U.S. Merchant Marine Acad-
emy. Dunbar concluded that Basia was a woman to be
reckoned with. While in Poland, Dunbar met several of
Basia's relatives and he confirmed when she desperately
insisted throughout the trial, that they were Polish aristoc-
racy.

DUNBAR: I have no doubt that her antecedents were a lot
    finer than those of Seward Johnson. I met Basia for the
    first time in Italy in 1971, before going to Poland. She
    was a strong and charming woman who gave Seward a
    lot of pleasure, but also I'm sure she was determined to
    be the wealthiest widow in Poland. Seward was patheti-
    cally devoted to her, an old man with someone who
    made him feel like a young one.

"Always I dream for a better life . . ."

In 1784 King Louis XVI commissioned Adam Weisweiler to create a black-and-gold, Japanese-lacquered secretaire with heavy gilt-bronze mounts. It was delivered to Versailles, and subsequently the King took it with him to the Tuileries when he was placed under house arrest before being guillotined.

On a humid July day in 1983, Basia Piasecka Johnson sat in the front row of Sotheby's frumpy, green-walled London auction gallery and outbid Versailles and the J. Paul Getty Museum for this secretaire, paying $1.5 million, the highest price ever recorded at auction for a single piece of furniture. Hidden behind one of the panels in the cabinet was a bonus, a sheet of eighteen lottery tickets from the year 1781. It was a scant eight weeks after her husband's death and Basia, slated to inherit approximately half a billion dollars, might be said to have won a lottery of her own.

The appeal of the lottery winner is deeply ingrained in the American psyche. In fact, the myth of striking it rich is a basic one in our culture, but then so is the opposing Puritan ethic deploring the vice of extravagance. We are a society in transition, still engaged in the battle between the stern values of our forefathers and our present worship of affluence and celebrity. Our compromise is to revel in opulence vicariously, but to relish tales of rich people who experience a comeuppance. We still need to hear that the rich are corrupt, unhappy, lead empty lives, and are plagued with misfortune, and of course the story of the Johnsons gratifies this need all too dramatically.

Media images present life in vivid primary colors that replace a more complicated and perhaps unknowable reality. The fundamental question on which this will contest centered was: Did Barbara Piasecka Johnson give her husband "a new lease on life," as her attorney suggested, or did she, as the children's attorney asserted, teach him "a new kind of servitude"? Was their life together "the dream" her attorney depicted or the "nightmare" the children's attorney said it was? This question was never answered. Perhaps that was because it was not a real question, but rather a legal construction having little to do with the reality of this complex woman and her relationship with her husband.

During the trial Basia understandably balked at the simplistic picture of herself as a Polish chambermaid raised to multimillionairess and fought the stigma by emphasizing her master's degree in art history. She remarked to one reporter, "I come from noble family." In probing beneath this easily accessible image, one finds less understandable contradictions in the personality of Basia Piasecka Johnson. In describing Basia, people who know her use the adjectives *headstrong, energetic, willful, vital, volatile, determined.* As far as the media coverage of the Johnson will contest was concerned, her history began in 1968 when she found employment in the Johnson household. But the shards of a much earlier history illuminate why she and Seward Johnson led the life they did and, ultimately, why she acted as she did, both in her marriage and in the court contest. From earliest childhood Basia Piasecka's life was one of striving and of disappointment and of harrowing experiences unimaginable to most Americans, who take political freedom for granted.

BASIA: My first memory is like a flash—somebody grabbing me and tearing away from me my father. My father was beaten afterward. They put us against the wall—my whole family, my brothers were there. They pointed machine guns at us as if to shoot us. We were standing there for hours.

I know from what my parents were telling me later that we were invaded. They bombarded the church, they killed the priest. The man who was taking care of the forest was tied to a tree and he was eaten by wolves. His flesh was completely eaten in two hours. I was two years, two years and seven months. That was when the Bolsheviks came, and the Nazis in 1939. They invaded Poland from the east side. The agreement between Hitler and Ribbentrop, and Stalin and Molotov, at that time was to divide Poland completely, and the east side of Poland will be Russian and the western part of Poland will be German. They have a plan that Poland will never exist on the map of this earth. And that is my first memory.

I have a second memory. We were under the arrest in our house, but we managed to escape. We were escaping. The peasants were shouting at us. They gave us hot, very hot coffee and it was an accident—he poured the coffee on my foot and I felt terrible pain. My mother was comforting me and I didn't cry. I was in a hospital with a huge room, but I was in a crib in the corridor because the hospital was very crowded. I was there to cure my foot, which still has a big scar which shows where it was burned. My brother Peter was there, he had pneumonia. My mother was spending more time with my brother than with me because he was very, very sick. I saw a woman passing by, in white. She looks like a nurse with the white. The white. When she pass by, I recognize her by her legs. She is surprised when I call out, "Mother, come." Then somebody show me two dead people. I see the dead people.

My next memories—I remember night and snow and forest. We are lying on the ground in the snow and I heard on the slope above us the horses' hoofs and the soldiers. It was Christmas Eve, we were escaping across the border. In Poland, Christmas Eve is the most important time of Christmas. We don't know where to go, so we follow one man and we found ourselves in a shelter, we came Warsaw on Christmas Eve. I remember the picture again: the woman dressed in white is coming toward with me with chocolate, and she says, "You say 'Heil, Hitler' and I will give you the chocolate." And my mother says very quietly, "Don't do it." And I say, "I don't like the chocolate."

We came as we were dressed—with nothing, nothing, you know. We begin many times. We had to escape the second time from the Bolsheviks in 1945. Begin again. Begin again. We spend the time in Warsaw. My father knew German perfectly, so he was a translator for the Poles and the Germans, and the ghetto was created for the Jews, and he managed to rescue many Jews because of his German language. After the war they gave a beautiful house to my father to repay him for what he'd lost in eastern Poland. For a year and a half we had that house. It was beautiful: great carpets, great paintings, and great furniture—a beautiful, beautiful house, very much like we have here at Jasna Polana, but maybe not that large. In 1947 they came and took it away—everything away from our house, from my father. Not everything, but many things. They took all the animals, they carried away the furniture, paintings. They came into my father's house and took away the piano. That is true. Many things they did. They made my home their headquarters. Always the Russians were after my father, all the time. In 1920 already the communists were there. My father was fighting not only for Poland, but for America. In 1942, in 1944, we were constantly persecuted by bad people, but I was persecuted here by bad people, in New York, in the United States. Here too there are bad people, I can tell you the truth of that. But when I was growing up, my father, he taught me I have a choice: you can do what is good or what is bad. My father taught me what is good and what is wrong and that I have a choice. That's what it is. My father was a very strong person.

After they took away our things, there was an agrarian reform, that there shouldn't be any more private ownership, so they left my father for a while with fifteen acres. But he couldn't do anything with that, so he gave away the farm. Not to sell it, he gave it away. In Poland he was a landlord. We come from one of the oldest families in Poland. During the partitioning of Poland they took away everything. Everything was taken away again and again.

I speak Polish, Italian, some Russian, some German. In university I took four years for my degree. All the art books are in German, they require German. I ask for asylum in Italy and I come here after. I was a refugee.

They portray me as an immigrant, a poor immigrant, which is not true. I didn't need to immigrate because of my poverty. My family was, you know, okay in Poland. I escape, I refused go back to Poland. If the political system was different, I would never come to this country. I would never need to.

I am a deeply religious person. I have religion in my heart. Always I dream for a better life, that I can create something. I felt that I'm full of energy and I can do many things which God gave me to do. I felt that all the time. I was never afraid of hard working and strong dreams.

According to her account, from 1958 to 1965 Basia Piasecka helped her father and brothers with the building of their house and the administration of the farm and attended Boleslaw Bierut University of Wroclaw. The subject of her Master of Arts dissertation was "Jan Stanislawski—Creator of Modern Polish Landscape Painting." After completing her courses, she received one of the first Vatican scholarships to study art in Rome and Florence. Basia's father then encouraged her to immigrate to the United States. She arrived on Labor Day of 1968, and through the Polish American Immigration and Relief Committee was placed in an inexpensive hotel. Friends in the Polish community in Perth Amboy introduced her to Zofia Koverdan, a cook at the Seward Johnsons' Oldwick, New Jersey, farm. Zofia had told Esther Johnson that she needed help, and Esther hired Basia as her assistant. Basia proved inadequate as a cook: "I could never figure out the timing of the meal so that it would all come together at the same time. I don't know how to cook American cooking and many things went wrong. Actually I wanted to resign from this position, but Mrs. Johnson made me stay. She asked me whether this work is too difficult, too hard for me, and perhaps I would prefer to do something else. I said, 'I will see, I will try.' She wanted that I take care of the grandchildren when they come. She knew that I have a very good attitude toward children, as well as toward the animals." Essie Johnson switched Basia to chambermaid and waitressing work, and occasional baby-sitting.

In her depositions Basia endeavored to paint a portrait of a somewhat sanitized courtship and an ideal marriage. She maintained that when she worked for Johnson he "was at home very rarely and he almost not have any communication with me." She declared, "I knew that he was a wealthy man, but I was not interested in how much money he owns." In an interview, however, Basia said that a few days after she started working at Oldwick, Seward Johnson came into the kitchen and introduced himself. "My wife told me we have a new, pretty cook. I hope you will be happy here." Basia recalled, "Because my English was not very good, I simply smiled at him." Then Johnson said, " 'With a smile like that you can conquer America.' He told me later that he had never gone to the kitchen before to introduce himself to the servants."

In another interview she declared that Johnson told her, "I fell in love with you when you were in our house working." Her reaction to that was, "I never expected because we could hardly talk to each other." And Basia stated that Jennifer told her that Seward nearly ran his yacht aground when he saw her walking on the beach in Chatham in her new $20 bathing suit.

One deposition reveals the sexual nuances of life in the Johnson household. Basia says that Keith Wold strolled into the kitchen and asked her to make him a cup of tea. At that point Essie stormed in and yelled at Keith that Basia had been working long, hard hours and that it was time for her to rest. Essie sent Basia to her room after warning her "to lock my door from inside." The next morning the Wolds left very early and everyone was talking about the incident. Later on, Basia stated that she assured Seward that Essie was overreacting and that Keith Wold was "not making passes" at her, but, according to Basia, Seward became angry at Keith. "My husband told me that a man who has such attitude toward women as Keith Wold had, the attitude which he demonstrated even in connection with me, because Mr. Johnson was informed by his wife about passes he had made on me in Oldwick. And also he expressed his disappointment about this man who has the profession of a doctor who is not working, but is taking advantage of his wife's wealth." Dr. Keith Wold, a retired ophthalmologist and head of several investment companies, says that Basia's assertions are "both venomous and groundless."

At the end of ten months Basia had saved over $3,000 from her $100-a-week salary and left to enroll in an English class at New York University. According to Basia, a few days before she was ready to leave, Seward Johnson came over to her on the beach at Chatham and told her that he hoped she would leave her telephone number with his secretary. When she did not seem enthusiastic about doing so, he jotted down her phone number himself. One week after she had left the job, she returned from a trip to find three messages from Seward Johnson waiting for her. On the fourth try, he implored her to come to his office, saying that he had "something very important to discuss," and he sent his limousine to bring her to his office at Johnson & Johnson. The office was an impressive one, decorated with half-models of his various sailing vessels, several abstract paintings, and a fine antique English desk.

Considering that Basia's English was extremely limited

at the time, one can make of the following account what
one will. "He explained the reason he had called me. He
said he was very impressed when he learned that I had
saved my money earned by hard work in order to under-
take my studies, that he respects me very much for this
reason. That I remind him of the American pioneers, and
that he's convinced that these kind of people deserve support."

He said he knew she was an art historian and asked her
opinion of the paintings in his office, a Franz Kline and
two Hans Hofmanns. Of the Kline, Basia said, "His painting is very good, and the stroke of his brush is very decisive and strong and expressive, and it expresses the way he
is making quick decisions." Evidently Basia was making a
quick decision of her own.

"Mr. Johnson agreed with my comments, and he said
. . . he felt exactly the same on the matter." Then Basia
severely criticized both paintings by the American master
Hans Hofmann, saying that they "do not have any artistic
value and they do not express anything specific." Again
Seward Johnson "agreed with my opinion and added that
this is exactly the reason why he needs my help." He characterized her analysis as "very brave and decisive."

By now one might perceive—even if Basia may not
have—the familiar music of the mating dance. Basia says
she told Seward, "So long as I am healthy and well, I will
be working. I am too proud to ask anyone for money." He
replied that it was his intention to collect art and that he
would like to use her expertise as a curator (subsequently
she received $12,000 a year for these services). He could
also foresee a future for her in his oceanographic institute,
he said, and he suggested scuba-diving lessons, with the
caveat that she must take them quickly because in a month
and a half he wanted to leave on a trip. He volunteered to

pay for the lessons, told her to travel to them in a car, and gave her a check for $2,000 to cover expenses. Basia "thanked him for his understanding and generosity. I promised that I will act accordingly to his wish and I will do my best to satisfy him."

Basia says she was then engaged to a world-class sailor, Peter Ejsmont, and that her relationship with Johnson at that time was platonic. Not until Ejsmont was lost at sea in December of 1969 did she become romantically involved with Johnson. Seward Jr., however, states that in the winter of 1968 he visited his father, who never drank or smoked, and found him with his feet propped up on the corner of the desk, leaning back in his chair, smoking a cigar, and sipping a brandy. Seward announced to his son that he was "going to take on a mistress." "My first thought was that because of Uncle Bob's death he felt completely adrift and also in a new way became aware of his own mortality. I also realized that he was probably confiding in me because he was aware of my resentment of Essie and it was his way of announcing his decision to loosen up from that relationship."

In November 1969, thirty-two-year-old Basia and seventy-four-year-old Seward left on the *Ocean Pearl* for the Bahamas. Captain Ray Gore testified that Seward instructed him that he was no longer to enter the names of the passengers in the ship's log. Basia contends that Seward brought a blonde girlfriend who played the flute, and Carter Nicholas brought his girlfriend, Lane Warfield. This was the first time Basia met Nicholas, who was Seward's nephew and trusted legal adviser. The trip marked the beginning of a life of glamour for Basia and was followed by trips with Seward to Rome, Paris, London, Ireland, where she was welcomed by friends, relatives, and directors of Johnson & Johnson. They'd visit art galleries, purchasing a $250,000 Mondrian, a $100,000 Picasso, a Cézanne for $250,000. Basia gave Seward "an oral analysis" on the spot when they were deciding on art. By 1970 she was ensconced in an apartment on Sutton Place, paid for by her benefactor.

When Joyce and Seward Jr. visited them there in the fall of 1970, Seward marched them into the bedroom to point to a nude painting hanging over the bed. "His retiring demeanor changed to an almost combative swagger," said Junior. Joyce Johnson concluded that her father-in-law was "gauche. He had a rather childish ego." For her part, Basia recalls, "I was very surprised because I had never heard about this son before. They were very impressed by the paintings that they saw and Junior was very happy that he had seen his father after a long period of time. They were very kind to me." When Mary Lea visited, she observed that Basia was pleasant, giggled a lot, and clung to Seward's arm. Mary Lea's father told her, "I found the ideal woman for me. She can't speak English, so I can't talk to her, and therefore I don't have to listen to her."

Several Johnson relatives speculate that had General Johnson not died in January of 1968, Basia Piasecka might simply have taken her place among Seward Johnson's extramarital affairs. According to several accounts, Bob Johnson was the one who had handled the women in Seward's life. "When they got too close or destructive or grabby, Uncle Bob would call them up and say, 'If you don't leave my brother alone, I'll disinherit him,' although of course he couldn't do any such thing," explains Seward Jr. "The General paid them off or scared them off," says another relative. In any case, Basia Johnson was not like the other women in Seward's life.

At Christmas, Seward gave Essie a locket, a gesture

that left her thinking the affair with Basia would run its course, but in January 1970 Seward moved into the Sutton Place apartment. Essie expected him to return, and he let her think he would, but on Basia's birthday, February 25, 1970, in São Paulo, Brazil, he proposed, she accepted, they drank a champagne toast. Seward bought Basia an exquisite oval amethyst-and-diamond ring, which she wore during the will contest with the large stone turned inward so that only a thin platinum band was visible to spectators and the jury.

According to Jennifer's testimony, Essie kept "hoping he would come back, but he didn't. Then his lawyer came over with the divorce papers one day, but she didn't know this [was going to take place]. She was upset, and said, 'Oh, I just want to forget it all.' My mother was devastated. She was depressed probably for three or four years. She never really recovered from losing my father. She was ill; she had terrible stomach pains off and on for a whole year. It just changed everything."

In May of 1970, while preparing to divorce Essie, Seward Johnson executed a will leaving the bulk of his estate to charity. On the same day he purchased the Sutton Place apartment for Basia for $110,000 and established a $50,000 trust for her. Basia recalls that Seward told her "that he would like to guarantee my financial safety and he wants to do it as quickly as possible." The wills were signed at the office of Seward's lawyer Robert Myers in Washington, D.C.

ELAINE: He sort of was getting out of one life into a new life. We invited ourselves to Ansedonia [Italy] about six months before they were married. That was when we saw Basia preparing to be Mrs. Seward Johnson. It was quite a shock. We met Basia's mother and father, and her brother, and none of them spoke a word of English. And so we smiled at all the family during dinner. It was a terribly uncomfortable feeling, but it was wonderful to see Dad, and the whole idea was to see Dad, even under these new conditions. Under any conditions.

I had never seen a person that wanted something so much or was so determined. I'd met a fanatic. I steered clear of her because I knew that there just wasn't any way I could understand her. If I could understand her, then I would know what the answers to a lot of these things were. I don't think anybody understands Basia.

KEITH: When we first went to Ansedonia, Basia and Seward were very good together. They were not married yet. They wore the same kind of watches, and each shared the half of a martini, and she was constantly looking after his needs and asking him if she could do anything. The next time we saw them, after they were married, she was yelling and screaming at him. The difference was like night and day.

In January of 1971 Carter Nicholas, thinking that Basia Piasecka should have her own representation, recommended Shearman & Sterling's Thomas Ford, who assigned the job to Nina Zagat. Zagat and Basia met for the first time on January 11, 1971, when the twenty-eight-year-old associate witnessed Basia's signature on her will. Simultaneously, Seward wrote a codicil to his May 5, 1970, will, leaving Basia nine thousand shares of Johnson & Johnson stock, worth $800,000. On November 3, 1971, Seward's divorce from Esther Underwood became final. On the 10th he signed an ante-nuptial agreement with Basia, granting her $250,000 outright plus the income from a $10 million marital trust. The following day Seward and

Basia were married. His children were not invited to the ceremony.

Once again Seward Johnson's patterns of behavior reasserted themselves as he fulfilled his needs with a love object he encountered in his own home. Once again there was the identification of someone else's strong interests as his own, and the use of his wealth as an enticement.

BASIA: It was always our destiny to meet. I believe it, this was my destiny. How can I come from a country that isn't free and how I come here and I could have taken another job. They wanted me in a library, but they paid so little and I didn't know enough English. So I said to myself, "It's much better to go to a place where you can save money. If I took another job, I'd have to pay room and buy my food. How could I do it? I'd have to work five or ten years to save, and this way I could save everything I earned. I have to do something with my life, and I think with this kind of job I can save money and I can work a year and then the next year I can go to school. I know that I am healthy, that I can work and save, and so I take this job." I didn't realize that they were rich people that live in that house. I didn't realize that they have millions and millions. The carpet on the floor, it was a poison green. I thought they were poor people. They had no evidence of taste, no evidence of wealth.

That's what is my destiny. You understand that? I never loved more anybody than my husband. I loved my father, but this is a different love. I mean, they were on the same level, but my husband was my husband, truly my husband. When my husband talked, sometimes I could hear my father talking. In philosophy my husband remind me of my father. That's why we were so close and we understand each other without words some-

times. It was great, great. Great times I used to have
with my husband because it was a continuation, you
know. I left my father, who was my mentor, and I came
here, and here it is again. I am very lucky. I am very
lucky and very happy. And very positive, even if very
sad things happened.

For the first time in his life, Seward had love. This
man doesn't live only by bread, and I helped him discover life. His other two wives, they did nothing for him,
neither the children. He said to me I was one of the best
Americans, the one who brought out the best in him.
Seward was my hero. He was the best kind of hero and
he taught me many things and I taught him how to live.
He told me I taught him the example of how to give.
Before me, he didn't know how to give.

Christopher Johnson, Seward's grandnephew, says Basia came into the quiet, meek Johnson family like a breath
of fresh air. She took Chris, who was then a teenager, for a
ride in her MG TF roadster, her blonde hair streaming out
behind her. She called her husband by the endearments
"Romeo" and "Sewardo." "There was no doubt that he
was crazy about her," says Spaulding Dunbar. "He'd tell
me, 'I can't believe my luck; someone like Basia—a beautiful young girl, and she's in love with me. She's sexually
attracted to me!' He couldn't get over it." Basia rejuve-
nated her husband; he took to wearing turtlenecks and a
Bulgari medallion. He sped along in his Jaguar convertible
as if he were a race-car driver.

The Johnson children all testified in depositions that
they did not know the contents of any of their father's
wills, nor, in the early years of their father's marriage to
Basia, did they seem concerned with this subject. When
Seward had divorced Ruth Dill, he had given her an in-

come of $12,000 a year. Esther Underwood received $20 million. When General Johnson died, he had left his widow, Evelyne, $20 million, while the remainder of his $1.1 billion estate went to the Robert Wood Johnson Foundation. Seward's children speculated that, like General Johnson, their father would leave a great deal to charity. Furthermore, in 1964 Seward had confided to his lawyer Robert Myers that when he'd set up trusts for his children, he'd expected to give them a third of his estate, to donate a third to charity, and to use the final third to "live it up."

At the time of his third marriage, Seward's stockholdings in Johnson & Johnson alone were worth approximately $400 million. The children assumed that the art would be put in Basia's name and that was one of the reasons why she bought so much. They were correct. Even under the Johnsons' ante-nuptial agreement, the stock of Fine Arts Mutual, which purchased art, and R.E.I. Company, which purchased antiques, was to go to Basia. Marty Richards recalls Seward taking him aside and saying, "For God's sake, don't talk art in front of Basia. Every time you mention the word, she goes out and buys another painting."

With each new will, Basia's share of the estate was steadily growing. On May 8, 1972, Basia's marital trust was increased from $10 million to $50 million. On January 17, 1973, the trust was increased to $100 million with the proviso that she receive the income but upon her death the corpus would go to a charitable foundation to be selected with Basia's approval. These wills were drawn by Robert Myers, Seward Johnson's personal attorney. On April 11, 1973, for the first time, Shearman & Sterling drew a will for Seward Johnson. In this will Basia still received a $100 million trust, but she was given the power to withdraw the entire principal.

Myers wrote Seward Johnson that this will could increase his federal and state taxes by $43 million. In a spir-
ited exchange Shearman & Sterling's Thomas Ford answered Myers in a manner that spotlighted the shift in
power inherent in these maneuverings and cut to what was
later to become the heart of the dispute. "Mr. Myers
seemed to have a completely different conception of what
Mr. Johnson wanted to do for Mrs. Johnson than we did.
Our instructions had been to give Mrs. Johnson as much as
possible. We therefore had expanded Mrs. Johnson's control over the disposition of the trust. We added the power
for her to withdraw funds from the trust and to make gifts
from it. Mr. Myers seemed to think that Mr. Johnson was
concerned about Mrs. Johnson's falling under bad influences after Mr. Johnson's death and possibly losing her
trust fund. We explained to Mr. Myers that since we had
been asked to basically represent Mrs. Johnson's interests
in the drafting of Mr. Johnson's will, we thought that he,
as Mr. Johnson's personal lawyer, should discuss the matter with Mr. Johnson."

It was Robert Myers who drew a codicil to this will
limiting Basia's power to invade the principal of the trust.
During the will contest, two witnesses testified that after
this episode Basia said that Myers posed an "obstacle" to
her plans. They also reported that Basia wished to replace
Seward Johnson's personal secretary, Fran Peree. In June
of 1972 Seward Johnson told Basia that he had fired Fran
Peree and removed her from his will. Actually, Seward
had switched Fran Peree to working for another Johnson
& Johnson executive and had instructed Robert Myers to
buy her an annuity that would yield her $116,000, which
was slightly more than the bequest he had left her under
his will. On July 10, 1973, Myers was fired.

Myers was to testify that he had gone to Seward Johnson's office and in the ensuing conversation "I told Mr. Johnson that I felt that I had no longer the confidence of Mrs. Johnson. I could understand her feelings because, as I told Mr. Johnson, she had caused a modification of his estate plan, then I had caused a reversal of that modification, and I could understand why her feelings for me might be somewhat less than enthusiastic. I don't believe we discussed the matter in greater detail than that. He told me that he felt that I had served him very well."

Now Shearman & Sterling became both Johnsons' lawyers and associate Nina Zagat began to do more and more work for them as well as for Harbor Branch. In 1971 this charitable foundation was essentially dormant, a philanthropic shell. Basia Johnson says that it was her spirit that breathed life into this organization. Donald Christ says of Harbor Branch, "In a way, it was the child of Seward and Basia Johnson." Basia says that it was her energy that gave her husband a purpose in the last years of his life.

BASIA: We considered it our future accomplishment of living together that we will promote art and science. His other two wives, they did not encourage him. I made Harbor Branch. It was not him, it was I. I said, "Let's go with that." Harbor Branch was to have a goal, I wanted it working for my husband. I said we could do great things, I told him that I will support Harbor Branch with all my heart. I didn't have to stay there in that place. It is not such a good place. I could have gone to Paris or done what I wanted. Instead, I was there, I wanted that for him.

Into the fabric of the life Basia and Seward Johnson increasingly shared, there would be woven the figure of Nina Zagat. She and Basia were near-contemporaries,

Zagat being only five years Basia's junior. Nina Safronoff was a graduate of Vassar, class of 1963, and Yale Law School, 1966. In 1965 she'd married a Yale classmate, Eugene "Tim" Zagat. She joined the firm of Shearman & Sterling as an associate in 1967 and was placed in the Individual Clients Group headed by Thomas Ford. This group of seventeen lawyers provided a wide spectrum of services: wealthy clients did not have to consult different departments coping with their various needs, such as taxes, trusts and estates work, litigation; one unit did it all. Soon Zagat was servicing one client in particular, and for Zagat an account as important as that of the vastly rich Seward Johnson was considered a plum.

Johnson was known as a "professional testator," and Zagat began to work on his numerous wills and codicils. But she became more than a lawyer, she became an all-service person, arranging for building material to clear customs, for a Sotheby's sale of Johnson artworks, applying for building permits and tax abatements, making restaurant reservations (she is co-publisher of the Zagat *New York City Restaurant Survey*), accompanying Basia on her European travels and art-buying tours, and even arranging the flowers for Seward Johnson's funeral. She partook of the Johnsons' life, visiting their estates, attending birthday parties and social lunches, and wore Basia's clothes and jewelry when her luggage was lost on a trip to Children's Bay Cay, the Johnsons' private Bahamian island. In February of 1975 Carter Nicholas died. One year later Seward Sr. asked Nina Zagat to become a co-executor and trustee of his estate. Nina replied, "I would be happy to," and Thomas Ford, in the Shearman & Sterling office, informed Zagat that as an associate she would be free to keep her fees and would not be required to turn them over to the firm as partners must. At that time, commissions on the

Johnson estate were limited to 1.5 percent, yielding approximately $2.5 million. Nina Zagat was to remain an associate of the firm.

Jeffrey Brinck of Milbank, Tweed, Hadley & McCloy terms Nina Zagat's eventual position with the Johnsons "the renegade-associate syndrome." He explains that Zagat had a client so powerful that, although she was not a partner of Shearman & Sterling, she began to wield enormous power within the firm and was allowed to proceed largely unsupervised. "Highly unusual" and "unprecedented" are the terms he uses regarding the methods by which Zagat had a hand in drawing wills in which she was an executor and trustee.

Seward's wealth and idiosyncrasies, Basia's energy and dreams would define this marriage. They set out to create a life together where money was no object. Neither of them was a member of a cultural group: Seward was a loner, Basia a "refugee." She says of her husband, "I rely on his views because I didn't know myself many things." With Seward as her "mentor," Basia learned quickly to implement her fantasies. Mervyn Nelson was to say that Basia had told him that "when she was a girl of fifteen she was lying in a field of clover, and she was hungry and her family was hungry and then she had this heavenly inspiration. She heard voices, heavenly voices, and they told her that she should go out and make her way in the world and buy up all this artwork and that she could try to help Poland."

"I wonder what it's like to wake up one morning and find that you have money beyond your wildest dreams. I wonder what you would do," a friend of Basia's said. What struck the Johnson children was the rampant luxury of their father's new lifestyle. At Oldwick, Seward had "lived a life that was very moderate. Now he stopped doing all the things he'd enjoyed. He stopped farming altogether," says Keith Wold. The Dodge cars were replaced by Mercedes-Benzes and Bentleys, the inexpensive Bordeaux by Château Haut-Brion and Saint-Julien. He purchased a private Bahamian island now valued at $7.5 million, two houses in Ansedonia, Italy (the second because its olive grove proved an ideal place to walk the dogs), and a $2 million house in Fort Pierce, Florida. Then, on 140 acres in Princeton arose the most expensive private home in America, a $30 million Palladian mansion, Jasna Polana ("Bright Meadow"). In the first six months of 1983 the estate cost $1,007,806 to run.

Jasna Polana took four years to build. Basia personally supervised the construction. Keith Wold says she told him, "All architects are stupid." Stories of her excesses proliferate. A lawyer in the case said, "She hired and fired scores of workers and craftsmen. She ordered entire walls torn down because she didn't like the color of a few stones." The interior ceiling was not high enough, so the roof was ripped off and replaced. A hotel was rented to house the Polish workmen imported to work on the wrought-iron gates and banisters of the mansion. Betty Johnson Bushnell says Basia was "never satisfied with anything. Never content. She doesn't know what she wants. Only that she wants more. Nothing pleases her."

During the trial the press descriptions of Jasna Polana emphasized luxury: a seventy-two-foot-long swimming pool surrounded by Greek and Roman antiquities, a $78,000 orchid house, an air-conditioned doghouse, heated marble floors, a twelve-foot-square marble bathtub with Jacuzzi, gold-plated towel racks, full-grown trees imported at a cost of $30,000 apiece, His and Her Italianate gardens, and a reflecting pool full of plump carp. They are all there, but the house is in fact an eccentric combination of grandeur and the prosaic. The small octagonal breakfast room is composed of 4,200 separate pieces of wood, yet it appears no grander than the breakfast nook in many a suburban home.

With unlimited funds, fantasies can become reality. Seward's security fears were deep-rooted, and Basia considered herself a political refugee. She was a supporter of Polish Solidarity, numbering among her servants political prisoners who had been incarcerated in Poland. Shortly after the first Tylenol-tampering death on September 30, 1982, Basia and Seward attended a dinner party given by an executive of Johnson & Johnson. The hostess recalls that after dinner the women withdrew to her dressing room, where Basia declared with solemnity, "Seward and I know who is responsible for the Tylenol deaths. Yes, Seward and I know. It is the Russians. The KGB. This is how they operate. They know how important we are to Solidarity." One guest thought this must be a joke and began to giggle, but Basia's frown silenced her.

The security system at Jasna Polana is strictly James Bond. All mail and packages are examined for explosives, cars are searched, every phone call goes to a central switchboard and is screened. Three logs are kept: a vehicle log, a phone log, and an activity log. The windows in the house are bulletproof glass. Two Johnson children remember their father telling them that in case of attack they were to run into the pool area because it would be sealed off from the rest of the house. Every resident of the estate is assigned a security number, employees have time cards, activities are monitored at all times by cameras in the trees and in plastic bubbles mounted throughout the house and grounds. There are electronic beams, sensors underground and under the floors and carpets within the house, panic alarm systems, and emergency telephones. These devices are tied to a central computer in a security room, where a staff of twelve security men monitors the cameras twenty-four hours a day. In the security department there is an arsenal of .38-caliber revolvers, 357 magnums, .45-caliber automatics, 9-millimeter automatics, M-16s and other high-powered rifles with scopes, 12-gauge riot shotguns.

And Basia's dream? "When I came here, I pick up tradition very quickly of American life to build a monument for the Johnson family, an art collection . . . like Mellon, Rockefeller, Frick." Although Basia insists that she is fulfilling the "vision and dreams" of her husband, the impetus toward art was surely hers. As Keith Wold testified, Seward Johnson's idea of art was the Durham bull painted on the side of a barn.

The art collection, estimated in value at approximately $100 million, concentrates on religious art and Old Masters, but the rooms are also chockablock with museum-quality furniture, Flemish tapestries, Renaissance bronzes, and antiquities. The price tags cannot fail to impress: $4.8 million for a 14⁵/₁₆-by-13¹/₂-inch Raphael black-chalk sketch; the $1.5 million Louis XVI secretaire; $935,000 for a Louis XIV boulle table with ormolu mounts; $375,000 for a pair of Louis XVI candelabra; a $203,500 pair of Louis XV armchairs; $550,000 for Zurbarán's *Saint Sebastian;* $1.75 million for Bellini's *Madonna and Child;* $1.5 million for Rembrandt's *Man with Arms Akimbo;* $3 million for Gauguin's *Maternité;* Botticelli's *Madonna and Child with Angels,* $1 million; Van Gogh's *Le Laboreur,* $1 million; Cézanne's *Allée at Chantilly,* $950,000; and Monet's *Pheasants,* $850,000.

But the quality is there, sometimes in gems such as an Orazio Gentileschi *Madonna and Child,* a painting by the Master of The Annunciations to the Shepherds, a Giorgione-Titian *Angel Pietà,* Lodovico Carracci's *Saint Peter,* and two Castigliones, *God the Father Creating the Animals* and *St. Francis of Assisi.* Six fourth-century South Italian vases are outstanding, as is the collection of Renaissance bronzes. Alan Rosenbaum, director of the Princeton Museum, asserts that this is the collection of someone who is going for the top picture in the same way that the Getty Museum is. It is also the collection of someone with unlimited funds and a vision. Rosenbaum says that Basia has "a noble ambition."

Basia plans to house much of her art in a twin-domed gallery still on the drawing board and a chapel already begun. Basia and her brother Gregory drove through Europe looking for historical precedents for the chapel and decided on a design by the sixteenth-century Italian architect Giacomo Vignola. She has commissioned a bell for the chapel inscribed on one side, "To the Greatest Friend of Poland, J. Seward Johnson, May 23, 1983," and on the other side, "Solidarity, 1980."

In envisioning their chapel, Basia said that her husband wanted the two Castigliones in it—the *St. Francis* and *God the Father Creating the Animals.* To Basia and Seward, St. Francis had a special meaning since animals assumed an important and beloved position in their life together. Seward Johnson particularly loved his dogs and owned five dachshunds and a mastiff as well as a favorite boxer, Prince. From several reports, Prince was to be buried in the chapel along with Basia and Seward. However, after the trial, reporters were shown Prince's grave under a tree at Jasna Polana and Basia denied that there had ever been plans to bury him in the chapel.

In June of 1983, one month after Seward Johnson's death, Maksymilian Kolbe was elevated to sainthood. On June

18, 1983, Pope John Paul II traveled thirty miles outside of Warsaw to the religious community of Niepokalanow to celebrate an outdoor mass in honor of Kolbe, a Franciscan priest who volunteered to die in the place of a fellow Polish man chosen for torture and execution at Auschwitz, saying that he was a lone priest while the intended victim had a family. During the mass the forbidden red logotype of the outlawed Solidarity union was unfurled, and at the end of the mass, after the singing of the religious and patriotic hymn "God Save Poland," the great majority of the almost half-million Poles gathered there raised their right hands, their fingers spread in the V-for-Victory sign that has become the unofficial symbol of Solidarity. Basia Johnson determined to dedicate her chapel to the memory of Maksymilian Kolbe.

Perhaps the clearest illustration of Basia and Seward Johnson's symbiotic mentalities is the building of a nuclear shelter beneath the chapel at Jasna Polana. Basia asserts that she and her husband talked "about the threat of the future war, and we even talked about the necessity to build the atomic shelter at Jasna Polana. We discussed the place which would be appropriate to construct a shelter, and we discussed the necessity to preserve not only human life, but also life of some animals and some objects of art and also some books to preserve what the human race created and achieved. He said that we have to fulfill this project." The completed shelter, designed for a nuclear holocaust, is stocked with five thousand gallons of water, ten thousand gallons of fuel, two electric generators, five freezers, an air purifier, and four periscopes—a reminder of the nautical Johnson.

Basia, like her late husband, is an individual of many contradictions. She is a woman who surrounds herself with opulent material possessions, yet she feels that Americans have been corrupted by their worship of wealth; a woman who lives the pampered life of an empress, yet she envisions herself a pioneer spirit who will lead a crusade back to basic values to create a simpler, greater America.

BASIA: In America, money is the God. Money is the only God. They worship money in America. But if you don't have spirit, money doesn't help you. I'd rather live in a free Poland today, because there I can do many things because they have spirit, not only money. We know money can be taken away. If you have spirit, nobody can take that away from you. What is money? I will use my money to make wonderful things, to make a contribution. What will those children use their money for? Nothing. They only consume things. They eat bread and go to the bathroom. They think only of themselves. Who are they? What are they? You have to understand that. They are absolutely the enemies of this country. Did those children ever give out of their own fortune one penny that was given them by their father to charity? They are so poor and so primitive. They are the most primitive people I have ever seen.

Look at the money they have. What would happen if you took that money from them? They wouldn't last five minutes. Do they have, as I have, resources to fall back on? Can they work as chambermaid? Do they have, as I have, an art-history diploma so they could work? If the money was taken from them today, what would they be tomorrow? They are *tabula rasa*. I have to achieve in life, I have to better myself, or else why should I be alive?

Self-criticism can be very productive. America is such a beautiful country. They came here and killed all the

Indians and said, "This is our country." And then they
turn and laugh at me as an immigrant. They are laughing at themselves when they laugh at me as an immigrant. They are envious because I am intelligent, they
envy that I get what I got, they envy that I am educated.
This country is typical of what we're going through, and
the establishment, everything should belong to them.
They only know to take. But if I criticize, I also mean it
that this is the best country to be here and to crusade.
Because this country is the future of the world, and this
country needs a lot of teachers, a lot of philosophers, a
lot of help. We cannot give up on this country. And I
will always be faithful to this country. I might not be
faithful to the people, some of them, but at least if I
found one-thousandth percent of the people who listen
to me and do something, that's enough. I am citizen first
of all of the United States and second a citizen of the
world, because I see this country has to be great again
like it was in the eighteenth century and nineteenth century.

Part
TWO

"I walked a tightrope . . ."

Basia knew little of her husband's relationship with his family. "Many times he told me, 'The children are my past, you are my future.' He did not want to see his children," she says. But Basia felt differently. "I do believe in family and I think that it is much easier to live when the family is on good terms—when the family lives in peace. I tried to bring them together, them who once were arguing. I invited them to all family occasions, I invited them to participate in our trips."

Seward Jr. had put his seal of approval on the marriage when he'd asked Basia to dance with him at the marriage of Betty Johnson's daughter, Libbet. "I'd resented Essie very much, and I'm afraid I was human, but I enjoyed the turning of the tables. It put things in perspective. Although I regret it now, I was not displeased by this turn of events." As a result of this gesture, Basia became Junior's strong ally and encouraged his relationship with his father. After Mary Lea and Marty Richards's wedding reception, they too began to visit Seward and Basia. Bert and Diana Firestone paid infrequent visits, but Seward and Basia did accompany them to Ascot. On the surface Elaine had been the only child who had never been, even briefly, alienated from her father. Betty Johnson Bushnell observed, "Elaine writes notes even if you don't write back. Elaine is always watering her garden." But Keith Wold seemed excluded from the new family situation. Almost every summer for many years Keith had raced his own sailboat at Newport and Seward had brought the *Ocean Pearl* as a tender. Nineteen seventy-two was the last time; after that, they saw little of each other.

KEITH: I could always count on seeing him, he and Captain Ray Gore, coming towards me in the *Ocean Pearl* as we went out to start those races. He was especially useful during one race when there was a great deal of fog and we were having trouble finding out where the starting line was and Seward was ahead of us with his radar going and we sort of followed him up to the officials' boat.

ELAINE: Dad went off with Basia, dropping the boat, dropping Keith, dropping Spaulding, and dropping all of the people without as much as a thought about any of them. See, it wasn't Basia. It was his change of life, that's the way it started.

KEITH: It was part of Basia's deposition that Seward told her that he would never cruise with me again because I had called Elaine a bitch or something like that.

ELAINE: We always felt that Basia turned Dad against Keith because she knew that he was the strong one, the only one that would stand up against her, and she knew that she had to get him out of the picture.

KEITH: In retrospect, that looks like a fairly decent bet. At the time, I was really just at sea about the thing. I felt he had this young girl, and he was rediscovering parts of his life which would be certainly, under the circumstances, the normal thing to do.

ELAINE: But, Keith, she knew she had to lock horns with you or be done with it.

MARTY: Seward and Keith were great friends, they were sailing buddies for years until he married Basia. Then Keith was cut off; his anger came after that.

In fact Seward Johnson's wary nature had long been disturbed by Keith Wold. As early as December 1966 Seward had written to his brother, Bob, "I am a little suspicious that the Elaine/Keith combination—principally the Keith side of it—would really like to replace and move the management of the trust from New Brunswick to Ft. Lauderdale." Says Elaine, "Dad saw virtually nothing of Keith after he married Basia. It was devastating. Keith considered himself a close friend."

Jennifer had also been alienated from her father when he left her mother to marry Basia, but, after four years, decided that if she wanted to see her father she'd better mend her fences, and she began to visit him three or four times a year. At various periods of his life Jimmy had not seen his father for years at a time. Now he would call and come by with his wife, Gretchen.

Elaine, Jennifer, and Mary Lea were included on several of Seward and Basia's trips. The Johnson children appreciated Basia's vitality and she seemed fearless—Mary Lea remembers that in Fort Pierce she had a pet alligator, Allush, and fed him every day. At Seward's request, Marty and Mary Lea took Basia with them on a trip to California, and the senior Johnsons attended a party with them for Frank Sinatra at New York's Waldorf-Astoria, where

Seward grew impatient with the festivities, left abruptly, rented a suite of rooms, and went to bed. They also attended a dinner for Pope John Paul II at the White House. Basia seemed to enjoy the company of her stepchildren. In a letter Seward Jr. referred to her as "the peacemaker."

When Seward Johnson, Jr., returned to Princeton in 1971, he was determined to reconstruct his life and to regain his father's respect and the power he had lost by resigning as a trustee of the 1944 trusts. In 1965 he had married Joyce Horton, a woman he deeply loved, and they had two children, John Seward Johnson III, born in 1966, and Clelia, in 1969. At a Boston art school he'd attended briefly, Seward Jr. discovered a talent for sculpture and founded in Princeton the Johnson Atelier Technical Institute of Sculpture, which was to grow into one of the largest art foundries in the world. His realistic, crowd-pleasing works depict people enjoying everyday pursuits: a man hailing a taxi, two tennis players discussing a match point, three teenagers gazing at a nude girlie centerfold, a man peering into his briefcase. He characterizes his sculpture as "the kind of work you bump into and say excuse me."

Basia promoted Junior to his father, who in turn involved him in the management of Harbor Branch. Seward's marriage to Basia, Junior's return to Princeton, the development of Harbor Branch all coincided. Seward Johnson and Edwin A. Link, the respected inventor of the Link Flight Simulator, had known each other casually because both had served as trustees of the Woods Hole Oceanographic Institute. In the late 1960s Johnson became interested in a prototype research submarine that Link was developing and reportedly asked Link, "Mind if I lend a hand?" Johnson, with his love of the sea, gadgetry, and tax shelters, and Link, with his inventive genius, were to prove an interesting pair.

In 1963 Seward had set up six charitable foundations, one for each of his children, in which he placed securities that would generate an income of over $100,000 annually for each to give to charity. Mary Lea's was named Harbor Branch, but at that time she was alienated from her father and she told him that if he did not want to speak to her, she didn't want to accept the gift. Johnson kept the foundation, which lay dormant until, in 1971 and 1972, he donated 121,000 shares of J&J common stock worth more than $20 million to Harbor Branch to propel his partnership with Link into operation. Eventually donations from an affiliated funding organization, the Atlantic Foundation, and another affiliate, the Harbor Branch Institution, would bring $130 million to this venture. The scope of the operation expanded; Link took charge of engineering projects, Johnson controlled the research. Harbor Branch funds supported the further development of Link's submersible, the building of laboratories, and the hiring of scientists to record underwater data.

Link and Johnson's dream almost foundered before it began when, in June of 1973, Link's son, Clayton, and a co-worker, Albert Stover, died after being trapped for thirty-two hours in the *Johnson-Sea-Link,* which had become entangled in wreckage 360 feet below the surface near Key West, Florida. This loss drove Edwin Link to invent the CORD (Cabled Observation and Rescue Device), a remote-controlled submarine that during the time of the will contest played a key role in the recovery of parts of the rocket engine of the space shuttle *Challenger.*

In 1974 Harbor Branch had become fully operational and somewhat of a family enterprise. Basia, Seward Jr., James, and Marilyn Link (Edwin Link's sister), as well as

Carter Nicholas, were appointed trustees. Nina Zagat handled the legal work. At a 1976 dedication ceremony of the Link Engineering Laboratory and the Johnson Science Laboratory, at Fort Pierce, Seward Jr.'s sculptures of Link and Johnson were unveiled.

Seward Jr., enjoying a renewed relationship with his father, had gradually assumed more and more responsibility at Harbor Branch. From 1974 to 1980 he served as vice-president, and in 1979 he was appointed financial director. In 1980 Junior told his father that the administration of the foundation was requiring a great deal of his time and energies, and that if he was going to devote so much of himself to this organization, he wanted to be sure that one day he would end up in control. To guarantee his son's continuing services, Seward instructed Nina Zagat to prepare a document granting him succession to an irrevocable Class A trusteeship which assured Junior of voting control of Harbor Branch effective upon his father's death. In the meantime Seward Sr. would remain as the sole Class A trustee.

One of the reasons Seward Jr. assumed increasing responsibility for Harbor Branch was his father's innate distrust of outsiders. Junior recalls, "My father purposely wanted me to be doing the investing because he felt that bankers always protected themselves so much they would never do a good investment. Also, he was against placing the money with outsiders, because he felt that money managers had an implicit conflict of interest." Acting on his father's suggestions, Junior began to divest the foundation of Johnson & Johnson stock and to diversify the investment portfolio. In an effort to "systemize my father's ideas," Junior began a computerized stock-selection program with the help of Michael L. Watner of Merrill Lynch, Pierce, Fenner & Smith. The widely diversified stocks were rapidly turned over. Junior estimates that under his direction the entire portfolio was renewed ten times annually and in the years 1980 to 1984 Merrill Lynch received $18 million in stock commissions from this account.

In 1982 Junior's computerized stock-selection program garnered $21.8 million in profits. He felt that he should be rewarded with at least half a million dollars for his atelier. As Junior recalls, Basia said, "Why not go for the whole million?" and Junior replied, "I won't argue," to which Basia said, "Don't worry, I'll talk to him." For emotional reasons, Junior wanted the million dollars earmarked not as a charitable contribution, but as what it was—a reward for his hard work. Finally, Harbor Branch accountant Lou Hewitt's tax advice prevailed and the million dollars was designated as a contribution.

Seward Johnson's policies were in the long run to affect adversely the financial management of the Harbor Branch portfolio and, after his death, place his son in legal difficulty. With this home-styled investment procedure, Harbor Branch would lose $12 million in the last six months of 1983 and another $10 million in the year 1984. This would provide formidable ammunition for Basia in the fight that was to come. Says Junior, "I did what I thought was best and tried to fulfill my father's long-term wishes. If I had known any of the consequences, I never would have assumed that responsibility."

In directing the affairs of Harbor Branch, both Junior and Basia held strong opinions and often they diverged, but they seemed to have established a good working relationship. In a letter to his father, Seward Jr. outspokenly characterized the various people involved with the organization. Of Basia he said, "Basia Johnson believes that if you have an opinion, it should be a strong one, and if someone else has a different opinion, they'd better be able to acquit themselves loudly and clearly. Basia has very good instincts and she also respects others who she instinctively feels know a particular subject better than she does. And, conversely, demands the same courtesy in return. Her fault is that Basia sometimes likes to reduce things to all black and white or the best and the unacceptable."

With time Junior began to feel that Basia totally controlled his father and provided the only access to him. He explained in a letter to General Johnson's widow, Evelyne, "I stood up to Basia on many occasions and encouraged my father, in front of her, to also stand up to her, which he did less and less. In his last years, as he became weaker and weaker, he totally gave in and became like moral mashed potatoes in her hands."

The transition, according to several relatives, had been gradual, but the adoring pupil had eventually vanished and a demanding master had emerged. Perhaps their perception was accurate, or perhaps they were observing the inevitable change that came as Basia assumed an increasing share of the responsibility for an old and infirm man. Junior, under the circumstances, began playing an uncomfortable role. "I walked a tightrope of honest confrontation at times and closing my eyes at other times."

DIANA: It came over a period of years. At first married life seemed to be fulfilling for both of them, and then it appeared to degenerate. They had periods of enjoying things, but then everything seemed to change once Jasna Polana was built. Mrs. Johnson suddenly got quite carried away with her power.

ELAINE: We weren't there that much. I didn't realize a lot of things. She did scream when we were there and sometimes she wasn't kind, but I didn't know the magnitude of what was going on.

During the will contest a Sullivan & Cromwell lawyer observed, "All Seward Johnson's life he was used to the full-service existence that vast wealth buys. Basia had to keep that going, and it couldn't have been an easy job." On a trip to Italy, Basia told Marty Richards, "You don't know how lucky you are to be in love. How sad not to share music and art and flowers and be romantic." Richards said, "Why don't you go out and get yourself a lover?" Basia replied, "You don't have any idea how cruel Seward can be. He threw Essie out. That is how he would throw me out. And he is insensitive sexually." And Keith Wold testified that after an argument with her husband Basia had said, "You'll never know how difficult it is to live with someone as stupid and cruel and crazy as your father[-in-law]."

During their infrequent visits the children noted Basia's uncontrollable outbursts of rage: a servant could be fired for putting a plate in the wrong position, a broken oven could inspire a tirade. When Seward spoke to Basia, he often used baby talk. Richards says, "She treated him like a mother." By the time Jasna Polana had its grand opening party in May of 1978, two witnesses were to testify that Basia sent her eighty-three-year-old husband to bed at 9:30. He protested that he was not tired, but she insisted that he leave the party. Later, according to the witnesses, she was seen with a Polish musician who caressed her breast and buttocks.

Ray Gore was to testify that at eighty-four the once-proficient sailor became confused and panicked at the helm of the *Ocean Pearl,* subsequently running the vessel aground. Estate manager John Stroczynski said that at the

same age Johnson, perhaps longing for his days as a
farmer, insisted on being taken to a farm where he might
purchase some livestock. In a parody of the once-profes-
sional farmer, Stroczynski recounted how Johnson walked
into the middle of a field of cows. "He said, 'I'd like to
have this cow.' And the girl, she said, 'This is my cow.'
And he said, 'But I want to buy it.' And she said, 'I will
not sell it to you.' So he pointed to another one. 'How
much?' he asked. '$3,000.' And then he said, 'John, we are
taking that cow.' Then he said it wasn't good to have one
cow in the barn, he needed two. And then he asked, 'Do
you have any horses?' and then he said, 'Never mind the
horses, as long as I'm going to have fresh milk and butter
and cheese, that's all I want to know.' "

At Jasna Polana, in June of 1980, Seward Johnson was
invested with the order of the Knights of Malta. For this
occasion, according to Marty Richards, Basia paid
$225,000 for china embossed with the Maltese cross and
$90,000 for crystal. The Peter Duchin orchestra played
while the guests spooned coddled eggs and beluga caviar
from eggshells. Richards estimates the cost of the party at
$1 million. A witness at the trial declared that Basia had
boasted she "spent more in a year than Queen Elizabeth."

ERIC: He was muttering through the whole thing, talking
to himself.

MARTY: She wanted to be the Knight, but when she found
out she couldn't, she wanted it for him. He couldn't wait
to get it over with. Gretchen, Jimmy Johnson's wife,
said that she and Jimmy had a big fight. They were in
the bathroom and she was complaining that security
people kept following her around like she was going to
something off the wall. And Jimmy said, "Stop talk-

LEFT: Robert Wood Johnson of Johnson & Johnson
Their father was no father.

BELOW: Seward Johnson weds Ruth Dill, July 14, 1924, St. James's Church, London: Bermuda's Attorney General Thomas Melville Dill is at the far left; Ruth's mother is next to the bride.
How amazing and fantastic it all seemed.

BELOW: Merriewold
Merriewold is still in my dreams.

The "first" family: Ruth with Seward holding Diana, Seward Jr., Elaine, and Mary Lea

I don't know how I stayed married to him as long as I did.

Diana at the hunt

Seward and Mary Lea at age nine
The incestuous father sees his child as his property.

BELOW, LEFT: Victor D'Arc
Accused of making a contract to kill Mary Lea

BELOW: Ruth with sister Fannie in front of garage/chicken coop
house
Dad lived so nicely . . . we had rats in our house.

ABOVE: Mary Lea, Marty, and Barbara (Basia) Piasecka Johnson at Frank Sinatra's party *We were such good friends.*

RIGHT: Elaine and baby Keith Wold, Jr.

BELOW: Elaine and Dr. Keith Wold

TOP: Diana and Bertram Firestone with their champion colt Flash of Steel

MIDDLE: The Firestones' Gilltown stud farm in Ireland
Horses, with the single exception of my family, have been the most important thing in my life.

BELOW: The Harbor Branch Research Vessel *Seward Johnson*
Seward Johnson loved Harbor Branch. Why would he cut it out of his will?

Esther Underwood Johnson

Jennifer Underwood Johnson

James (Jimmy) Johnson

Seward, Jr., with his sculpture of his father

Barbara Eisenfuhr Kline Bailey Maxwell Johnson and dog, Ebenezer
The divorce was a protracted and bitter affair.

The General, left, and his son, Robert Wood Johnson, Jr. (Bob), right
The General was an egomaniac and he destroyed his own son.

Basia and Seward
Basia's a beautiful young girl and she's in love with me. She's sexually attracted to me!

RIGHT: Seward and daughter Mary Lea with Johnson's private jet decorated by Pierre Cardin

BELOW: Basia rubs Seward's feet on Children's Bay Cay, their private Bahamian island. *Seward was as selfish and self-occupied as King Henry VIII.*

Edward Reilly

Alexander Forger

ABOVE: In the courtroom. *Front row:* Joseph Duke, James, Marty, Keith, and Elaine. *Second row:* Joyce and Junior

RIGHT: Junior zips his lips about the settlement.
Hall conferences, black coffee, and all-night negotiations

Surrogate Marie Lambert
Part Portia, part Tugboat Annie

Nina Zagat with Basia
Accused of "fraud, duress, and undue influence"

Basia with Frederick Lacey

Robert Osgood
Accused of "bribing and intim-idating" witnesses

Donald Christ,
Basia's chief lawyer
*Nine lawyers could not save
Basia's reputation.*

Jasna Polana
1. Tennis court 2. Orchid house 3. Rose garden and reflecting pool 4. Garages 5. Security 6. Indoor swimming pool 7. Dog pavilion over breakfast room 8. Dining room 9. Cast bronze door to art gallery and $100-million art collection 10. Basia's bedroom

and dressing room 11. Sunken master bathtub 12. Seward's bedroom 13. Living room 14. Guest wing 15. Front reflecting pool 16. Wrought-iron gates from Poland 17. Basia's hidden Italian garden 18. Seward's rock garden 19. Chapel over atomic-bomb shelter

Basia's hidden Italian garden

The bulletproof glass swimming pavilion

The indoor swimming pool

The outdoor reflecting pool

Basia's "two bedroom house"

Basia with her Renaissance bronzes

ing, don't you know there could be cameras in the bathroom? Don't you know there could be microphones in the bathroom? My father will find out that you're saying these things." So they had a real fight.

During 1980 Seward Johnson's New Brunswick office at J&J was gradually closed. The files were transferred to Shearman & Sterling. The office work now emanated from Jasna Polana. None of the children knew what their father's financial arrangements were. Nina Zagat was the conduit through whom the Johnson's legal wishes were conveyed to Shearman & Sterling, and she became fully involved with their financial affairs, arranging for transfers of money, loans, eventually paying bills for art, real estate, and the maintenance of their estates, as well as taking care of a great deal of detailed paperwork relating to their various activities. In 1980 Jennifer had lunch with Basia and Zagat and listened as they discussed some expensive French furniture Basia had purchased at auction. After lunch they went to Zagat's office, where she paid for the purchases by transferring funds from a Citibank line of credit. Jennifer realized that "when they would spend more than their income, Nina Zagat would make a transfer of funds from my father's loan at Citibank. I was quite surprised and shocked because I had always thought that my father never spent more than his income. It was so different from anything he'd taught us. We would never borrow money or live beyond our income."

The "tightrope of honest confrontation" that Junior walked began to collapse with Seward Johnson's final illness. In October 1980 the eighty-five-year-old Johnson checked himself into Peter Bent Brigham Hospital in Boston. He told Nina Zagat to say nothing to Basia, who was in Europe. According to Zagat, Basia telephoned her and kept asking Seward's whereabouts. Finally she revealed the truth to Basia, and afterward when she told this to Seward, he said, "Oh, good, I'm glad that she knows." But in March of 1983, when Basia told Junior of this incident, it confirmed his growing fear that Nina Zagat was representing Basia's interests rather than his father's. However, he could not have realized that there may have been a reason for his father's request. Johnson was seeking aid "for increasing impotence . . . with regard to difficulties with erection." Seward returned to Jasna Polana with a clean bill of health and a pretty young nurse in tow. Basia returned, the nurse left.

Shortly after Seward returned from the hospital, Zagat met with him to discuss his will. She was to testify that at that time she asked him "if he was sure that his children understood that they were not going to be receiving anything under his will." According to Zagat, Senior said "his children knew. I told him that I thought it was extremely important that they know so that there wouldn't be any problems in the future. Mr. Johnson said well, that the only one that he thought would create any problems might be Keith Wold, but he said, 'I don't think Elaine would ever let him do that.'" It would seem consistent with Seward Johnson's pattern to take the easy way out by answering in this manner.

By the spring of 1981 Basia had become dissatisfied with Nina Zagat, who she said had performed her duties too slowly in securing the necessary permissions for the construction of the chapel. Basia says that she told Junior, "I didn't want that she represent me as a lawyer any more, that I would like to have another lawyer." Junior says that Basia wanted to hire a second-rate Perth Amboy firm and that he jumped in and advised Basia not to make this change. Junior now says that at this point Basia never seriously intended to fire Zagat, but was "twisting Nina's knickers to assert power over her."

On May 19, 1981, Seward Johnson checked into the Medical Center at Princeton and was diagnosed as having cancer of the prostate. Five hours before his admission he signed a codicil to his May 1976 will which lifted the cap from the executor and trustee fees, escalating them from a potential value of $2.5 million to $30 million. At the same time, according to Alexander Forger, "For all practical purposes, Basia was to receive the entire estate outright . . . this will not only defeated the charitable interest totally but added to the tax burden." Basia's bequest included a Fund B which had previously been remaindered to charity. Basia could now take this money outright.

Zagat testified that Johnson's thinking was influenced by the fact that she had advised him that Congress had passed a bill effective January 1982 under which the portion of an estate one could leave to a spouse tax-free was increased from 50 percent to 100 percent. Zagat further testified that Seward said that was "wonderful." Forger was to term this will "a highwater mark" in the Basia Johnson/Nina Zagat conspiracy.

DIANA: I began to suspect something was wrong in 1981 when he first was in the hospital for cancer. I was a little bit confounded by all the flurry of Basia and Nina. They looked very distraught, as if they wanted something done at that point. I'm sure my father didn't have time to read that draft when he was being rushed to the hospital. In the hospital he was withdrawn. I think he was a little frightened.

Four days after his admission to the Medical Center at Princeton, Seward Johnson underwent a bilateral subcap-

sular scrotal orchiectomy, in which all his testicular tissue
was removed. When Johnson returned from the hospital,
according to Basia, Dr. James Varney told him he could
live a year or three years. Basia was angry. "I consider it
improper to tell things like that to a patient." Her husband
told the doctor "that he is going to struggle; that he is
strong enough to beat the illness." By May of 1982 Dr.
Allen Yagoda of Memorial Sloan-Kettering Hospital pronounced Johnson free of cancer, and Seward and Basia
went to the Four Seasons restaurant to celebrate. However,
within six months the cancer had reasserted itself and Dr.
Yagoda ordered a series of cobalt treatments.

". . . she knew what was in the will, and I didn't."

On a brisk autumn day in 1986, Bertram and Diana Firestone invited me to use their Falcon 50 jet to visit them in Waterford, Virginia. The Firestones' Catoctin Stud farm encompasses two thousand acres of staggeringly beautiful rolling meadows, and the trees were ablaze with fall colors. Here Diana is in her element, expansive about this place and knowledgeable about their horse operation.

The Firestones have owned several of the finest race-horses in the world: General Assembly, Cure the Blues, Optimistic Gal, Honest Pleasure, and the 1980 Kentucky Derby winner, Genuine Risk, the first filly in sixty-five years to win this race. The Firestones also are the owners of Gilltown Stud in County Kildare, Ireland, formerly owned by the Aga Khan. Bert Firestone drives us on a tour of the farm. One hand is on the wheel; in the other is a walkie-talkie over which he carries on a dialogue with his office staff. A slight man with a diffident manner, Firestone was an amateur show rider for many years. He and Diana knew each other on the horse-show circuit and, according to Diana, made their "big plans" in Deauville and married in 1974 "about five minutes" after her divorce from Richard Stokes.

The Firestones' unfinished new home is designed by Robert Dean, an architect who worked on the restoration of Williamsburg, Virginia. This residence has been under construction for three years and approximately eighty men report daily as the work continues. Bertram Firestone, who is also a commercial-real-estate developer, dismissed the original contractor and has taken over the job with his own crew. The construction headquarters, housed in three air-conditioned trailers, is equipped with computers to track expenditures and materials. The house, still a year from completion, has every detail and luxury imaginable. Diana's bathroom has a square twelve-by-twelve-foot marble tub with Jacuzzi under a skylight; there is a sauna, a steam room, an indoor pool and gymnasium, a massive media room, a commodious kitchen with fieldstone walls and an open hearth, an Olympic-size outdoor pool with pool house and electric barbecue. This incomplete house has both grandeur and charm. Normally taciturn, Diana talks freely about her passion for the breeding and care of horses that started when, at twenty-six, she bred her mare to Nashua to produce a stakes winner.

DIANA: My father sort of encouraged me. He bought me a horse when I was in high school. At [the Madeira] school you could just fox-hunt by hacking. You didn't have to put the horses in a truck. I hunted every weekend, and even when some of the school went in to see the Inauguration, I said, "That's a fox-hunting day, I'll hear about it later on the radio." Kennedy wasn't President, it was before that. I don't remember.

As I got ready to graduate, I asked my father for a brood mare, which he gave me, and I left her in Virginia and went on to junior college. I came back to Virginia to train the foals and I've been here ever since. When I came back, my father was wondering if I had the right approach and he asked me to write a neighbor who was a good horse breeder and tell him what I was planning to do. I explained the two projects I had in mind and he wrote my father, "I have nothing to teach Diana." That was James Cox Brady, the father of Nicholas Brady [Diana's trustee who became her adversary]. In view of what happened, I think that's ironic.

In the spring of 1982 there occurred yet another incident in the intertwined financial and legal machinations of Johnson life, in which the damage of the past was to influence present events. Junior relates how he was summoned by his father to Jasna Polana, where his sister Diana and her husband, Bert, were visiting. The Firestones complained that the trustees of her 1944 trust were withholding a loan to their horse operation—the latest incident in a series of escalating hostilities between the Firestones and Diana's trustees that was destined for a courtroom confrontation. Although Diana received a distribution of approximately $3.5 million annually from her trust, their horse operation cost more millions to run. In June of 1981 Diana had advised her trustees that she would not be able to pay back a $3.9 million loan because one of her horses, Cure the Blues, valued at $8 million, had taken ill. That prompted Nicholas Brady, chairman of Dillon Read & Co. and one of her trustees, to state that he did not think the 1944 trust should be tied to the Firestones' horse operation, since the business was really "a tax game." Diana and Bert became incensed at that remark. Diana said, "Horses, with the single exception of my family, have been the most important thing in my life."

By 1982 the long- and short-term debt of their horse operation was estimated at $25 million by Diana and at $35 million by her trustees. In a deposition Diana stated, "We were experiencing a tight cash flow problem because of the interest rates. We were getting a little worried at that point." A loan from her trust, since the interest would revert to her, seemed most advantageous to the Firestones, but Diana's trustees did not agree. Also, as Judge John Keefe was to state, Diana "sensed, from comments and attitudes, that the trustees were not happy with her husband Bert, and somehow saw themselves as protecting her from him." Bertram Firestone's father had changed the family name and he was not a member of the Firestone rubber family. He had been married twice prior to his marriage to Diana—first briefly to Lynn Belnap and the second time to Dariel Henderson, the Avon-products heiress.

Echoing the past, Diana requested that her brother, Seward Jr., become her new trustee. In a letter of April 21, 1982, Diana wrote her trustees that her brother had been forced to resign "against his will" and added, "It is now time for these past deeds, which affected my brother, my trust and myself, to be corrected and the original intentions of my father to be carried out." Junior too became distrustful of his brother-in-law after an incident that he described in an affidavit. "I told Bert and Diana that if I was going to be of any service to them and to the trustees, I was going to have to be educated rapidly. They agreed that I could send down my accountant (a partner of Main Hurdman) to go over all of their books and records. While he was down there, Bert Firestone called and told me he was very impressed with my accountant and would it be all right if he hired him. I replied 'absolutely not,' that as far as I was concerned that would compromise the weight of his findings for my purpose. Frankly, his suggestion upset me." Junior says that he became even more concerned when he later told Bertram Firestone that it was now all right to hire Junior's accountant but Firestone was no longer interested in doing so.

Later that month Junior met with James Pitney, the very lawyer for the 1944 trusts who had, seventeen years earlier, offered Junior the disastrous *"quid pro quo"*: Junior's resignation of the power of the vote for a divorce settlement. By June of 1982 Junior observed the same pattern evolving when Pitney offered Diana and Bert a loan of $2 million in return for not opposing her trustees' choice of a new trustee. After protracted and antagonistic negotiations, a $2 million loan was granted, but only with Seward Sr.'s signature of indemnity. The trustees didn't understand her "standard of living," Diana claimed. And they didn't understand the business she was in. Subsequently Albert W. Merck was appointed as the new trustee.

In February of 1983 Basia was in Princeton, so Junior "filled in" in Florida, taking his father by helicopter from his Fort Pierce home to the Boca Raton hospital for a transfusion. Junior said that his father could not sleep, so he sat up all night with him and had "one of the most meaningful conversations of my life." Among other matters, his father expressed to Junior his wish that his son be reinstated as Diana's trustee. Junior was later to testify in *Firestone v. Merck,* an action brought one month before his father's death, that during that conversation his father was "acute," "responsive," "challenging," and "imaginative."

The outcome of this New Jersey action depended on proving that Seward Johnson Sr.'s "intent" was that his son be reinstated and that he was in total control of his faculties at that time. In the New York will contest, however, the children's lawyers were to contend that Seward Sr. during the same period of time was senile and lacked testamentary capacity. Seward Jr., who was deposed in both actions, said that for the New Jersey litigation he quoted things his father had said to him during the helicopter ride, but in New York he responded to questions with answers like "I patted his knee." Sullivan & Cromwell lawyers noted this discrepancy and soon issued a brief on "the two-faced Johnson children." Junior observed of this astounding dilemma: "Those damn lawyers. Don't they ever talk to each other?"

Between 1981 and 1983 Seward Johnson was hospitalized five times as his condition deteriorated and the cancer metastasized to the bones. On several of his hospital admission forms he listed himself variously as "Johnson & Johnson—President" and as "Retired Johnson & Johnson—President." Basia Johnson recalls that during this difficult period her mother was ill, Edwin Link, co-founder of Harbor Branch, died of cancer, and, of no less importance to her husband, his beloved boxer, Prince, also contracted cancer. Basia felt that her husband identified with the dog and did everything possible to save his life. Prince was sent to Cornell Medical Center, but to no avail. "I only see my husband cry twice in his life. When Princie died and when Junior take the Class A trusteeship away from him."

This rich man attempted to stave off mortality with vitamins provided by Johnson & Johnson, massages, special diets, and a faith healer, Clive Harris, whom Basia imported from England. Basia volunteered Harris's services to other family members (who nicknamed him E.T.). He relieved a tremor in Joyce Johnson's hand, and Seward Jr. felt intense heat emanating from Harris's hands when he touched Junior's head, but Seward Sr., in the middle of a treatment, called for a Tylenol.

At the Johnson household the pattern of sickness and

death continued. At two a.m. on November 6, 1982, Seward Johnson collapsed on his bedroom floor and lay there for two hours until he was able to crawl to the phone and call security, who in turn called Basia. The next morning he was admitted once again to the hospital. During hospitalization the following month, his medical records indicated that the cancer was causing secondary maladies such as hardening of the carotid artery and colonic diverticulosis as well as "altered mental states" and "severe transient episodes of dysarthria and confusion, which cleared promptly." The first week in January, Basia's mother died at the Princeton hospital.

On January 23, 1983, Johnson, weak and dehydrated after a bout of extreme diarrhea, entered the hospital for a transfusion. His doctor, Jacqueline Mislow, noted, "The patient was weak and pale with sluggish speech which was uncustomary in this formerly dynamic eighty-seven-year-old gentleman." The following day Basia removed her husband from the hospital for the last time. According to Seward Jr., Clive Harris, "the soothsayer," had recommended the discharge and an immediate trip to Fort Pierce. Mislow noted, "His wife requested that the patient be transferred back to Jasna Polana as soon as possible for a trip to Florida, possibly the next day, and although I cautioned them about the inadvisability of the air flight in such an unstable condition, they were adamant about his discharge. On the following morning, the patient was much more alert, in jovial spirits, and most anxious for discharge, to arrange his flight to Florida as soon as possible." But Junior felt the removal had been peremptory and remarked to Nina Zagat, "This won't look good if there's a will contest." According to Junior, she replied, "Do you think there will be one?" Junior said, "I've heard rumblings. If it's a cold fish in the face, I'll be in the thick of it." Junior says he realized that "Nina and Basia were in control, and they would be most wise to design a will that was not so flagrant." Zagat later denied that this conversation took place and said that in January she had no suspicion of a will contest. In his deposition, however, Thomas Ford admitted that she had informed him that Junior told her there might be a will contest if the will were "a cold fish in the face," although he did not recall when he first heard this phrase.

BERT FIRESTONE: When we visited Seward in Fort Pierce, no one spoke English and he couldn't drive an automobile by himself any more. As we left, I remember turning to Diana and saying, "He's a prisoner in his own house."

SEWARD JR.: I knew that Basia was totally dominating him, there was no question in my mind about that, but I thought things still might work out all right. I knew Nina Zagat was in Basia's pocket at the time, but I had two suppositions: one was that Basia might somehow be satisfied to take a civilized share and so I was waiting for the will to find out. That's what I told them both. I said, "I'll wait and see. I'll tell you what when I see the will." The other supposition was that my father, who was a cagey sort of person and had learned to stand up to his brother by being cagey because he could never confront him, possibly had another lawyer stashed away. I thought every time he would write a will with Zagat, maybe he was writing another one with somebody else that would make it null and void and letting Basia think she was getting away with it. This was a way not to confront her. But then I began to realize that he wasn't getting to see other lawyers because she was controlling that.

Basia and I were fencing all the time. We would have fights, you know, just to let each other know that we were willing to fight. We'd scream at each other and my father would hold his head and cover his ears and shake his head, he'd rock back and forth, and I'd say kiddingly, "Come on, Dad, it's fun, get into it," and Basia would laugh and say, "Come on, Seward"—you know, that type of thing. But it really was that we were positioning psychologically with each other, so when I said that thing in January of '83 about a will contest, then in February, all of a sudden, I found myself in the will for the first time for a million dollars.

Will contest—the phrase had surfaced. In the waning days of Seward Johnson's life there was played out a scenario of suspicion, secrecy, subterfuge, and colossal misunderstanding.

On February 18 Seward Johnson signed another codicil to his May 1976 will granting Junior property in Chatham, Massachusetts, and $1 million outright. The property had formerly been bequeathed to Junior's half-brother, James, which seemed logical, since it adjoined James's mother's property. Alexander Forger was to assert of this will, "For the first time, Seward Johnson, Jr., and perhaps other family members, began to suspect that neither family nor Harbor Branch had any significant interest under Seward's will. They came to realize that Nina Zagat was not Seward's lawyer but Basia's. The response of Shearman & Sterling was to depart markedly from the earlier estate plan in a way which can only be rationalized as an attempt to buy off the family and forestall any contest of Seward Johnson's last will."

At the trial the charges against Basia and Zagat would be of exerting "fraud, duress and undue influence" on a senile old man to pry away his wealth. But during the period prior to Johnson's death, the question of Basia's control was not at issue. All of Johnson's children acknowledged this control and the empirical question seemed to be how the estate was to be divided. Nina Zagat, who was also the lawyer for Harbor Branch, told both Marilyn Link and Seward Jr. that it would be well provided for, and the children relied on Basia's sense of fairness and friendship. In 1981 Nina and Basia had spent ten days with Elaine as her guest at the Maine Chance health spa. "They were so warm and friendly. I said to Keith they couldn't be like that unless they are doing the right thing for Harbor Branch."

SEWARD JR.: I appreciated the number of things Basia had done in my behalf and I wanted to do things in her behalf, but all of this led up to the inevitable, which was the will. It was a matter of how she handled that: whether she handled it with noblesse oblige, or whether she went for broke. That is why I had to take a double position, because I felt she knew what was in the will, and I didn't. I think sometimes he used me as a check against her. I didn't know whether I could trust either one of them. I think I was beginning to wonder at that point, because I felt he was continuously giving up authority over his life and I didn't know where it was leading.

Basia's art-buying continued unabated. In January of 1983 alone, she purchased the Zurbarán *St. Sebastian* for $550,000, a pair of Louis XVI candelabra for $375,000, a pair of sixteenth-century horses by Giambologna for

$250,000. During the same month Zagat wrote five letters to Raquel Filamor, an assistant Citibank vice-president, requesting transfers from Seward Johnson's line of credit totaling $3.35 million.

Seward still rode in his golf cart, took walks along the Fort Pierce waterfront, dined with the family, but he was growing weaker. Dr. Fred J. Schilling was flown in by helicopter from his Boca Raton office to attend him. Dr. Jonathan Wideroff lived at Fort Pierce from April 13 to May 20 and would frequently administer blood tests. (He didn't tell Johnson that he was a doctor and Johnson thought him simply a technician named John.) There were around-the-clock nurses who often became the target of Basia's rages. One of them was fired after Johnson complained that she had forced orange juice down his throat; another, Judith Abramovitz, after she had allowed Johnson to drink papaya juice, which had been expressly forbidden by Basia. During Basia's tirade against Nurse Abramovitz, Seward goaded her on from his bed. According to Abramovitz's testimony, when Basia's fury would "simmer down," Johnson would "get her going again. He would say, 'She's dumb,' meaning me, 'she never should have done that. You're absolutely right, Basia,'" and the tirade would begin again. Basia admits that nurses were a problem. "My husband was a very big perfectionist, and they were sloppy in their work, and sometimes they behaved as if they were giving a favor when working. . . . Some of them acted dumb and they didn't know how to behave in the capacity of a nurse . . . some of them were wearing perfume that my husband was allergic to . . . that even I am allergic to this kind of perfume."

On February 24 Nina Zagat returned to Fort Pierce and they celebrated Basia's birthday the following day with a cake and champagne. During that visit, Zagat says,

Seward asked her to prepare a new will for him as well as a letter to Junior assuring him that he would succeed his father as Class A trustee of Harbor Branch. This letter was to be given to his son upon Seward's death. On March 10, Zagat returned with the letter and the will, which specified that Basia's long-standing marital trust remain intact but that in addition she was to receive the right to appoint $20 million during her lifetime to "the descendants of her father as she may choose," which, in its peculiar wording, did not exclude Basia herself. Of the second trust, Basia was to receive income only, while the remainder interest was assigned to Harbor Branch. Zagat testified that at this time Seward asked if there were any way his will could be challenged. She answered that there were three possible grounds: improper execution, lack of capacity, and fraud. "Do you think you want to review it with Seward Jr.?" Seward Sr. asked. "No," Zagat replied.

When she returned to New York, Zagat stated, she consulted with Shearman & Sterling partners Thomas Ford, Henry Ziegler, Werner Polak, and others and they decided to expand the language of Article Eleven, the disinheritance clause, so that "the children will understand." They also decided that Zagat, who was a trustee and executor of the will, should no longer serve as a subscribing witness, because in the event of a will contest "a subscribing witness could be deposed before a will objection is filed."

On March 18 Seward Johnson was so ill that Basia summoned a priest. "He is dying," she announced as she emerged from his room. "He is not going to last until dinner." Four days later, however, Seward signed another will. In this will was the elaboration on the disinheritance clause which Zagat had discussed with her colleagues at Shearman & Sterling. The new language now read, "I have intentionally made no bequests in this will to my descendants, other than my son, J. SEWARD JOHNSON, JR., not because of any lack of affection for them. It was my wish to provide my children with financial independence at an early age and, accordingly, I created a substantial trust for each of them during my lifetime. It has been a source of pleasure to me to see my children pursue their interests independent of me and in a way that would not have been possible if I had not provided for them in this way." The addition of this language was the only change between this and the previous will of March 10, and for the first time Zagat did not act as a subscribing witness.

ELAINE, April 10, 1983: Keith asked him about the boat and he looked like he didn't recognize him, and Keith went over and said, "Seward, I'm Keith," and Dad said, "Oh, yes," and smiled, but Keith felt that he didn't know him.

JAMES, Spring 1983: Basia had told me from time to time he would lapse into a coma or something, where he couldn't distinguish his reality around him. He thought he was a little boy. He recalled events of his childhood. He would close his eyes a lot, his voice was shaky, he would have difficulty recalling people close to him.

JENNIFER, April 1983: I remember him saying to me how he had to eat to get better so that he could go out on the *Ocean Pearl*. And then we did go out on the *Ocean Pearl* . . . he was carried on the boat and he was just so withdrawn he didn't say one thing the whole time that we were there. The only thing I remember him saying is "We can go home now."

In view of the overwrought atmosphere at Fort Pierce and his father's failing condition, Junior became increasingly worried about the future. Although Junior had devoted most of his time to carrying out his father's wishes, Seward Sr. had not substantially altered his behavior toward his son. Junior reported that one evening when Basia began to show him a photograph album, his father remarked, "I thought company was leaving." Basia says that when Junior arrived at Fort Pierce in May, his father said, "Why did you come? Do you want more money?"

This insensitivity was not limited to Junior. Basia says that on several occasions when Jimmy visited, her husband refused to see him, and that he disliked Jimmy's wife, Gretchen, so much that she made him physically ill. Junior began to feel Basia too was becoming increasingly antagonistic toward him. In criticizing a planned Harbor Branch mission to Russia, she screamed at him over the speakerphone in his father's bedroom for forty-five minutes, saying such things as *"Our will* says no money will be given to communist countries." On another occasion, when he misunderstood the fact that Basia wanted him at the house, she said he had the brains of a "soft-boiled egg."

Then there was the matter of John Peach, a Harbor Branch employee who had become increasingly involved with making Seward Sr. comfortable—arranging nurses and ordering special hospital equipment for his room. By mid-March of 1983 Peach was spending practically all his time, even weekends, at the Johnson home, and he accompanied Seward on each of his four trips to the Boca Raton Community Hospital. Peach, whose salary was $51,600, informed Junior that he'd had another job offer that paid $78,500 and told Junior he had twenty-four hours to meet the offer or Peach would be forced to leave. At Harbor Branch a 9 percent raise was occasionally given for out-

standing performance, but never more. When Junior told
Basia that the foundation could not justify the raise, she
again began to berate him, saying that John Peach was
making Seward Sr. comfortable and that he should be paid
whatever he wanted for that. Junior asserts that Basia said,
in front of his father, "John Peach is like a son to us. He is
more than a son to us!" Later that day Nina Zagat told
Junior that she'd arranged for the personal part of Peach's
raise to be paid by the Johnsons.

Junior felt that his father, "who had been dominated
by his own brother, wanted a bit of the credit for Harbor
Branch. He wanted to make it his monument." Junior, not
knowing of the existence of the March 10 letter that assured him sole control of the Class A trusteeship, recalled
that at one point Basia had expressed an interest in sharing
this trusteeship with him. Unsure of his position, he began
to think about how Zagat had broken confidence with his
father when she had told Basia of his admission to Peter
Bent Brigham Hospital. " 'Ah,' I thought, 'my father
doesn't have a lawyer and I don't have a lawyer.' " Junior,
realizing that Zagat had drafted the Class A trusteeship
papers, and not trusting her, promptly queried Gary
Hehrer, a Princeton lawyer and friend, who pointed out a
minor technical discrepancy in the trustee assignment. Junior then tried to reach Nina Zagat to ask her about the
discrepancy, so that when he spoke to his father he would
have her explanation, but Zagat was vacationing on Children's Bay Cay, and the phone was broken. Had they communicated, the unfortunate scene which Basia alleges led
to the final will change might have been avoided.

On March 31, while his father was in the Boca Raton
hospital receiving a blood transfusion, Junior asked him
for his resignation as Class A trustee so that Junior would
be assured of control of Harbor Branch. He later admitted,

"It wasn't the most beautiful time to bring it up. I don't know whether he felt that resigning was giving up life." After the conversation, Junior offered to his sister Diana, who had not eaten all day, a cup of soup from a thermos Basia had brought. His father snapped, "That soup is for my wife, not for you," inflicting yet another slight hurt. Junior left the hospital room angry at his father for not giving him what he felt he deserved and angry at himself for being put in this position. The Johnsons returned home from the hospital, and that evening Junior, on a piece of memo paper, wrote a resignation for his father to sign: "I John Seward Johnson hereby resign as Class A trustee. . . ." Basia says she asked Junior why he could not wait until the following day and have the resignation typed, and adds that even his wife, Joyce, thought his handwriting might be illegible, but Junior insisted that he had to leave for Princeton the next morning.

SEWARD JR.: The lawyer in Princeton found a problem: the board had given my father discretion to give a *revocable* appointment, but he gave me an *irrevocable* appointment. The lawyer said, "There's only two ways to straighten that out. One is to have a board meeting, the other is to have your father resign now." I went to him in the hospital and I said, "Dad, there seems to be this problem," and I told him the two ways out of civility. Because he was too sick for the meeting, that option didn't really exist. But Dad said, "Well, I kind of like having the trustees and directors' meeting," which was saying to me, "I don't want to resign." And I said, "Well, that's impossible." I was going to have the A Class trusteeship, otherwise I wanted to spend my life sculpting and running my own organization.

I decided, "What's going on here? Who's the person I

fear the most?" It was Basia. So I said, "Well, I'll find out. Might as well go right to the lion's mouth and find out." When we got home, I said, "Basia, the deal was that I was supposed to have this and it's under threat. What do you think I should do?" She said, "I think that you should have it, you've done a fantastic job at Harbor Branch. You're doing everything right and you should definitely have it and I'll talk to him." She talked to him about four minutes and he was ready to sign away anything. It was just like that. He called me into the bedroom and signed away this thing. After he signed it, he patted me on the head. Then Basia and Joyce and I sat in the living room and talked for a couple of hours while he fell asleep.

If my father had been angry at me, why would he have left me as an executor and trustee of his will? Why would he have left me property and a million dollars? It doesn't make sense.

What does make sense is that Basia ended up with what Harbor Branch would have gotten. All that maneuvering by Basia and Nina was about cutting out Harbor Branch, a charity everyone admits my father loved. Basia's story gives exactly the opposite impression of what actually happened.

JOYCE JOHNSON: We were visiting just literally when he was dying. My husband had asked him if he would sign. He was so reserved and hesitant and deferential to his father he could hardly bring himself to do it. And so his father signed something and said, "Yes, of course I should, and you are running this." It all took place in about ten minutes. Now, Basia had said at the time, "After all, you are running it. You deserve this. Come on, let's do this, we'll get this done." And she did. In her own officious kind of aggressive way, she got the whole thing done. Now Basia is saying my husband seized power from his father.

BASIA: His father was very sad, very angry, I could see that, but he took those papers and he signed them. Junior asked me to sign them as a witness. Immediately after the signing of the resignation, Junior was very excited. He said, "I hate that old father of mine. I hate him with all my heart, the most I can, because he should make this resignation a long time ago, at least two years ago, but he wanted all the power for himself." I was paralyzed after what I have heard. I have heard it before, but I never treated it seriously. I never consider it serious what he was talking about his father, that he hates him.

My husband was very upset about that and he cried and told me, "My son is awaiting my death." He demand that Nina comes immediately. He asked me to call her and make her come, and he said that he absolutely has to change the part of his will that those money that after my death were supposed to go to the Harbor Branch foundation will not go there automatically.

Before my husband was dying, a month and a half, Seward Jr. says, "Give me that Class A trusteeship." Why? He would have had it anyway. It broke his father's heart. He couldn't wait, he just took it away from a dying man. It was terrible, and that is what he was like.

On April 11, Basia says, she was the one who called Zagat and told her of Seward's determination to change the Harbor Branch provision in his will. On April 14 Zagat, accompanied by Shearman & Sterling associates

Jack Gunther and James Hoch, flew to Fort Pierce with a new forty-eight-page will complete with ribbons and seal. This will was truly to be Seward Johnson's last, although there would be more legal documents to come.

The will granted to Basia a limited testamentary power, the right of assignment of the trust's remainder to Harbor Branch, a charity of her own choosing, or to Seward's children. The inclusion of the children in the choices was, according to Zagat's own testimony, an inducement to them not to contest. But this added precaution was to backfire. According to Nina Zagat, Seward asked, "Why did you include that? I don't want to leave more money to my descendants." Zagat answered that "since you had asked me whether there was any way your will could be challenged, we had thought a lot about that and it might be a good idea for your descendants to realize that there's always the possibility that Basia may decide to leave them some money later on." "Well, let's talk about it with Basia," Seward replied. Zagat said she then asked Seward if he wanted to write a letter to Basia asking her to give first preference to Harbor Branch, though, from a common-sense point of view, this suggestion would seem to contradict the reason for a new will. At the trial, when Zagat was asked what Seward had replied to her suggestion, seemingly unaware of the irony, she'd answered that he'd said, "No, we will just end up with a lot of lawyers." After lunch Seward Johnson was wheeled into the living-room/dining-room area, where he signed the will in the presence of Gunther and Hoch.

During lunch Zagat and Basia had discussed the fact that Basia wanted to write a letter to her husband assuring him that the residuary interest would go to Harbor Branch. Zagat wrote out the basic letter on a legal pad, Jack Gunther refined it, and then Basia copied the letter in her own hand. When she told her husband of the letter, according to Zagat, he said, "Basia, you don't have to do that," but she replied, "I want to." She asked the lawyers, "Can I sign it 'Love, Basia'?" After Seward read the letter, Basia asked him to countersign it and Zagat asked him to write "acknowledged."

On April 14 Johnson also signed a revocation of his ante-nuptial agreement. Zagat said this was done to tie up "loose ends . . . it tidied up Mr. Johnson's files and affairs." Later that day Dr. Schilling arrived by helicopter, examined Seward, and signed a legal paper Zagat had prepared. Said Basia, "I think it was time for a routine checkup."

ELAINE, April 29, 1983: Keith and I and Diana flew up to see him. Dad didn't talk a great deal. I think he was in pain. . . . I said, "Dad, this is Diana," and he said, "Oh," and smiled, and I thought he didn't recognize her.

JIMMY, Spring 1983: I don't think he could read, he couldn't look at television, so I assume he wouldn't have a clear understanding of his assets and estate.

He was regulated by Basia and doctors, and had very little free will. He was a sick man, he needed this, of course, but I think if you're accustomed to being told what to do all the time, you lose track of what you have, your possessions. Over the past five or six years of his life, he lost all initiative in controlling his life and the affairs around him. . . . He was often falling asleep, and most of our conversations were in short sentences where I would say something and he would nod in agreement. I felt it was nice just to be near him at the time.

JENNIFER, May 1983: He seemed pretty weak. He had to eat slowly and he would cough. His stomach was very distended. He wasn't eating all that much and his arms and legs were extremely emaciated. His face was swollen because he was taking steroids at that point. It was terrible. . . . He was kind of going in and out of a sleeping state. He wasn't in a coma, but he was just drifting, and he wouldn't know where he was, and then he would come back and see where he was. He was talking about some sort of fish. And I came later and said, "What's your favorite kind of fish?" And he said, "I'm hallucinating and I'm trying to control it." He was telling Basia about riding on donkeys or something. She said, "Isn't it lovely that your father is in such a happy place in his mind? He's in Italy, riding in a donkey cart with his mother, and the flowers are blooming." It was just—he was gone.

On April 28, Nina Zagat reported, she received a phone call from Junior saying that two of his sisters were considering contesting the will. According to Zagat, Seward Jr. apologized profusely and said that he would try to talk them out of it. Seward Jr. says that this conversation never took place and that Zagat invented it as an excuse for her next financial maneuver. Junior says he did speak to Keith Wold in January after a will contest was mentioned, and at that time Wold consulted a Florida attorney. Now he spoke with Keith again.

KEITH: When Seward and I talked, even the grandchildren were never mentioned because we felt that Harbor Branch should be funded and we knew that this was his desire. And this is what we were preparing for. I don't remember what I said to Seward Jr. in those conversa-

tions, but I do know that we felt that there was some
hostility between Barbara Johnson and Seward Jr. over
the management of the foundation, that she had alluded
to the fact that perhaps either she would take over or
that she would make sure it was not funded if young
Seward took over.

Seward Jr.'s phone call set into motion another legal
flurry. Measures were being taken. Zagat testified, "I discussed it with Mr. Ford, Mr. Reilly—Mr. Reilly of our
office—Mr. Gunther, Mr. Field." They warned her that a
common tactic in a will contest was to tie up the estate so
that the widow would have insufficient funds to fight. It
didn't matter, they told her, how good a case Basia had
unless there were financial means at Basia's disposal to
fight a possible will contest. Immediately Shearman &
Sterling began to prepare papers to take $9.4 million in
tax-exempt bonds that Seward Johnson had kept as what
he termed his "anchor to windward" (a nautical safety
precaution) and transfer them to a trust for Basia of which
Zagat was the sole trustee.

Nina Zagat's May 3 to 5 visit to Fort Pierce was particularly frenetic. On May 3 Seward signed the "anchor to
windward" trust, as well as a document increasing his $24
million line of credit at Citibank to $25 million and an
unrestricted power of attorney; he was allegedly present at
directors' meetings for four of his closely held corpora-
tions: R.E.I. Co., Fine Arts Mutual, Children's Bay Corp.,
Barbara Piasecka Johnson Foundation. The afternoon of
May 3 Dr. Schilling arrived and spoke with the family,
which then included Jimmy and Gretchen, who were visiting, about not applying heroic measures to save Seward
Johnson's life. Basia says that Gretchen "made a demand
that Dr. Schilling would inform my husband that he is

dying. He was outraged: 'My duty is to maintain my patient's hope, and I know what I'm doing.' He [James] was completely quiet, and he did not have courage to say a word against her."

JAMES: I have this vision of him lying in bed, and thinking to myself, as I walked out the door to leave from my visit, that it might be the last time I'd see him alive.

"All the time it was lies."

The *Queen Elizabeth II* was passing through the Panama Canal when the Richardses and the Wolds, aboard for a three-month vacation cruise, received a call from Basia that Seward was near death. They hurriedly left the ship by descending a rope ladder into a launch while both vessels were moving at ten knots. They arrived in Fort Pierce to find a moonfaced Seward, swollen from prednisone, barely able to lift his head from the pillow, and hallucinating that he was on his subchaser during World War I. Mary Lea contends that while her father was dying, Basia was in the next room, pen in hand, checking off the antiques she planned to buy at a Sotheby's auction. She later received a bill from Sotheby's for $2,203,185.19 for items purchased sixteen days before her husband's death.

On May 20 Seward was in such pain that, according to Marty Richards, Basia wanted to inject him with powerful painkillers. He took her outside and said, "Think of the horrible things that are going on with the von Bülow case. You are not a normal lady married to a normal man. Don't be a fool. Don't assume these responsibilities yourself."

Basia's version differs slightly: "He advised me that I shouldn't make any decision myself, that I should consult the doctor. He added that he is giving me this advice against himself and against his family out of a great respect and love which he has for me. I thanked him, but I said that I do not understand what he says, what does that mean? [He replied] "Don't you? What I have in mind is Seward's will.""

On May 23, at four a.m., there was a knock on Basia's door. It was John Peach. Basia threw on a long woolen robe and ran downstairs. When Peach entered Johnson's bedroom a few minutes later, Basia was holding her husband's hand and murmuring, "Seward, I love you. I love you." Then she brushed Johnson's hair and told Peach to hold off a few minutes before calling the undertaker.

The following afternoon the family assembled in a nearby chapel.

MARTY: He was laid out in a tuxedo. They all walked in. Diana was always the lowest-keyed of all and rarely shows emotion of any kind; I've always heard from Keith and from Seward Jr. that she was the most bruised because she was the youngest and had no real life before her parents' marriage was over. When they closed the casket, Diana ran out of the funeral chapel and she was sobbing and sobbing, and then Seward ran after her and he started sobbing and he was hugging her. Mary Lea stood over in the corner crying. And Elaine just looked at everything like it was total devastation. But it was Diana who totally broke down, and she was the furthest one anyone would have ever thought to have shown that much emotion. She tried to take it away privately, she was so destroyed. It was as if she was saying, "Where did this whole life go? Why did all this have to happen? Why was our family like this?" It was as if a floodgate had opened. I felt it was so many tears for what could have been and never was in their lives.

To avoid publicity, there was a private funeral at six a.m. on Wednesday, May 25. Basia says that Keith Wold and Marty Richards and Gretchen Johnson all inquired if the will was going to be read and Gretchen insisted "that the will should be read today. The house was full of people, but she came and whispered in my ear." At eleven there was a memorial service attended by officials of Johnson & Johnson, Harbor Branch personnel, and friends of the family. After the clergyman finished speaking, Seward Jr. gave a short speech which included these sentiments: "Our father lived in the future. He wanted to serve the future by sending man into the sea to fully reap the benefits of our planet. The day before yesterday my father's future became eternity and at the same time the hardest day of my life. We are here today to celebrate the peace that comes with final surrender. . . . It is up to us, Basia, and the rest of the family to fill that empty place in our beings with the stuff of ourselves that is most like him." The ceremony concluded with taps and then three blasts of the foghorns of the R/V *Seward Johnson,* which were echoed by blasts from the *Ocean Pearl.*

BERT FIRESTONE: We went to the funeral and Nina was standing at the door passing out pictures. You know, glossy PR pictures of Seward, and the *New York Times* obituary. It sounded like "Goodbye. Don't come back."

After brunch Jennifer kissed Basia. "I told her I loved her. I said something to try to be supportive." James expressed to her the view that Basia took better care of his father than his own seventy-six-year-old mother could have done. The Richardses invited Basia to their Southampton estate to stay as long as she pleased. Then they all departed.

Three days after the funeral Nina Zagat arrived at Seward Jr.'s Princeton home at four in the afternoon. He had been assigned to serve as executor and trustee of his father's will, along with Basia and Zagat. As Zagat explained the will's provisions, he became increasingly upset. He was the only child to receive a bequest—$1 million and his father's boathouse in Chatham, Massachusetts. According to Zagat, Seward's wife, Joyce, came in and announced dinner, so Zagat volunteered to explain the will to each member of the family and left. Junior made a quick calculation and told Joyce, "It looks like they're trying to buy me off for $5 million to betray my family." (In fact, Junior had miscalculated: his fees alone totaled a $30 million value. Basia Johnson and Nina Zagat, the other two executors and trustees, would receive the same enormous fees.) "The minute I knew what was in the will, the relationship with Basia was severed . . . cut like a knife. I no longer relied on her fairness," Seward Jr. recalls. Within the week, Basia says, she received a call from Marty and Mary Lea's secretary, who relayed the message that they were "stupefied" by the provisions of the will and that Basia was no longer welcome at Southampton.

ELAINE: I felt that no friend of mine would do such a thing as this, and I was dumbfounded. With Nina, it was a general feeling of good will that she wouldn't do anything. I mean, she never said as much as "I will take care of the will" or "I am doing right by you," she never worded it, but her attitude of being a friend, and living in harmony and coming to Maine Chance, was there. She was being friends with all of us, yet underneath the table she was planning, and even working on the probate at that time. That's not a friend. And the executor's fee that Nina got at the end of the will, that was almost a joke, an obscene joke. All the time it was lies.

Junior had created a massive, poetic, semi-abstract sculpture—a figure of King Lear—totally unlike his other works. It had been inspired by his father and he'd placed it at Jasna Polana so that a committee from Lincoln Center might see it in a natural setting. After his father's death Junior became obsessed with the idea of reclaiming his sculpture.

SEWARD JR.: I spent all night working on this King Lear and to me it's my best piece. I told my father about it and I said, "This piece was inspired by you, do you know the story of King Lear?" and he said, "I can't remember it." I said, "Well, King Lear signed over all of his kingdom to someone else and then he was kicked out." And that was the closest I came to telling him that he had jeopardized himself.

I brought it out there, but Basia didn't want it where I wanted to put it in the courtyard, so she put it outside the gates. I said, "Basia, that's right in line with the story." So I had him with his back to the gates, thrown out of his kingdom.

Immediately after his death Basia was off to Europe spending money. I thought, "My God, my King Lear is still at the house and they have so many guards there, how the hell am I going to get my sculpture out of there?" I called up Jasna Polana and said, "I'm afraid the sculpture is nickel and it'll get bronze disease if we don't put the coating on it and I must get the sculpture immediately to put this bronze coating on it." It wasn't true. Then I sent in a crew from the Atelier and I told my group, "It's going to take a while to get it on the truck and they may get hold of Nina Zagat and Basia over in Europe and stop you from getting off the property. What I want you to do is take a camera with you and take a picture of it. Immediately take your film out of the camera, put it in your pocket, and put a new film in the camera because the guards are instructed to take cameras away from everyone and destroy the film." They did all of this. I had another truck outside the gates just in case, if my men got to the electric gates and they closed them, they could take a crane and lift it over the gates and get it out of there. It turned out not to be necessary.

Based on the family history and on the manner in which General Johnson, who frequently set the pattern that his brother, Seward, followed, had handled his own financial affairs, at least some of the Johnson grandchildren had expectations from the will. However, in 1961 and in 1963 Seward Johnson had set up charitable trusts that in the year 1997 would grant the grandchildren of his first marriage a total of $40 million. In the year 2014 the grandchildren of both his first and second marriages were to receive an additional $35 million. There are twenty-two Johnson grandchildren. Presumably, Johnson thought that this had taken care of their financial future. In his final will, and in fact in every will he executed, the Johnson grandchildren had not been included.

ERIC: It starts with an "I wonder what" kind of game, and then you start to play with figures and you come up with some reasonably educated guesses. When we grew up, we were really close to two second cousins of mine, Billy and Keith Johnson, both of whom are dead, who were Bob Johnson, Jr.'s sons and the General's grandsons. Those boys at twenty-one were worth about $4 million apiece, at twenty-five another $2 or $3 million, and then at thirty-one they were worth like $15 or $20 million apiece from various testamentary devices by their father and their grandfather. The male side of that family received the General's money. He left his daughter, Sheila, out; it was his attitude toward women.

In any event, we grew up with our playmates in the mirror position, and these kids, you know, had a whole lot. And when the two boys died, they left their entire estates to their surviving siblings. It wouldn't surprise me if my cousin Woody were worth $300 million. That's not a farfetched figure at all.

We were of course aware that it was a different situation with my grandfather, inasmuch as he'd remarried and things like that. But I would say that the expectation ran somewhere in the neighborhood of not less than $1 million and probably no more than $7 million for each of the grandchildren. In my own sort of calculations we were applying a multiplier for the wives and for the fact that we were third-generation. Attorneys that we would be in contact with would kind of go along with the idea that this was not an unrealistic expectation.

The Tuesday after Memorial Day the Johnson children met at New York's Metropolitan Club. As the family assembled, the elements that would make the will contest inevitable were already in place. Seward Johnson's tactics of secrecy and divisiveness had left open wounds. The deprived childhood of Seward Jr. and the later events surrounding his divorce and resignation of power in the '44 trusts had been followed by the long climb back in which he sought his father's recognition and the approval he never fully received. These circumstances would make him the unofficial leader of the will contest.

Through his incestuous relationship with his daughter Mary Lea, Seward Sr. had damaged her and set the pattern for the events which were to follow. In speaking of the will contest, the words Mary Lea most frequently used were "abused," "excluded," "unfair." These words surfaced again and again, suggesting her perception not only of the will but also of her life.

Jennifer had been alienated from her father when he had left Essie to marry Basia. According to Mary Lea, Jimmy's wife, Gretchen, was very angry because her husband was not included in the will while Junior was, and Gretchen had said that "Jimmy was a kind, sweet, human being and she couldn't understand why he wasn't better liked by his father." Gretchen asked whether anyone had inquired of Seward as to the contents of his will while he was alive. They all agreed they had not. Jennifer later said she was "too chicken to ask," and in a deposition stated, "It was a taboo subject." Marty Richards says, "Mary Lea wouldn't use the bathroom in her father's house without asking permission. How could she ever ask about a will?"

The emotions generated over a lifetime ran strong. Seward Jr. felt his father was responsible. "He was deceitful. He shouldn't have seen us, he shouldn't have had anything to do with us, if that's what he was going to do. He deceived me entirely . . . he was buying his comfort, his youth, at the price of his obligations." Junior thought that eventually the money would go "to a bunch of Polish people my father had never met."

Mary Lea reacted most strongly to the specific disinheritance clause. "You know that clause. The one that says 'not because of any lack of affection for them . . .' and so forth. Elaine said, 'It was as if he'd turned around and slapped us in the face after he'd died.' Everybody went through a deep hurt that nothing had been left to us. It was as if he'd had no children or grandchildren . . . we thought we should get something, if not for ourselves, then for our children."

Harbor Branch had been included in Seward Johnson's penultimate will for a trust remainder of $72 million. In his final will Basia controlled the assignment of this money. The children decided this could not have been their father's intention, that he would have taken care of his beloved Harbor Branch. This provided them with an altruistic reason to fight, and they were determined to prove that they were not weak, that they would not endure this final indignity. Their father's estate had been cleaned out—lock, stock, and barrel—and they were convinced the presumption was that they would not have the strength to protest. Joyce Johnson recalled that Basia's two favorite phrases were "Strike while the iron is hot" and "When you see an opportunity, take it." Joyce felt Basia had taken it, all right—nothing for the blood kin, nothing for the charity, all for Basia.

JOYCE: Everyone felt that the family honor was at stake. That a great wrong had been done and the family had been, through Basia, manipulated and the Harbor Branch foundation had been denied what they were expecting. Everyone was shocked and scandalized that Harbor Branch was not mentioned, and they felt that this was the love and main interest of my father-in-law and that a terrible wrong had been committed.

DIANA: I had hoped that he would make a mention of us, or his grandchildren. I just think it is a natural thing. I would be pleased to be included. I was surprised that Harbor Branch was left out, and that his family was substantially left out. It doesn't seem a will that my father had a part of.

ELAINE: We were all astonished! We wondered if it was a document that my father would have prepared. I feel that I have an obligation to my father to do what would be right and just. I believe it would be right and just to know that we're seeing his dreams fulfilled.

JIMMY: My objective would be that some of his grandchildren might be beneficiaries . . . He was too ill to read a document like that and too ill to have a full consciousness of all that was in there.

MARY LEA: Nobody expected very much, but just something. "I am your father," that kind of acknowledgment. I would have liked to have said to my children, "This is what your grandfather left you."

JENNIFER: I guess I thought that he was going to leave everybody a little something. I thought, a picture maybe. A memento of something from his life. He was in my will, so I thought maybe I was in *his* will. I thought he wanted to have some of his money eventually going to the Harbor Branch foundation. I remember him telling me that it is very important for us to be very public-spirited people because we have received so many advantages from this society we lived in.

SEWARD JR.: Well, what gets me is that it was so perfunctory. It was such legalese. We'd been robbed of our history, an acknowledgment of bloodline. It should have returned to the family blood and the family charity, not to the Polish, and not scattered to hither and yon, according to her wishes. The only thing that you can do is fight to prove that you're worthy in the fight, that you're not just going to lie down and let it happen. To win that dignity.

ERIC: It's more psychodrama than anything else. I think it's really much more tied up in the personalities involved. Wills aren't contracts, it's not like you do this and you get this. I think that what really got my mother and her siblings together was that it wasn't just money, that it was a sense of family honor, that, damn it, if they're going to take it all, we're going to fight. I believe that my mom really felt that the wills didn't reflect her father's true interests or intentions, and I think that that was an important decision for her to come to in terms of being able to justify her participation in the contest. I think that Mom could just have swallowed her pride and said, "Well, I guess we weren't as close as I thought we were," or said, "I guess he left me well enough off during my lifetime." Before my grandfather died, Mom said she wouldn't be a bit surprised if she herself didn't receive anything if we did. I really think her pride was hurt that none of the grandchildren were remembered. But even if the money had gone to a couple of charities that my grandfather had set up, my mom and her siblings would have felt they could walk away from it.

But, from a psychological perspective, here they had an advantage of fighting not just as greedy kids but fighting for the charity, fighting for their own children, that sort of gave them a sense of cause. And for my uncle Seward, I think he felt he had a lot of shame to live down. It was more like trying to earn back his father's respect.

Mary Lea says everyone decided to go forward, with the exception of James, who said he was sorry but he had his own life to lead. He asked the others, "How can we be sure that this was not Daddy's wishes?"

"There's no way we can be certain," Seward Jr. replied. "However, Jimmy, do you think your father was not senile?"

"No, I think he was senile," James answered. (In his deposition James said that he thought his father was "slightly senile.") James too fell into line.

Elaine declared, "As a group, we should all stand together and fight with firm conviction and no doubt whatsoever in our mind, heart, or soul. To sleep with it and get up in the morning and go ahead with it. Fight the good fight with all thy might."

At the end of the meeting Joyce Johnson said, "When we go home tonight, we all have got to search out our hearts and really understand why we are doing this and the purposes we are doing it. That they are moral purposes and not greedy purposes." The emotions about their father were transmuted. This had become an affair of honor, and with the battle for honor came lawyers, lawyers, and more lawyers.

The next day the family met again for a second session that lasted ten hours. This time Alexander Forger, the managing partner of Milbank, Tweed, Hadley & McCloy, and Jeffrey Brinck of its trusts and estates department were on the scene to discuss the possibility of a will contest. At that second meeting the raw emotions of rejection and ill-use were summoned into something more tangible—a legal premise. Brinck recalls, "I could see the children were emotionally appalled. When we began to discover what had gone on, we became legally appalled."

What had begun with feelings of unfairness, deprivation, and unfocused rage was rapidly transformed into a colossal legal battle with related actions in three states, bursting forth from the main contest like a paramecium in fission. All this litigation eventually generated four hundred thousand pages of documentation (Basia paid $119,415.95 for transcripts of the New York will contest alone) and involved 210 lawyers from twenty-two law firms.

ALEXANDER FORGER: I met them for dinner at the Board Room. I had not even read the other wills. I also got a sense through that meeting of the interpersonal dynamics within the family as the different personalities emerged. Jimmy being the youngest, maybe being most sensitive about Father's memory, and let's not do anything that's going to stir up any problems. Keith being the professional with some medical background. Marty being genuinely open, friendly, funny. Elaine being sort of the family unifier; when I think of Elaine, I think of let's get everybody together thinking good positive thoughts. Diana, very quiet. Bert was there, as I remember. Mary Lea, very charming, but Marty reciting many of the instances of mistreatment of Seward. Seward Jr. was sort of the spokesperson for the family.

There was mention that nothing was there for grandchildren and nothing for themselves, but that wasn't the point of it. The point of it was that the principal charitable object of Father's attention during his lifetime was seemingly out of it. I'm not certain that at that point there was anything to say except that here's a will presumably giving almost all the benefit to a wife. Wives always exercise influence over husbands, not necessarily undue influence over husbands, and that's sort of a fine line. Unquestionably there was a lot of medical care and attention given. With a major firm like Shearman & Sterling involved, not very likely that there was a basis for invalidating instruments or want of testamentary capacity or maybe even for undue influence with such high-standing professionals in the picture. I mean it wasn't the local druggist who gave the decedent a will form to fill out. It surely appeared on those facts that it was going to be a very great uphill struggle to get any evidence. I was corresponding with Tom Ford and said, "Send me the wills that you've got. And, by the way, how big *is* the estate?"

The Metropolitan Club meeting was followed by meetings on Nantucket with Forger, Jeffrey Brinck, and litigator Edward Reilly. Alexander Forger warned that it would take at least a year of discovery proceedings before they knew if they had a case. These children, who had never communicated, now gathered together, each contributing a piece to the puzzle. Elaine Johnson Wold commented, "You know, this might be a very good thing for all of us, in that it is time we got to know each other better. We have been, as a family, kept apart from half of our siblings, and we really got to know them, during the few meetings we have had, as real people. It is lovely that we are all getting together to know each other." There on Nantucket the family resolve coalesced. According to Nina Zagat, Nantucket marked the first time the children had ever compared notes. Said Zagat, "I think after their father's death, for the first time they got together and compared how they felt about their father. That was the first time, I think, they ever expressed their feelings, and that's what brought them together." Seward Jr.'s determination led the way. As he observed, "This was not a group of soldiers charging over the hill in a line. All of them were peeking out from behind the front ones."

ELAINE: The whole thing was a lie, but it's all so legally confused. All I know is when you get down to the legal part of it, I don't get involved in it.

ALEXANDER FORGER: I was just astounded. Midsummer is when I looked at the major testamentary instruments that were executed within fifty-six days. The maze of highly complex, very substantial numbers of weighty legal documents, with an estate plan that said to me somebody has been gearing up for a will contest, started to excite me as I looked at that as a professional. To see what happened in the course of two or three months, it defied one's belief as to what could transpire in these last days. I didn't know how this could have come about. Could this have been an eighty-seven-year-old man who was changing his mind every three weeks of every four weeks and getting into some pretty sophisticated sort of provisions? Could this guy really have been engaged in all of this high-intellectual, legal activity?

We started charting out all the wills back to 1971 and saw a progression from a $10 million to ultimately the whole thing. It seemed to me that within about ninety days, we concluded that there was enough there on the surface to warrant going forward and looking below. This cried out for explanation.

"One will too many!"

The legal battle ranks
formed. The first skirmishes began. News drifted back to
the children's camp that Nina Zagat and Basia were in
Europe spending in excess of $2 million on antique French
furniture. During the first week in August 1983, Nina and
Basia appeared at the Harbor Branch offices in Fort Pierce,
an unusual time of year for them to be in that vicinity.
Methodically, they went through the offices and removed
the financial and business files.

John Peach was fired by Seward Jr., who stated that his
raise was not justifiable. Basia Johnson claimed that Peach
was fired because the Milbank lawyers ascertained that his
loyalties were to her. The following day a security guard
was stationed at the Harbor Branch gates, and when Peach
tried to get to the Johnsons' residence, he was denied access to the property. Basia says, "That is what started the
war. He [Junior] barred me from my own house." In fact,
it was this one ex-employee who was barred, but in September Basia brought an access suit against Harbor
Branch. Peach also lodged a suit over his dismissal. Junior
says, "Basia saw me as the kingpin in the will contest. She

knew the only way she could give me trouble was through Harbor Branch. I told everybody to expect it." The legal clock was beginning to run. The access suit alone cost $3 million.

Jeffrey Brinck of Milbank, Tweed was chagrined to find that in preparing to attack Seward Jr., Basia Johnson's attorneys were using the Shearman & Sterling files accumulated over a decade. Junior, now in control of Harbor Branch, replaced Shearman & Sterling with Milbank, Tweed and removed the files. In a Sullivan & Cromwell brief, Milbank was accused of a conflict-of-interest position in representing both the children and Harbor Branch. "Objectants stood to gain as distributees only if *all* of Mr. Johnson's many prior wills were denied probate, while Harbor Branch could benefit only if the March 22 will, or some other will, was admitted to probate." Therefore, Dewey, Ballantine, Bushby, Palmer & Wood were retained to represent Harbor Branch in the will contest. Lawyers, lawyers, and more lawyers.

Three days after Junior's deposition was taken in the access suit, Basia Johnson filed suit in the Chancery Division of the Mercer County Superior Court of New Jersey against Seward Jr., charging Junior with mismanagement of Harbor Branch's investment portfolio and the loss of $24 million in assets. She petitioned that Junior personally be surcharged for these losses. Junior's net worth was then $23 million.

More legal maneuvering, more money, more lawyers: Seward Jr. amended the bylaws of Harbor Branch to hold an annual trustee election and Basia Johnson was voted off the board. Since Junior could not remove her from an affiliated organization, the Harbor Branch Institution, he drained funds from the institution, reducing its capital from $10 million to $2 million by building roads, housing, and making other physical improvements on Harbor Branch land.

Basia had recovered from her initial reaction of "surprise and hurt" that the children had turned against her and began to take action. If there were to be a will contest, obviously Shearman & Sterling could not represent Basia and Zagat because of the firm's involvement in the drafting of Johnson's wills. Therefore, partner Thomas Ford recommended that they contact Donald Christ of Sullivan & Cromwell, who was known for his tact in negotiating out-of-court settlements. Christ—Choate, Yale, Justice of the Peace of Oyster Bay Cove and Mill Neck, Long Island, the son of a New York State Supreme Court judge—is a low-key, laid-back man whose idea of a perfect vacation is fly fishing, and who ties the flies himself. Christ is possessed of social poise, a wry sense of humor, and an affability that displayed itself in small ways during the trial: when asked to turn on a tape recorder to play a tape damaging to his client, he declined, saying, "Remember what happened to Rose Mary Woods." When Edward Reilly grew agitated and red in the face after a heated argument, it was Christ who put his hand on his opponent's shoulder and whispered *sotto voce,* "Take it easy." On a day when depositions were being taken in three states simultaneously, Christ, feeling that he couldn't do the job unaided, enlisted the services of Sullivan & Cromwell partner Robert Osgood.

Christ seemed the perfect choice for Basia Johnson. In fact, the children themselves had discussed the possibility of retaining Christ, and might well have approached him had Forger refused the case. The choice of lawyers may not have seemed so crucial at this time: none of the lawyers anticipated that this case would end up in a courtroom; logically, Basia Johnson, with an estimated half-billion dollars at stake, could easily part with a token amount to the Johnson children and grandchildren and restore the bequest to Harbor Branch.

But, from the start, the late Seward Johnson's mixed messages pervaded the proceedings. Basia felt that she was carrying out her husband's "vision." She said that on repeated occasions he had told her, "Basia, everything is for you." Just as he had told Junior that he would take care of Junior's children, who were "the poorest of the cousins," and that when he died Harbor Branch would be endowed with $300 million. Just as he had told Keith Wold that a third of his wealth would go to his family.

Another example of Seward's divisive behavior seemed to concern his ante-nuptial agreement with Basia. Both Mary Lea and Elaine testified that Basia had told them that her husband had torn up the agreement, yet at the trial the signed original document turned up in the safe of Carter Nicholas and a duplicate signed original was provided by Robert Myers. Nina Zagat stated that toward the end of Seward's life both Seward and Basia told her that the ante-nuptial agreement had been revoked, but since she could find no such revocation document in her files, she prepared another one, which was signed on April 14 along with Johnson's final will. And Basia testified that she had never seen a revocation document prior to April 14, or ever discussed the agreement with her husband. Seward Johnson had left behind a volatile legacy of unresolved issues and unexplained intentions.

KEITH: You know, for want of a nail, the war was lost. Before we went to court, if Basia had said that she was going to restore the Harbor Branch trust fund, a non-invasive portion of it, and to have separate trustees other than just herself and Nina to insure the fund remain intact, I don't think anybody would have said anything. I think that we would never have gone to court. But I guess Basia didn't want to lose any of it.

BASIA: Always I was willing to give to Harbor Branch, they always knew that. But right away they kick me off the board, get rid of me. Without me there would have been no Harbor Branch. Now Seward Jr., it is in his hands.

NICHOLAS RUTGERS: There are a lot of things Seward could have done so there wouldn't have been a will contest. He could have made clear what his intention was toward Harbor Branch. He could have spoken to his children. None of them are greedy, but they needed to understand. The real crux of the matter is that Seward was just out there playing with his toys and he didn't know what life was all about.

On September 30, 1983, Milbank, Tweed filed an objection to the will. But, even so, it seemed inconceivable that Milbank, Tweed really intended to take on the combined forces of Shearman & Sterling and Sullivan & Cromwell in a serious way. That would violate the rules of the game. These lawyers are all members of an elite fraternity and, for all their courtroom histrionics on behalf of their clients, they rarely indulge in real war against their brethren. The lawyers at Sullivan & Cromwell who represented the widow Johnson regarded the Milbank challenge with a combination of annoyance and disdain, and could not believe that this was anything more than a capricious nuisance action.

ALEXANDER FORGER: At the time of the filing, there was a notion that we were just sort of making waves and

posturing. Courthouse people, lawyers for the widow
saying, "How can you file an objection with somebody
of this stature? You're accusing the widow of undue influence and you're saying the law firm and the doctors
permitted him to execute documents when he didn't
have the capacity to do so. Come on! The kids have
enough money, the charity's got money. What is this?
Some kind of strike suit, a vendetta? You're going
through some sort of a charade here."

I think as the thing went along, it was pretty clear
that Sullivan & Cromwell thought you can't go forward
with building your case in a way that's going to dispar-
age or reflect badly on any of the things that we have
done here. It was in spades a sense of arrogance as to
"How dare you question what we're doing with our witnesses, or the fact that we didn't produce the prenuptial
agreement for you, the fact that we didn't produce the
letter of April 14?" And it was a progression of an ero-
sion of that attitude, month after month after month,
not so quickly the first year, but then at an accelerated
pace, and the last four months on a roller-coaster.

Although, as Robert Osgood commented, the extent of
discovery was like an immense anti-trust suit, the documents in this case were in the form of the detritus of human life: telephone records, menus, bills, diaries, photograph albums, appointment calendars, guestbooks, letters,
thank-you notes. During the period from September of
1983 through February of 1986, fifty-five motions were
filed, several as thick as a New York telephone book, concerning such matters as Milbank, Tweed's contention that
the widow should be compelled to answer the question
"Did you drive a farm machine in Poland?" or whether the
widow knew what to do to obtain a scuba-diving license.

On the other side, Sullivan & Cromwell demanded the elementary-school records of the six children. Surrogate Marie Lambert says, "They made each of these motions seem monumentally important, as if the entire case rested on the outcome." In a decision on one of these motions Lambert wrote that discovery proceedings had deteriorated from *This Is Your Life* to *Trivial Pursuit.*

Depositions were taken. With the exception of Diana Firestone, who said, "I would be pleased to be included," the children asserted in their depositions that they wanted nothing personally from a suit. Basia's lawyers moved that since the Johnson children wanted nothing from the estate, they had no right to contest. That motion was fought all the way to the Appellate Division before it was finally denied. In actuality, throughout the trial and in a final press conference, Seward Jr. freely admitted that one of the goals always had been to keep some of their father's money in the Johnson bloodline.

The legal house of cards kept building. Based on documents and an affidavit obtained from Ruth Dill Crockett, Milbank, Tweed, on behalf of Seward Johnson's first four children, filed a separate claim to one half of the Johnson estate. This action, if successful, would leave Jennifer and James, the children of the second marriage, out in the cold. At a Metropolitan Club meeting in January of 1984, the first four children, one after another, used the device suggested by their lawyers of standing up, turning, and facing the wall as they expressed such sentiments as "If we win this claim, we would think it right and fair to share with Jennifer and Jimmy." In effect, this pact kept the family united in their mission, but could not be attacked by Basia's side as a legal agreement. When asked during depositions if a legal agreement existed, the children answered, accurately, no.

During the will contest Surrogate Marie Lambert held this claim aside, deciding not to rule on Milbank's request for a summary judgment until after the trial. Therefore the Sword of Damocles of losing half the estate, irrespective of the validity of the will, hung over Basia Johnson's head during the will contest itself and provided a potent bargaining tool for the children's side.

Harbor Branch entered the fray and allied itself with the children. Sullivan & Cromwell charged that it had exceeded the statute of limitations and could not join the contest. The foundation replied that it had not known its vested remainder interest had been removed until September of 1983. It was permitted to join the suit. The Harbor Branch involvement was to lend the proceedings a good appearance. Harbor Branch was perceived as the White Knight and the children as fighting for a disinherited charity. Basia's lawyers did not bring out the fact that where Harbor Branch was concerned, in actual dollars $5 million not $72 million was at stake. As a lawyer explained, "If you went to an insurance company and said, 'I am a forty-nine-year-old woman in good health and I want someone to get $72 million *when I die,*' they would sell you a policy for $5 million that would guarantee that. Therefore, the worth of the bequest in today's dollars is $5 million."

Another pertinent fact that never surfaced in the courtroom, that the children and Harbor Branch had divergent interests, was pointed out by Marilyn Link, a representative of the independent Harbor Branch directors' litigation committee formed to avoid a conflict of interest now that Junior controlled this organization. Said Miss Link concerning the choice of children *or* Harbor Branch as recipients under Johnson's wills, "Essentially we were competing for the same bucks."

At Milbank, Tweed a massive battle campaign was being mounted. What made this case different from most was that, because of the vast amounts of money involved, the law firms could investigate every possibility and utilize unlimited personnel. The children's bill from Milbank, Tweed through June of 1985 was $6 million, and during the trial period the law firm's services ran $300,000 a month. In the six months prior to the trial, fourteen Milbank lawyers were working full time on the case.

ALEXANDER FORGER: The other side, I guess they believed they had an unlimited treasury. They lawyered this in a way that was designed to cause the objectants the most possible expense and time. Not that they thought our folks would run out of money, but maybe, they thought, the longer it is stretched out, the more expensive it becomes, the more impatient people might get and maybe they would go away.

ERIC: A friend of mine suggested that we should go to the attorneys and offer them a flat $5 million if this case was settled in six months and have it declining from that point on. The more hours they put in, the less they'd get. That seemed like a wonderful idea. But you could never get the Bar Association to go along with it.

In Milbank's trusts and estates department, thirty of Seward Johnson's wills, dating back to 1966, were carefully analyzed. After Basia's $100 million marital trust was established in 1973, each will granted her this same amount. According to Jeffrey Brinck, Johnson's complex forty-eight-page last will and testament, signed April 14, also seemed to grant Basia the same $100 million. However, the will was divided into two sections, and Article 9 of the latter section provided a complicated formula by which virtually the entire estate was kicked back to Basia. This formula, Brinck concluded, was employed simply for purposes of obfuscation. "There was a clear and simple way to state the same thing. There is little possibility a lay person could figure out that formula, no matter how sophisticated he is, much less a dying eighty-seven-year-old man." Alexander Forger too began studying the pattern of Johnson's wills, and he drew his own conclusions as to what had transpired.

ALEXANDER FORGER: One will too many! If they had stopped with the next-to-last will, Harbor Branch got $72 million. Yes, it was the widow who was getting life benefit, yeah, the kids were not included, but Seward Jr. is an executor, Seward Jr. is a trustee, and if they had been real smart in that will, they would have given $100,000 to each grandchild. They would have been home free. It's a common thing that you see people get carried away. The most important thing you have as a lawyer is independence of judgment, and when the day comes that you start doing things and giving advice because you think that's what the client wants to hear—you're finished. This is my major grievance with some of the lawyers.

How do you rationalize this slalom that went on—the numbers of documents, the unexplainable changes in provisions, except bearing on the will contest? What it came out to is that all of the players got obsessed with the notion of getting everything covered. They could have stopped 90 percent of the way. I mean, the gifts at the end, the trust, everything. Clean it out. It was the lawyers. They had to show how brilliant they were.

At Sullivan & Cromwell, self-confidence ran high; the case was a shoo-in. The children had not been in thirty wills dating back to 1966 and, anticipating a will contest, Shearman & Sterling had tightened up the language of the disinheritance clause. Although in the penultimate will Harbor Branch was bequeathed $72 million upon Basia's death, it had received nothing in previous wills for a decade. Finally, Zagat had obtained properly executed wills and Dr. Fred Schilling had signed a certificate stating that Seward Johnson was of "sound mind and memory" on the day he signed his final will.

EDWARD REILLY: I've had a number of cases I'd put in the St. Jude category—the patron saint of hopeless causes. A will contest is a very difficult kind of case to win, and particularly with children of prior marriages, but I do remember very plainly feeling personally that there was something wrong with this will. And, also importantly, I felt that we had an obligation to our clients as a family—they're not just like six stockholders who happened to have purchased Go-Go Industries at the same time based on the same quarterly report.

Edward Reilly was chosen to head up the children's litigation team. Reilly had been brought up in a New York suburb, the son of a lawyer with a strong ethical code and sense of morality. Two of his sisters are nurses, one of whom, Peggy LaMassa, recalls that their father, in sharp contrast to J. Seward Johnson, gave his children "nothing but everything." She also recalls the day in November of 1964 that "Eddie" called her at her Flowertown, Pennsylvania, home, where their father, who had suffered three strokes, was living. "Wheel Daddy to the phone," he instructed Peggy, and when she did, Reilly said, "Dad, I owe you so much and I wanted to thank you. I wanted you to be the first person to know that I've been made a partner of Milbank, Tweed."

In 1946, at the age of seventeen, Reilly had enlisted in the Marines and, after an eighteen-month stint, used the GI Bill to help finance his education at the University of Pennsylvania's Wharton School of Business and Yale Law School. He always excelled and supplemented his income by grading papers, waiting on tables, and teaching seminars.

In 1954 he was hired by Milbank and credits "luck and timing" for his rise in the then expanding litigation department. Today Reilly is in charge of this department, overseeing seventeen partners, forty-two associates, and about thirty paralegals. At Milbank, as in childhood, his reputation was that of a hard worker. A partner says that when people arrive in the morning and find the conference-room table littered with books, they say, "Reilly's been here." Reilly admits that he has no trouble working eighteen to twenty hours a day, although he discourages his young associates from following the same pattern and ignoring their families. He recalls that once, in the middle of an anti-trust trial, he was walking to his car when his six-year-old son ran up to him, took his hand, and said, "Daddy, you're my best pal." Realizing how little time he spent with his family, Reilly was both touched and abashed.

In common with Robert Osgood of Sullivan & Cromwell, Reilly most frequently litigated cases concerning large corporate matters, although he has also litigated such cases as that of Jacqueline Onassis enjoining the use, by Christian Dior, of a look-alike model. Asked by a reporter if he had won the case, Reilly replied, "We win 'em all." In his desk drawer he keeps a piece of paper on which is written Queen Victoria's statement to Lord Balfour: "We are not interested in the possibilities of defeat."

In the initial stages of the battle, Reilly and associates Charles Berry and Paul Shoemaker conducted depositions. Reilly refused to attend any of Basia Johnson's depositions, and entered the courtroom with his legal construction of her unobscured by contact with the individual herself. However, he was anxious to be at Zagat's depositions.

EDWARD REILLY: I wanted to study the pattern of her testimony. Very often lawyers make what I consider to be a mistake in depositions—they're more interested in each other than in observing the client. Also, they sit next to the client, so they can't see the visual reactions. I watched Zagat very carefully. There were times when the red flush would start at her neck and rise up her face like a fever thermometer.

Reilly was to refer to the case he presented as a "mosaic," and the image was to prove apt. The Johnson children had rarely seen their father on the same occasions, and what one of them might deem to be an isolated incident was to emerge as a pattern. Servants were deposed, and one after another they made similar observations about Basia's behavior toward them and toward her husband. Medical records were studied. "I was lucky," said Reilly, "I had almost two years of medical records and nurses' notes in detail to work with." And work he did, familiarizing himself with complex medical terminology, drafting a chronology of Seward's last days, and forming a thesis about Basia's behavior toward her husband.

Throughout March and April of 1984, Alexander Forger spent many evenings in his forty-sixth-floor office at 1

Chase Manhattan Plaza studying depositions and the testamentary pattern of Johnson's wills. At sixty-three, the strikingly handsome, six-foot-four Forger was possessed of the urbane and doctorly demeanor one has come to associate with a trusts and estates lawyer. But, just as the old family doctor has metamorphosed into today's medical specialist, so Alexander Forger is an example of a new breed. Forger has never tried a criminal case and rarely appears in the courtroom, but he was the *éminence grise* behind the Johnson will contest. Over the years, he has honed his mediating and bargaining skills, often working in a *pro bono* capacity for federal and local governmental agencies. Although dignified, he is not reticent about joining in the fray.

Forger, the son of the secretary-treasurer of Julius Forstmann Corporation, woolen manufacturers, attended Princeton University and served with the 75th Infantry Division during World War II, where he was awarded the Bronze Star for "heroic achievement," before attending Yale Law School. Forger, determined to move his firm into the competitive present-day legal environment, had attracted many new clients to Milbank, and was responsible for getting Jacqueline Kennedy Onassis a $20 million settlement when she had been left a $250,000 bequest under her husband Aristotle Onassis's will. Since that time he has handled several problems for the Kennedy family, including the arrest of one of Robert Kennedy's sons on drug charges, Mrs. Onassis's property dispute on Martha's Vineyard, and Joan Kennedy's divorce from her husband, Senator Edward Kennedy. The privacy Milbank affords these clients is greatly valued. Jacqueline Kennedy Onassis is never referred to by name on client matters or billing statements, but is identified simply as "Special One."

After ten weeks of study, on May 10, 1984, Forger

says, he "fired the first salvo" of the legal war in the form of an affidavit that laid out the essential terms of Milbank's case. Forger charged the widow Johnson and lawyer Nina Zagat with "fraud, duress and undue influence," as well as asserting that Seward Johnson was senile and lacked testamentary capacity when he executed his final will and testament. Forger carefully analyzed the testamentary pattern, but it was the personal-background section of his affidavit that was to affect irrevocably the tone of the litigation. The Forger affidavit contained a virulent attack on Basia Johnson's motives and reputation.

ALEXANDER FORGER AFFIDAVIT: She [Basia], then 31 years of age, arrived with but modest means. Almost immediately, she found employment as a chambermaid in the household of J. Seward Johnson Sr. Notwithstanding the language barrier and her lack of facility with English, she did succeed in communicating with Seward, who was then well into his seventies. Within a year of her arrival on the scene, the domestic tranquility of the Johnson household had been shattered and the marriage of Seward and Esther destroyed.

On November 11, 1971, Basia and Seward were married. She had then reached the age of thirty-four, and he, having passed the age of seventy-six, had already achieved an actuarially determined full life expectancy. The wide disparity in their ages was paralleled by the vast differences in their educational and cultural backgrounds, in their financial resources and business interests and in their philanthropic, recreational, and social interests. What then was the attraction that caused Basia to embark on matrimony? One is drawn unmistakenly to the conclusion that the real attraction for Basia was the money . . .

As tools to achieve her goal of dominion over Seward's entire estate, Basia relied not only on her ability to enchant and captivate Seward, but also on her violent temper and fierce outbursts which Seward, by nature a reserved person, became too weak to resist as time wore on. Against his will, or without his realization, he placed virtually his entire estate under her control. A few weeks short of his 88th birthday, Basia succeeded to virtually his entire estate, undoubtedly becoming one of the world's richest women.

The insulting words and phrases struck Basia's Achilles' heel: "modest means," "already achieved an actuarially determined full life expectancy," "real attraction . . . was the money," "shattered" and "destroyed," "enchant and captivate," "chambermaid."

BASIA: They say terrible things. They accused me that I was just waiting for my husband to die and that he didn't die soon enough. That's the worst possible thing anyone could ever say. I did everything, everything. I was fighting for his life as long as I could.

According to Sullivan & Cromwell lawyers, the reaction at the firm and on the part of their client was one of rage and shocked disbelief. Seward Jr.'s statement "I think they were surprised by the vigor of our response" was an understatement. For years Basia had lived with the elevated respect and protection that great wealth affords. With the filing of the Forger affidavit, powerful emotions entered into the proceedings. Basia Johnson felt her reputation and motives were under severe attack. As the assault on her character continued through a series of legal maneuvers, both sides became increasingly angry and bitter.

On December 17, 1984, Robert Osgood answered the Forger affidavit with one of his own, more virulent and destructive than his opponent's. Osgood alleged that the children had brought suit through "disappointed greed and envy" and that Seward Johnson did not want them to have any more money because the vast fortune he had bestowed upon them had not been used wisely. To bolster his point, Osgood annexed to his affidavit twenty-five exhibits that were composed of tabloid headlines, divorce petitions, depositions containing innuendos of emotional disturbance and suicide attempts—in short, inflammatory material that was undoubtedly meant to serve as a warning that if the children pursued this case, a lot of dirty linen would be washed in public.

Often the connection between Osgood's exhibits and his expressed purpose to demonstrate Seward Johnson's disappointment in his children was tenuous. Exhibit 6 contained Seward Johnson, Jr.'s amended divorce complaint, which set out in the most graphic and lurid terms his distressing experiences. Exhibit 10 contained excerpts from James's depositions, about which Osgood asserted, "Yet another of the decedent's children, James L. Johnson, appears to have exhibited severe emotional disturbance during his father's lifetime." Exhibit 14 was the Mary Lea "troublemaker" letter. Exhibit 15, referring to Mary Lea's divorce from Victor D'Arc "in unusual circumstances," was the article from the *Daily News* with the headline "Spouse, Hitman Hit It Off, Heiress Says." Osgood's rationale for including this exhibit was "Her father was aware of this divorce." Exhibit 16 was a letter from Seward Ryan to his grandfather that contained the sentence "It's too bad about all this god damn money—if it were not there, maybe we could be a closer family." (That sentence was to provide an irresistible tag line to many members of the news media.)

If the Forger affidavit had been strong in its criticism of Basia, the character assassination of the Osgood affidavit was brutal. Soon after, according to Edward Reilly, carefully highlighted copies of the affidavit found their way from Osgood's office to members of the news media. On June 18, 1985, *The New York Times* published an article that utilized much of this material, including Exhibit 6—Seward Jr.'s 1962 divorce petition in which he'd alleged that he'd served his wife breakfast in bed and that she had a lover. The article, garbling this information, stated, "He was subjected to such humiliations as serving breakfast in bed to his wife's lover." Subsequently the *Times* printed a correction, but the repercussions had been felt. The news media, who were to play a significant role in the contest, had been alerted: the upcoming Johnson will contest held the promise of steamy revelations, of sordid doings amidst unheard-of luxury.

At the time of the *Times* story, Seward Johnson, Jr., and his wife Joyce, who had been married for twenty years, were vacationing at their Nantucket home. Their two teenage children, John and Clelia, knew little of their father's first marriage. A friend of John's showed him the *Times* article and teased him about it. Then someone stopped Joyce and said, "Oh goody, we've been reading all about the von Bülow case and now we'll be reading all about you!"

EDWARD REILLY: That document hurt a lot of people, but if Osgood thought it would make us back off, he was wrong. He not only prepared an affidavit to which he annexed a lot of scurrilous and, as the court later ruled, irrelevant material, but then he distributed it to certain representatives of the press in a way that assured that there would be no way that they could avoid seeing what he wanted them to see because he attached a pale green or yellow plastic marker. It was a pretty sorry thing to do. The other side was not only disseminating things to the press, but doing it in the most reprehensible way. It was terrible, not so much for the people involved, because they'd learned to live with bad publicity and they knew what they were risking by bringing this case, but the way it was done touched their children. That was particularly painful.

SEWARD JR.: At the beginning, all the questioning that was done of us was to try to prove how close we became to Basia and to our father during their marriage. But then later their tactics changed and they tried to say that the reason we were rejected in the will was that our father felt we were all so terrible. That dichotomy has to be noticed: truth ekes its way out through this myriad of lies, this structure of lies.

"I'm going to bury Robert Osgood."

*E*dward Reilly, during the discovery period, had become increasingly dismayed at the methods employed by Sullivan & Cromwell's Robert Mansfield Osgood. On the surface, Osgood seemed an unlikely villain. His clear blue eyes and direct manner were engaging. The son of a Methodist minister from Rome, New York, he'd served as a minister himself for a year before entering Syracuse University Law School. Sullivan & Cromwell was his first place of employment and he had progressed steadily upward. Osgood served as Sullivan & Cromwell's hiring partner, and young lawyers in the firm respected his tenacity and the time he spent with them, furthering their careers. Osgood had been involved in a great deal of corporate litigation and was known for his adroit handling of anti-trust cases.

But this was no anti-trust action, this involved human emotions, and Osgood's affidavit had been lacerating. When Osgood deposed Joyce Johnson, she found him to be unnecessarily harsh. According to her account, Osgood grilled her for three hours about the conversation pertaining to Seward Sr.'s Class A trusteeship resignation. Finally

Milbank petitioned to stop her from being further deposed. Seward Jr. felt keenly that Joyce was being persecuted, and he balked at the fact that Sullivan & Cromwell lawyers had read her his love letters to his first wife.

JOYCE: You can't believe the way he treated me, he was so bullying and insulting. He wouldn't dare do that in a courtroom, and as a result I reacted badly. I didn't handle it at all well. Basia was there, smirking, laughing at me.

But it was when Reilly went to Florida in search of witnesses that his rage really grew. The observations of medical personnel, especially the private-duty nurses who had attended Seward Sr. during his waning days, were crucial to Reilly's case, but he found that "it just reached a point where I felt nurse after nurse and other people would turn away. I knew there was something wrong." Again and again the names of Robert Osgood and John Peach surfaced. Through documents obtained by court order, Reilly discovered that John Peach was employed by Sullivan & Cromwell, working closely with Robert Osgood, visiting various nurses who had attended Mr. Johnson. At that time Reilly had no idea of how much Peach was being paid. Eventually, through another court order, he was able to document almost $25,000 paid by Sullivan & Cromwell to Peach "to assist them in their litigation activities" and $100,000 paid by "Mrs. Johnson and the Estate for caretaking and related work." The monies paid to Peach over a twenty-eight-month period would finally total $161,000.

EDWARD REILLY: It made my task absolutely hopeless. There was no way that I could get someone who had been made part of the Sullivan & Cromwell litigation

team to testify for us. I mean, when you combine what
Peach has done for Sullivan & Cromwell and what he's
done with respect to all these nurses—I think there were
half a dozen nurses he would take to dinner or take to
lunch and entertain them—it made it increasingly difficult for us to get nurses even to talk to us. But eventually we did get to some. There were a few, like Bonnie
Weisser, who had the strength of character to resist the
importunings of Sullivan & Cromwell; she just said,
"Get lost. I'm not going to sign your affidavit."

Of all the nurses who attended Seward Johnson, Bonnie Weisser was one of the most respected for her knowledge and her calm command; the other nurses looked to
her for guidance. In January of 1984 Weisser had received
a call from Osgood and agreed to meet with him, but from
the first she felt uncomfortable. Mr. Osgood volunteered to
send her résumé to Johnson & Johnson with a letter of
recommendation from Basia Johnson. He told her he had
already done this for Fran Cioffi Adams, another of the
nurses.

On March 22, 1984, Robert Osgood appeared at Weisser's Orlando, Florida, apartment with an affidavit and
asked her to sign it on the spot. When she demurred, he
reluctantly left it with her. The next day he called and
"was very angry," demanding to know whether Bonnie
Weisser had spoken to "the other side." She told Osgood
that his affidavit was not accurate and refused to sign it. By
the time Weisser met Reilly, her ire matched his own.
Reilly discovered that Osgood had extended an offer of
help not only to Weisser and Adams but also to nurse
Sheril Bennett. Adams had been told "that Mrs. Johnson
was in a better position to get her a job at the company
than were the objectants." To nurse Patricia Reid, who

had noted Johnson's confusion, Osgood had written, "Please do not worry about getting involved. We will keep you out of it." Eventually Reilly was able to document these and other examples of Robert Osgood's *modus operandi.*

BONNIE WEISSER AFFIDAVIT: I felt [Robert Osgood] was pressuring me in an improper manner and telling me inappropriate things about the case. He didn't simply ask questions about my knowledge of Mr. Johnson's treatment and condition, but in an effort to persuade me of the merits of Mrs. Johnson's position, gave me an explanation of the reasons for the provisions in Mr. Johnson's will, and told me that the children were trying to show that Mr. Johnson was a "lunatic."

Although I said I had no interest one way or the other, he went on to say that Mrs. Johnson had been loving and devoted to her husband and he explained why she had been the primary beneficiary of Mr. Johnson's will. He treated me as a salesman would and asked questions that seemed to be designed to get answers he wanted, or to persuade me about particular facts. For example, he asked, "Isn't it true that Mr. Johnson read three newspapers every day?" My response was that it was true three newspapers were delivered to his room every day and Mr. Johnson spent some time looking at them, but he would often stare at one paper for a very long time and never gave any indication that he understood what he was looking at.

Mr. Osgood also tried to inject an inappropriate personal note into his dealings with me. . . . He passed along greetings from Mrs. Johnson and after our initial meeting, called me from her house at Ft. Pierce and urged me to come down in a private plane to meet with him, have a swim in Mrs. Johnson's pool and draft an affidavit.

SHERIL BENNETT AFFIDAVIT: I am a nurse who attended the decedent, J. Seward Johnson, for five days in late March 1983. . . . I am making this statement to advise the Court of the intimidating manner in which one of Mrs. Johnson's attorneys has dealt with me so that the Court may be able to take whatever steps are necessary to prevent such treatment of other witnesses.

I initially met with Mr. Robert Osgood, an attorney for Mrs. Johnson, sometime in the first few months of 1984. He was accompanied by John Peach. . . . I answered their questions fully. After I told them all I could remember about my time working for Mr. Johnson, Mr. Osgood told me that I could not be of any help to the other side in the lawsuit and that if I was contacted by any attorneys for the other side to let him know so he could tell them not to bother me.

At the same meeting Mr. Peach made a comment that struck me as very strange and made me uncomfortable. He said something to the effect that "if there is anything you ever need help on, Mrs. Johnson would be glad to give it." I was surprised by the remark because I had just finished telling Mr. Peach and Mr. Osgood about the unpleasant circumstances in which I quit working after Mrs. Johnson rudely insulted me in front of her husband and others. I told them that it was very unlikely that Mrs. Johnson would truly want to help me in any way or that I would expect any help from her. Mr. Peach responded that Mrs. Johnson "feels sorry about the way she treated many people and wants to make up for it."

Several months after meeting with Mr. Osgood and

Mr. Peach, I met with an attorney for Mr. Johnson's children and went over my recollections of working on Mr. Johnson's case. . . . Last month I got a telephone call from Mr. Osgood. . . . He asked me if I had met with any attorneys for Mr. Johnson's children, and when I told him that I had, he insisted on knowing what I had told them and whether I was going to come to New York for the trial. . . . Mr. Osgood then became very intimidating. He told me that I "certainly had nothing pertinent to contribute" and that he did not think I had any business being a witness at the trial. He said that if I came to New York for the trial I would have to undergo his cross-examination and that he really did not want to have to do that to me. He also told me that he would have to take my deposition, and he made it clear that he would make it unpleasant for me if I were to testify. . . . I could not believe that a witness with no interest in a case could be treated like that in the real world. I thought that kind of thing only happened on television or in soap operas.

About ten days after speaking with Mr. Osgood, one of the attorneys for Mr. Johnson's children called me and renewed his request to have me appear as a witness at the trial. I told him how upset I was about the intimidation. . . . I informed him that I had decided I do not want to get involved.

DANIEL C. MALICK AFFIDAVIT: I was the pilot of jets and other airplanes for J. Seward Johnson for approximately fourteen years. During that time I logged thousands of hours of flight time with Mr. Johnson and his third wife, Barbara Johnson. . . . I submit this affidavit to set forth certain communications that I have had with attorneys . . . particularly to bring to the Court's attention statements made to me by Robert Osgood . . . which I feel were designed to dissuade me from being a witness or to influence any testimony I might give.

Early in 1984, I was requested to meet with Mrs. Johnson's attorneys in New York City. I met with Mr. Osgood and other attorneys, answered all their questions and signed an affidavit prepared by them. . . . In early November 1985 I received a call from Mr. Osgood. . . . He wanted to know whether I had been in touch with any attorney for Mr. Johnson's children, and I told him that I had. He then asked if I had been asked to be a witness at the trial in New York, and I told him that I understood I might be asked to do so by the attorneys for Mr. Johnson's children and that I was willing to appear if asked.

Mr. Osgood's conversation seemed aimed at dissuading me from testifying. He told me that I had nothing particularly pertinent to contribute to the case and mentioned a number of things about the contents of Mr. Johnson's will and the contents of prior wills which were clearly intended to persuade me of the merit of the last will in question. He told me that under the will in question, Harbor Branch was to receive $130 million. He also said that roughly one-half of Mr. Johnson's estate was to go to charities selected by Mr. Johnson and that Mrs. Johnson was to get approximately one-third of the estate but would only control it during her lifetime. . . . Mr. Osgood generally made a big effort to engage in friendly conversation with me not relevant to the lawsuit. He even mentioned that he used to be a Methodist minister.

The description of Mr. Johnson's will seemed reasonable to me and I felt that there might be little purpose in testifying at the trial if the changes in the will were as minor as Mr. Osgood said and the provisions were as he described. . . . I had some doubt, however, and therefore I decided to check with Marilyn Link, who was one of Mr. Johnson's closest friends. Marilyn said that . . . under the will Harbor Branch received no gift at all. I met with Mr. Osgood again. . . . I confronted him about my doubts about what he had said and . . . he backed down . . .

I am surprised that Mr. Osgood went to such lengths to try to keep me from testifying at the trial. I am also concerned that he misrepresented facts to me about the case and only acknowledged the true facts when I confronted him with what I had learned elsewhere.

Another incident of money intertwined with a potential witness surfaced. Seven months after Seward Johnson's death, Judith Smith, who had been a well-liked nurse at the Johnson establishment, was in an automobile accident in which her niece was killed and both of Smith's legs were shattered. Basia Johnson paid her a visit, bringing her roses and a wheelchair that had belonged to Seward Johnson and, as Miss Smith was later to testify in a deposition, "her love." In Robert Osgood's presence, John Peach made offers of assistance to Miss Smith in connection with her medical bills. At first, Smith said, she did not think she would need help, but eventually she accepted a $23,000 payment from Mrs. Johnson toward her medical expenses. During her period of employment Judith Smith kept nurse's notes on Mr. Johnson. Now, when she was deposed by Milbank lawyers, her testimony went as follows:

QUESTION: Why did you make the entry of "disorientation" [on May 18, 1983] at 3:45 a.m.?

ANSWER: That's what I assumed it was. I should have used the word "appeared" or "assumed." I found out I was wrong.

QUESTION: Would you read the entry for May 19 at 4:30 a.m.?

ANSWER: "Awake, was disoriented, mentioned being on a train." Yes, I found out what that was. That was his air mattress. I thought that was disorientation. That was the motor of his air mattress. Shut off the air mattress, you have Mr. Johnson without a train going by, that is natural. I mean, I didn't realize what it was at first.

QUESTION: Did you ever make an entry in the notes that reflected Mr. Johnson had been confused at any time?

ANSWER: What I mistook for confusion was [that he was] plain exhausted.

Judith Smith went on to state that Seward Johnson's episodes of confusion and disorientation were "not prolonged" and did not occur "frequently." Reilly pounced on this as an inadvertent admission that Mr. Johnson had at times been both confused and disoriented.

BASIA: She had broken legs, two hips, she was in a very difficult situation at the time. I decided to pay part of her medical expenses for the hospital. If I am not wrong, it was the sum of $23,000. I have spoken with my lawyers about that, they have some reservations, but I do not care about what somebody can think about my actions in the situation when here is a person who had to be helped.

DONALD CHRIST: We didn't think it was a good idea in view of the litigation, but it was a generous and human thing to do and it's grossly unfair that it should be otherwise interpreted.

Edward Reilly documented the connections between Basia Johnson's potential witnesses and the power of her money. This, coupled with the conduct of Sullivan & Cromwell and Robert Osgood in preparing Basia's case, in effect disqualified witnesses who might have been most helpful to her. Only a small portion of John Peach's deposition was admitted into evidence. Nurses Fran Cioffi Adams, Patricia Reid, and Sheril Bennett did not appear. Pilot Dan Malick did not appear. Only Judith Smith came forward to testify for Mrs. Johnson. Bonnie Weisser appeared as the children's witness.

Reilly twice petitioned Surrogate Lambert to depose Osgood on matters relating to "bribing, intimidating, and otherwise improperly influencing material fact witnesses." Twice he was denied. Finally, on June 24, 1985, Reilly filed with Surrogate Lambert a thirty-seven-page brief accompanied by a forty-nine-page affidavit documenting Osgood's activities and again requested that he be deposed. The following day Lambert expressed the widely held view of the legal fraternity: "If you want to attack the other side's clients, that's fine. But I don't think you ought to demean lawyers." Lambert denied Reilly's motion, and the incensed Sullivan & Cromwell lawyers fought back.

SULLIVAN & CROMWELL MEMORANDUM, July 18, 1985: This latest motion is a sign of desperation. The six unhappy Children were all made multimillionaires by their father at an early age. Together they have squandered tens of millions of dollars, with nothing to show for it but broken lives. And they still have plenty left: none of them is in any danger of going on welfare. The value of their trusts when their father died should have been over $660 million.

But they seem to want more, more, MORE. Not content with their father's gifts of great wealth, the Children have laid siege to his estate. The desperation reflected in their current motion comes from a failure to make any headway against a long line of wills, stretching back before the third Mrs. Johnson, in which their father said repeatedly: "No more for my children. I have given them enough."

And so with fourteen weeks to go before trial and the key facts lining up against them, the Children have thrown a little tantrum. They call the lawyers rude names; pound on the table; demand to take lawyers' depositions; and suggest that if they lose this contest their defeat will result from the undue influence of lawyers on witnesses—not because their father saw no need to heap more millions upon them.

This motion does, however, try one novel tack: the primary targets of this cross-motion are now not adversary *parties*, but adversary *counsel*.

DONALD CHRIST: The children's motion is pitched at such a low level that it says much more about them than those whom they slur. It is unfortunate when litigation descends to such an uncivilized state. But the children will use any excuse to avoid trial. Scurrying from the merits, they fabricate delays, dirt, and diversion.

ROBERT J. DELAHUNTY, July 25, 1985: The children's reply memorandum is a cheap shot aimed at one of the attorneys in this case. As the children's case lurches from disaster to disaster, their invective grows more bitter and their accusations grow more irresponsible.

Mighty law firms lined up in an unprecedented, no-holds-barred war. Behind the accused Nina Zagat stood Shearman & Sterling, one of the largest of American law firms: it has 146 corporate lawyers, 74 litigation lawyers, 29 banking lawyers, 28 tax lawyers, and 22 real-estate lawyers. Dewey, Ballantine, Bushby, Palmer & Wood, the representatives of Harbor Branch, also belonged to the exclusive legal fraternity. A partner, William Warren, when asked exactly what his role in the litigation was, answered, "I'm the Alexander Forger of my firm."

Sullivan & Cromwell, who were engaged to defend the widow Johnson and Nina Zagat, is a firm of seventy-five partners and over nine hundred employees. The firm represents the Mellon family, such corporate clients as Exxon, Kodak, General Foods, and the National Football League. They have worked on mergers and tenders for the First Boston Corporation, Goldman Sachs & Company, Kidder, Peabody & Company, and Merrill Lynch, Pierce, Fenner & Smith. Ironically, given that eight courtroom litigators from Sullivan & Cromwell were to present Basia Johnson's case with approximately twenty-eight others involved in back-up work, the *American Lawyer* noted, "This firm has a reputation for lean staffing of client matters. Client teams rarely involve more than three or four lawyers and most cases do not involve more than three lawyers."

Milbank, Tweed, Hadley & McCloy might be regarded as the Princeton to Sullivan's Harvard. No less prestigious, social, or powerful, Milbank, Tweed is known as the Rockefeller family's firm, and as such is one of the chief advocates for keeping the cap firmly on the size of executor fees. Large estates provide Milbank with a "loss leader."

For example, a Milbank partner was an executor of John D. Rockefeller, Jr.'s estate. The executors' commissions in 1960 on this $160 million estate were $800,000.

What had taken place in an unprecedented manner was the growth of acrimony between the opposing lawyers and between their respective firms. There were to be two battles fought at the Johnson will contest, and one was a colossal struggle within the heart of the legal establishment. Noted Harvey Corn, Surrogate Lambert's able law secretary, "In this case the lawyers and law firms involved assumed the personalities and grievances of their clients." And well before the court battle began in February of 1986, the word was out—Edward Reilly had vowed, "I'm going to bury Robert Osgood."

JOYCE, September 15, 1985: Basia is simply literally trying to destroy Seward in every direction of his life, his work, his personal life, everything she can do. It's become a seven-day-a-week vendetta all the time, every single day. For instance, last spring, Basia would have a letter delivered at nine o'clock at night, hand-delivered so it wouldn't arrive during the day, telling us her next move or her next threat. This would happen week after week. At night someone would ring the doorbell and she'd be telling Seward the next thing she was going to try to do to him. Something she was trying to pull or threaten. It's like the Mafia, what she's doing, constant non-stop behind the scenes. When we first started, it seemed a question of honor, it seemed a question of strength to simply not allow something that should not happen, happen. Now it's simply a question of survival.

As the legal battle escalated, on another front there were personal casualties. By the fall of 1985 Junior had been deposed for 356 hours and Basia had attended most of the depositions. Basia herself was deposed for 120 hours. Her migraine headaches, dormant for several years, reasserted themselves. She had practically no social life. Her lawyers advised her not to be photographed. The estate money was tied up and she sold a Giacometti, a Maillol, and several other artworks in order to purchase a $4.8 million Raphael black-chalk sketch, a study for an apostle in *The Transfiguration*. She stated that she had done this because her husband had always wanted a Raphael in their collection.

By October 4, 1985, when I had lunch with Seward Jr. in Lahière's, a cozy French restaurant in Princeton, he'd been involved in a Laocoön tangle of litigation for two and a half years. Wearing a soft flannel shirt and corduroy pants, Seward Jr. looked every inch the country squire. He has an unaffected, self-deprecating manner, a boyish smile, but the legal imbroglio that occupied his life had taken a tremendous toll. Junior was the only one of the Johnson children in financial danger: if Basia won the Harbor Branch suit she had lodged against him, a surcharge of $24 million, as Junior pointed out, was $1 million more than he possessed.

Seward Jr. confided that he had no time for his sculpture any more, "except when they come to do television shows and then I pretend to sculpt for five or ten minutes on camera." On New Year's Eve he'd been at his desk studying his depositions and Joyce had come in at two a.m. and said, "I just wanted to tell you, it's another year."

In fact, with two cases behind him, Seward Jr. was still involved in three cases at once. In New Jersey there was the mismanagement suit as well as an appeal in *Firestone* v. *Merck,* the suit his sister Diana had lodged to replace a

hostile trustee. In New York the discovery proceedings for
the will contest were still going on. It was a legal orgy.

Seward Jr. recalled a recent day when he'd been in the
Middlesex County Superior courtroom, listening to testimony in the Firestone case, while Joyce was in New York
giving her deposition to Robert Osgood. He felt Joyce
needed him in New York. He felt Diana needed him in
New Jersey. Sitting in that New Brunswick courtroom as
the lawyers were saying "Johnson Jr. said this and Johnson Jr. said that," he suddenly had the feeling, "Why don't
they ask *me?*" He was so distressed that tears began cours-
ing down his face. "That's the worst it got."

Junior ordered a bottle of Haut-Brion to accompany
our omelets. (Once, in assuring his father and Basia that he
had not taken sides in their lunchtime dispute over which
one was the more extravagant, Seward Jr. had confessed to
them that he had treated himself to an $800 bottle of
wine.) Four days previously, Judge John E. Keefe had
ruled against Seward Jr. and his sister Diana, stating that
Seward Jr.'s testimony did not have the "ring of truth." At
Sullivan & Cromwell that morning, lawyers were preparing a memorandum incorporating Keefe's decision and
pointing out that Junior's testimony of his "memorable"
conversation with his father in regard to restoring his
trusteeship was in direct conflict with his New York depositions that his father was senile during the same time period.

But, once again, who was the villain? The case was
based on the "probable intent" of J. Seward Johnson, Sr.,
and it had been lodged before his death, but Judge Keefe
noted that Senior's wishes at best seemed "ambiguous." In
his decision Judge Keefe stated, "It would seem to have
been a perfect opportunity for [Seward Sr.] to have pre-
served for the record his belief that there had been an

oversight in the original instrument and his desire to fill that gap by Seward Jr.'s appointment. . . . [Seward Sr.] was a man of wealth and intelligence. . . . If [he] was then harboring such thoughts, it seems reasonable to conclude that a way would have been found either to express them or preserve them."

Junior appeared to have suffered yet another blow because of his father's not taking a firm and direct stand. Seward Sr.'s "ambiguous" attitude would provide lawyers with a forum for costly debate as they tried to determine the intention of a man whose life's pattern clearly demonstrated that his intention was to let people believe whatever they wanted to believe. Legal fees for *Firestone* v. *Merck* are estimated at $6 million.

SEWARD JR., October 4, 1985: Lawyers always like things not to be clear, because it makes a lifetime work for them trying to clear things up. It's devastating to me not to be believed. Emotionally, I needed to be Diana's trustee. I needed to be told that by my father. To be a trustee is a vindication, and that's why it's so important, and to have it denied to me is deeply troubling to me. But as for personal jeopardy, it's the Harbor Branch case I fear most. Basia just zapped me. At first the lawyers told me there was no danger, that it was just a nuisance suit, but now I know I'm in real trouble. I don't know if I can make it, I don't know if I'm going to get through this. If Basia wins, I'm wiped out. It really scares me. I tell everyone my energy must be here in New Jersey, not with the will contest. This is the one that makes me lose sleep.

My only hope is that Basia's losing as much sleep as I am. In six months I've only slept three or four hours a night. I just lie there. I try to do calisthenics to get the

endorphins going. I'm running out of gas, I don't know
how to recharge. At this point it's really beginning to
concern me. I don't know how much longer I can go on.
The trick is to realize that this thing must be lived like a
war. It's learning how to adapt to war and siege conditions.

I'm glad I didn't know what was going to happen. I
don't see how I could have made the decision to do it,
but I don't see how I could have not done it either. I
don't think I could not do it, but I think I'd jump off a
bridge if I ever had to make the decision, knowing what
I know today.

On the first day of the New York will contest, Seward
Johnson, Jr., was asked how he felt. He answered, "Like
an emasculated runner who has not yet begun the race."

Once the lawyers had appeared on the scene, inevitably,
direct communication between the widow Johnson and her
stepchildren ceased, and the necessity to build their opposing cases created an irreparable rift. During her marriage
to Seward Johnson, Basia had enjoyed a cordial relationship with her stepchildren and they hadn't disliked her
until they realized she'd been willed everything. Early on,
Marty Richards wanted to go to Basia to effect a settlement. He felt they were close and he could say to her,
"This will is not fair, it's not fair to take everything. Give
each of these children some of their father's money so they
can have their family dignity. We all love Harbor Branch,
he would have wanted them to have something too. Let's
not argue, let's move on as a family." Richards was advised by Forger against such a direct approach. Then came
the mudslinging, the publicity that opened old wounds and
inflicted new blows. But, despite this, approximately three

weeks before the trial began, Mary Lea and Jennifer still
wanted to drive out to Jasna Polana to try for a settlement
with Basia. Again, Forger warned them not to pursue this
course of action. Undoubtedly, by this time Forger was
correct. Donald Christ continued to advise an out-of-court
settlement, and although Basia Johnson indicated her will-
ingness to consider giving $20 million to Harbor Branch
(with strings attached, including the demand that some
way be found to monitor the actions of Seward Jr.), when
settlement with the children was mentioned she instructed
Christ and Osgood, "Slam the door in their face, and give
them not the dust from a penny."

Part
THREE

"Let's go to woik!"

February 27, 1986: The final battle—the will contest itself—is about to begin. I stand on the Chambers Street steps of the Manhattan Surrogate's Court and watch as Basia Johnson's blue, bulletproof Mercedes pulls up. She alights with Nina Zagat and Arnold Bauman, a partner of Shearman & Sterling. Suddenly a bodyguard appears at her side, two others stand on the steps speaking into walkie-talkies, a fourth brings up the rear, carrying a large hamper inscribed "21." A crowd of reporters rushes forward, glaring lights and television cameras snap on, Basia Johnson's gray-green eyes look glazed. There is a fixed smile on her face. She bows her head and clutches Bauman's arm as she proceeds across the vast, marble-floored rotunda and disappears into the elevator.

Mary Lea and Martin Richards arrive in their maroon stretch limousine. As Mary Lea dashes up the steps, her bodyguard endeavors to throw his coat over an intruding camera. Richards remarks, "There's got to be a better way to handle things—this isn't a felony trial." Somehow Seward Jr. and his wife, Joyce, slip in unnoticed. I intercept them. "Do you think the truth will come out in this courtroom?" I ask. Junior, who has been besieged with this litigation for the past three years, replies, "I doubt it. A court really doesn't deal with truth at all. It deals with two possibilities as far apart as they can be."

In the upstairs hall are five camera crews and about twenty members of the news media. "Which one's a Johnson?" they ask. When I point out Diana Johnson Firestone (net worth, $56 million) and Jennifer Johnson Duke (net worth, $100 million), a cameraman exclaims, "Jesus, they don't look rich."

The Johnsons have image problems. What appearance should you project when half a billion dollars is at stake and you are being judged by a sanitation man, a secretary, a corporate travel agent, a management consultant, a mother of two, and an Exxon financial analyst? I thought about the problem during the two weeks of jury selection preceding the so-called opening day, when almost simultaneously I heard a prospective juror say, "I can't live on twelve dollars a day, I have a granddaughter to take care of—her mother's in the streets," and behind me I heard from the Johnson camp, "I think people who keep their pools at eighty-nine are crazy. If you want to swim, then you keep your pool at eighty."

Seward Jr., aware of the problem, asked his sister Elaine not to wear her Buccellati gold necklaces and to leave her limousine at the back of the courthouse. The first two weeks during jury selection all the Johnson women shivered in thin cloth coats until Surrogate Marie Lambert swept in in a black mink and the fur-coat barrier was shattered. The following morning Basia appeared in a three-quarter-length sable. In the courtroom Basia Johnson's light brown, blond-streaked hair was most often rolled into a severe bun anchored in place with tortoiseshell combs.

As soon as the trial was over, she literally let her hair down to float in a cloud of curls around her face.

On this bright morning there are important things going on in the world, even things tangentially related to this action. This is the week that more poisoned J&J Tylenol capsules have been found on pharmacy shelves, that the *Johnson-Sea-Link II*, a submarine perfected at Harbor Branch, has found a crucial section of the Delta rocket of the ill-fated *Challenger*. But in this courtroom there is an atmosphere hermetically sealed, as if no other world existed.

Every seat is occupied. Reporters jam the right-hand aisle and crowd onto the steps of an interior stairway. Behind Basia sits a bodyguard; I see the outline of a gun strapped to his ankle. The Johnson children, their Hermès-tied husbands and tweed-skirted wives sit in the front row in old-fashioned mahogany school chairs; only one seat separates them from the enemy camp—Nina Zagat, Basia Johnson, Arnold Bauman. Although Shearman & Sterling cannot represent the proponents, Zagat says that Arnold Bauman has been involved behind the scenes since the inception of the litigation and has played a major role in planning the court strategy.

The seventy-two-year-old, lanky, soft-spoken Bauman had achieved an impressive career as an outstanding trial lawyer and former president of the Federal Bar Association. In 1974, after only two years, Bauman had resigned as a federal judge from the Southern District of New York, citing as his reason the inadequate pay of $40,000 a year. Bauman had been present when Basia's and Nina Zagat's depositions were taken. In the courtroom he served as Basia's constant escort and Cerberus to guard her from the news media, who referred to him as Basia's personal adviser. Whenever an arcane legal point was in dispute, it was Bauman to whom litigators and spectators alike turned for a clear explanation.

In the center of the room, at a wide, thirty-foot-long counsel table littered with attaché cases, file boxes, thermoses, and glasses, sit squadrons of lawyers from some of Wall Street's most prestigious firms. The image they project is one of self-assured respectability, of infallible integrity; their hair is crisply cut, their suits are Dunhill, their ties are predominantly the new power color, yellow. Watching them, I am reminded that this contest gradually has been transmuted into a battle among lawyers, about lawyers, for lawyers.

Surrogate Marie Lambert walks slowly down the red carpet that stretches from chambers to the judge's podium. Lambert's black robe is draped over her shoulders like a cape, revealing a bright red dress. She is matronly, her freshly hennaed hair severe and short. The daughter of an Italian barber, Lambert attended Brooklyn College and obtained a scholarship to New York University Law School. She has served as president of the New York State Trial Lawyers Association, the only woman ever to do so. The accents of New York hang heavy on her tongue: "Let's go. Let's go to woik!" was a frequent reprimand. Part Portia, part Tugboat Annie, Marie Lambert was the most colorful of judges, and when, in the tenth week of the trial, she was accused of not having "a judicial temperament," even those observers who thought her effective could not disagree. Early on, Lambert seemed to catch Edward Reilly's moral fervor, and several reporters began referring to her as his "co-pilot." Her frequent outbursts were aimed at Sullivan & Cromwell lawyers: at the sidebar, after lawyer Sherryl Michaelson asked an improper hypothetical question, Lambert boomed out, "If this is amateur day, I'm telling you I don't want it. Do you want me to tell this jury that a first-year law student wouldn't have asked such a question?" When Donald Christ conducted a prolonged, detailed cross-examination, she admonished him, "Go right ahead, Mr. Christ, you don't mind if I do some paperwork, do you?"

Martin Richards referred to the huge amounts of money involved in this case as "telephone-book numbers," and at the outset Lambert instructed that no transactions under $10,000 should be mentioned. By the second week she was heard to remark, "Only $300,000? What's that?" Then, catching herself and slapping her forehead, she exclaimed, "What am I saying, that's almost four years of my salary!"

Immediately it became apparent that Lambert's first priority was to her jurors. "Can everybody hear me without the microphone?" she inquired. "Because the jurors can't see me if I have a microphone in front of me." After brief instructions, Lambert got the day off to a quick start as she deferred to Basia Johnson's chief attorney, Donald Christ, who strolled to the podium. From the outset Christ's affable demeanor seemed better suited to a gentlemen's clubroom than to the bitter contest taking place in this courtroom. In describing the Johnsons' marriage, Christ presented it not in human terms, but as a media image of the American Dream. He made their marriage sound like an episode of *Dynasty,* a column by Suzy: ninety servants, a private island, private airplanes. "They owned homes in Europe, in the Bahamas, in Florida, and in New Jersey. They amassed a collection of beautiful art and beautiful antiques, a fleet of beautiful automobiles." Christ seemed to be asking, "Aren't you wowed by this? Isn't this a life to be envied, the one you wish you had?" Basia Johnson was described as if she were a combination of a high-society Katharine Hepburn in *The Philadelphia Story* and a devoted Florence Nightingale, a wife who "cared for her husband twenty-four hours a day, day after day," a "vital, vibrant, exciting, and interesting person" who gave her husband "a new lease on life. . . . The Johnsons lived a dream."

Reilly was to take this description and use it to deride his opponent, characterizing her lifestyle as profligate, extravagant, excessive. If Basia had been presented as a volatile woman of Polish background who expressed affection through attention to food and emotional reprimands, she might have seemed more sympathetic. Had Donald Christ described her marriage in realistic terms as one in which there were ups and downs but which was ultimately a close relationship, she might not have been so vulnerable to attack.

Christ stated that Seward Johnson's will reflected his intention: "He did what he wanted and he knew what he was doing when he did it," and that as a result of their father's largess the children had all been made multimillionaires during his lifetime. Christ's opening concluded on the lighthearted note: "I think you'll find the real question that the children are asking of their father in this case is, 'What have you done for me lately, Pop?' "

Donald Christ was a lawyer with a client. Edward Reilly was a man with a mission. He rose from his red leather chair and slowly approached the lectern. There is a stiffness to Reilly's gait, as if his joints are not well oiled. His manner has the same careful rigidity, but his pent-up rage at Basia Johnson and her lawyers channeled itself into a powerful, emotional opening statement. Far from being a "dream," the life Basia Johnson created for her husband was a "nightmare." Reilly asserted Basia had "bullied and terrorized" her enfeebled husband. "She did not give him a new lease on life, she taught him a new servitude. Her tirades were terrifying and lasted literally for hours. She often shrieked in anger for so long that she became hoarse and could barely even talk." She "manipulated and controlled" her husband and "exerted a psychological influence over him. She threatened him with abandonment, public humiliation, with the most common fears of all elderly and infirm people regardless of their wealth—isolation, loneliness, and embarrassment in front of others." She called him "ga-ga," "stupid old man," "senile old fool," "stupid American."

When Christ jumped to his feet to object to this characterization of his client, Reilly shot back, "What I have to say is going to be a bitter pill for some people in this courtroom. I don't feel I have to sugarcoat it—it's going to be very graphic, explicit, and the jury's entitled to know what it is."

Basia Johnson listened impassively, a slight smile, a mask of vague amusement, concealing her emotions. Jennifer Johnson began to cry. Her half-sister Elaine reached over and held her hand.

BASIA: What upset me was Mr. Reilly, what he said about me. That was the worst. I never knew what was going on. I didn't understand. Right away they start to throw mud on me.

JENNIFER: We knew all that, but in some way we didn't know. Mr. Reilly's opening was so much more emotional than we had ever expected, it put it all in perspective for us.

Reilly then introduced the theme of what he deemed to
be the flagrant misbehavior of Shearman & Sterling's Nina
Zagat. He asserted that Basia Johnson "had one fixed purpose and she pursued it with single-minded resolve: the
acquisition and control of Seward Johnson's vast wealth.
Over the years she enlisted the essential assistance of her
lawyer, Nina Zagat, to achieve her goal." Zagat was depicted as presenting Johnson with documents to sign that
he had never previously seen and was incapable of understanding. Reilly alleged that Johnson signed his final will
at a time when he was hallucinating and too confused to
recognize his own children. "The contents were dictated
by someone who hopes to become one of the richest
women in the entire world if this instrument is accepted
for probate by this court. That woman, Barbara Johnson,
was assisted in her scheme to dictate the terms of this will
by Nina Zagat, who herself will become an instant multi-
millionaire if this document is admitted to probate. We
shall all listen with interest when Nina Zagat tries to justify this extraordinary arrangement."

During jury selection Reilly had conveyed to Judge
Lambert his moral indignation concerning Zagat's fees.
When Lambert inquired about this issue, Reilly told her,
"The cap was actually removed in May of 1981 as Mr.
Johnson was being wheeled into the operating room and
Nina Zagat had him execute a codicil which had the effect
of increasing executor's commissions from approximately
$1.5 million to $2 million to something like $24 million."
Although Donald Christ was present, he said nothing and
did not challenge this shocking explanation to the judge.
(In fact the codicil had been executed five hours before
Johnson was admitted to the hospital and he was operated
on four days later.) This passivity on Christ's part was
indicative of much that was to follow.

BASIA: I tell you the truth—I don't know about courtrooms or lawyers, so I didn't know what to expect. But I
never expected what happened. I had such a good case,
such a clean case.

LAMBERT: She thought she came in here with a perfect
case. What did she come in here with to start with?
Number one, all of her witnesses had been obtained by
John Peach. Peach had earned a tremendous amount of
money working for her and for Sullivan & Cromwell, so
the witnesses came into the courtroom with a taint.
Number two, one of the main nurses that she brought in
was a nurse who had received what, for the nurse, was a
tremendous amount of money. The most important
thing is that one must recognize the weakness of one's
case, and one's got to tell the client.

REILLY: I thought we were going to win from the moment
I said, "May it please the court." I had no doubt when I
finished the opening statement. As soon as Christ finished his opening, from then on we were in complete
charge and complete control.

Although Basia Johnson and her lawyers had been certain of a quick and easy win, at Milbank a strong case had
been constructed from elements that were not immediately
apparent and from others that did not exist at the start of
the battle. By the time the Johnson will contest reached the
New York Surrogate's Court, there were so many documents in the fourth-floor Records Room that the belea-
guered workers hadn't filed them all; most of the three
hundred thousand pages were stacked three feet deep and
spread out across the entire surface of an eight-foot
counter. Before the trial began, I'd sat there week after
week sipping Diet Pepsi while I studied depositions (sev-

enty witnesses had been deposed), affidavits, motions, briefs, exhibits, claims, and counter-claims. I was drowning in material.

One day I read of an incident where the elderly, infirm Seward Johnson wanted oatmeal at six in the morning. The cook was not yet awake, so Basia told him to make do with oatmeal cookies. Seward Johnson sent one of his security guards out to buy him a Crock-Pot so his nurses could make oatmeal whenever he wanted it. When Basia found out, she was furious and had a temper tantrum. "Wait a minute," I thought, "are they kidding? Is this what those multimillion-dollar lawyers are going to be arguing about —oatmeal versus oatmeal cookies?"

As it turned out, I wasn't completely off the mark. A great deal of the most damaging testimony about Basia involved food: when Basia forced her husband to finish his oatmeal, denied him dessert, put him on the Stillman diet, threw a fit when he was given papaya juice and another over orange juice. One day a nurse testified that Johnson had been given puréed eggplant for breakfast. Lambert covered her mouth with both hands to stifle a laugh while her legal assistant Harvey Corn looked at her questioningly. Then she and Corn entered into an intense whispered discussion at the bench. Lambert later said, "I guess everyone thought we were having an erudite judicial discussion, but I was explaining to Harvey about the color and consistency of eggplant purée." There was so much of this kind of testimony that the thought occurred to me, not entirely in jest, that had the Johnsons never had a meal together, Milbank, Tweed might have been hard put to build a case against Basia Johnson. After the trial, on a press tour of her Princeton estate, Basia, indirectly alluding to this testimony, led reporters to a room and, smiling broadly, announced, "And this is the famous breakfast room."

Reilly's strategy was to not concentrate solely on Johnson's wills but to try the conduct of his wife during their marriage, or, as Basia Johnson announced one afternoon mid-trial, "This is not a will contest. This is a divorce case after someone has died." Finally, what was to make the children's case so strong had less to do with Basia's treatment of her husband than with the ethics of the lawyers who prepared his wills and his widow's case. In these areas Basia Johnson's "clean case" had become sullied. In the courtroom Nina Zagat would be put on trial; in the Surrogate's chambers Robert Osgood too would be subject to Reilly's attack.

". . . a personal attack . . . a smear . . ."

*S*urrogate Lambert ruled that the scandal concerning the children's lives would be inadmissible evidence in her courtroom, but that didn't inhibit the news media. During the week prior to the trial, the Records Room had been crowded with reporters who, daunted by the mass of material, simply headed straight for the Osgood affidavit. Several reporters dropped quarters into the Xerox machine and ran off copies of the letter to Mary Lea from her father that began, "You are turning out to be a troublemaker beyond my imagination."

Mary Lea, finding herself besieged by reporters, spotlights, microphones, said, "I just try to be myself and tell them that I'm not allowed to comment on the case," but the strain showed. At night she'd have dinner in bed and watch TV, where accounts of the purported attempt on her life and accusations about the conduct of her children were repeated over and over.

On Thursday night of the first week of the trial, Marty Richards spoke with me on the phone. "Have you seen TV tonight?" he demanded. "That troublemaker letter about Mary Lea's been on eight times! They don't even know

what it's about, they don't even say that her uncle apologized for it and said he was wrong. I want to sue somebody. I said, 'Mary Lea, let's stop this whole thing right
now. What do we need it for?' But she said, 'That's just
what Basia's hoping we'll do, so we have to go on.' "

Friday, after a long day in court, Marty and Mary Lea
got into their stretch limousine and started up the FDR
Drive. The phone rang; it was Mary Lea's sister Elaine
Wold. "Where are you?" Mary Lea inquired. "Right behind you," Elaine answered. They talked about the week
and how Mary Lea and Marty should accept their sister
Diana's invitation to spend the weekend at the Firestones'
vacation home at Lyford Cay in the Bahamas. Marty and
Mary Lea decided it would be good to get away. They
went home, packed their bags, and boarded the Firestones'
private jet. It rained all weekend. On Sunday they returned
to the plane, which a steward had loaded with lunch and
other supplies. His final touch was to put on board the
Sunday papers. Mary Lea opened the Miami *Herald* and
saw the headline, "FORTUNE SETS OFF A FAMILY FEUD."
The article described how her second husband allegedly
had forced her to have sex with other men while he
watched, and how he had taken out a murder contract on
her.

The emotional events of the week, Reilly's unexpected
opening, the memories of her life and her father all welled
up and she began to sob uncontrollably. Her husband tried
to comfort her, but there was little he could do. In the
limousine heading home from Teterboro airport to New
York City, Richards suddenly felt a sharp pain in his chest.
He was sure he was having a heart attack and he was
rushed to New York University Hospital. As he lay on a
table in the emergency room awaiting treatment, a gray-
haired woman with an intravenous needle in her left arm

kept staring at him. She asked, "Don't I know you? Are
you in the garment business?"

"No," he replied.

Then she said, "Oh, I know where I saw you. You're
married to that rich woman. Your picture was in the paper
today."

When the doctor examined Richards, he said it was not
a heart attack but an anxiety attack. "Are you under any
strain?" he inquired.

LAMBERT: Everybody was trying this case in the press to
   begin with, and that's the way it operated, by trying the
   case in the press.

The Johnson will contest had all the elements of a big
story. It involved wealth, a sumptuous lifestyle, hints of
nefarious deeds. It had the fascination of a fairy tale: was
Basia Johnson Cinderella or was she the Wicked Stepmother in the same story? And it had an image too com-
pelling to resist—the myth of striking it rich. That first
week Basia Johnson smarted under repeated descriptions
of herself as the immigrant Polish maid who hit the jack-
pot. In hallway conferences she emphasized the fact that
she was an "art historian" and complained to reporters,
"Tell me, is it a crime in America to be a maid and work
hard? Is that a crime?" Every evening, television covered
the story of the "disinherited" Johnson children, who were
pictured climbing in and out of their limousines, and "the
billion-dollar widow," who smiled into the cameras and
murmured, "I am sad, so sad." Basia Johnson's adroit
public-relations representative, Jack Raymond, handed out
pictures of Basia and Seward in smiling poses on sailboats,
beaches, a terrace in Capri overlooking the Mediterranean.
The children's representative, James Mitchell, a specialist

in society clients who like to see their names in Suzy's column, sat in a trench coat and dark glasses looking bewildered. At the end of the first week he handed out a Xeroxed release noting the remains of the space shuttle rescued by the Harbor Branch CORD and *Johnson-Sea-Link II*. Reporters went directly to Seward Johnson, Jr., who regularly briefed the press on the children's point of view and recent discoveries. Mitchell was soon replaced by John Scanlon, who had represented CBS in the CBS/Westmoreland libel trial.

By Tuesday, March 4, there was a media blitz as one scandalous article after another appeared. On dismissing the jury, Lambert added to her usual directive that they not discuss the case with anyone, or allow anyone to discuss the case with them: "There's been a great deal of excitement here today with newspapers and with photographers and so forth. I know it is going to be irresistible for you not to look at television, but please close your ears when you look. If you want to see your pictures, turn it on without the sound." Seward Jr. shrugged: "It's like an earthquake. Lambert said all this stuff has no place in this proceeding." But what was banned in the courtroom had become a free-for-all in the press. The *Daily News* that morning carried a vintage Jimmy Breslin article headlined, "LET THE MAID CLEAN UP." In a typical plague-on-both-your-houses Breslin ploy, he'd interviewed several sanitation men (one of their number, Jose Santana, was a juror) and asked them how they felt about the will contest.

JIMMY BRESLIN ARTICLE, *Daily News,* March 4, 1986:
"She was the maid. Then she married him. The wife was 34. He was 76. Do you think $400 million is right?" "All the homeless we see in the street all day, you could take care of them," a guy named Tony said.

I told them that nobody in the courtroom had worked for the money, and that the law companies involved in the case, one lawyer told me, are going to take about $20 million in fees, and in doing this without showing a twinge of conscience, they reveal that their minds are infested with the same ideas as that of their clients, and thus they become as common as the clients, a task which people who work honestly for a living might find extremely difficult. The clients consist of the widow—the former upstairs maid—and then the six Johnson children who are considerably older than children but have done so little to distinguish themselves since childhood that all in the courtroom refer to them as "the children."

Breslin also repeated information from the Osgood affidavit. An angry Marie Lambert marched the lawyers into chambers. "I just read the Jimmy Breslin article and I think it's so prejudicial. I don't know what you want to do about it." Reilly said, "I know my clients are very upset about it, and some of the reporters never would have had the material but for Mr. Osgood's disseminating it to them."

Harvey Corn, on whom Lambert relied, endeavored to bring calm to the situation by suggesting that the reporters could have gotten the material out of the papers that had already been filed. Reilly shot back, "Could have, but didn't!" Corn then interjected, "The interesting story from the press angle has been the interplay of sex and money. In fact, a Channel Seven reporter last night said, 'This story makes *Dallas* look like *Romper Room.*' " Lambert sighed, "I must tell you, I feel sorry for all the parties in this case, every one of them."

* * *

It was later that morning that Reilly struck Osgood a blow
by filing a fifty-page memorandum that alleged, "The objectants are aware of seven material-fact witnesses whose
testimony proponents and their counsel, particularly Robert M. Osgood of Sullivan & Cromwell, have improperly
attempted to suppress or influence. . . . They perpetrated
this scheme by paying extraordinary sums of money to
some witnesses who became beholden to them and by
threatening and intimidating others who did not." In a
detailed summary, complete with affidavits, exhibits of
bills, canceled checks, and letters, Reilly documented his
charges that $161,000 had been paid to John Peach for his
work for Basia Johnson and for his help in recruiting witnesses; that $23,000 in medical expenses had been paid for
nurse Judith Smith; that there had been attempts to silence
or sway nurses Weisser, Adams, Bennett, Reid, and pilot
Malick.

Donald Christ then stepped forward and asked that
Lambert keep Reilly's memorandum from the press, and
Osgood chimed in that this was "a personal attack . . . a
smear that should be kept in chambers."

"Never once has Mr. Osgood denied any of the conduct attributed to him," said Reilly.

"That doesn't bear a response," replied Osgood.

Lambert pointed out how serious this attack was, and
Reilly acknowledged it, saying, "It is indeed a serious attack. It is not an attack solely on counsel, it is an attack
basically on the two proponents [Zagat and Basia Johnson]
and the vast sums of money they have paid to influence the
testimony of witnesses. . . . In their blind desire to win
this proceeding at all costs, proponents and their counsel
have not only corrupted fact witnesses but have also corrupted their own case." Expressing his indignation at the

Osgood affidavit, Reilly said, "I simply point out the contrast in handing out material to the press and making sure that there is wide dissemination of things that were devastating to infants, while at the same time what may affect Mr. Osgood, by God, let's put it under the rug."

Lambert answered that she would take it under advisement whether or not to release Reilly's affidavit, and later that month Sullivan & Cromwell's Marvin Schwartz appeared with S&C partner Robert MacCrate, president-elect of the American Bar Association, to argue that the document be sealed. This was Marvin Schwartz's initial foray, and when Basia Johnson read the transcript of the heated battle that followed, she became impressed with him. Schwartz and Reilly went at it *mano a mano* while MacCrate and Forger stood by, lending their prestigious visages but saying nothing.

REILLY: This is the third time, if not the fourth, that these matters have in some way surfaced on motions before your Honor—never once did anyone from Sullivan & Cromwell see fit to submit an affidavit in opposition, taking issue with anything that we said. Their position, basically, is that there is nothing wrong with it. Well, if there's nothing wrong with it, then of course there is no need to seal the record.

SCHWARTZ: The prejudice of not sealing to our clients, to Mr. Osgood, and to my firm is immense. By my count, may it please your Honor, Mr. Reilly has chosen to use the word "corrupt," directed at Mr. Osgood, seventeen times in fifty pages of his brief. . . . He has elected to use the word "bribe" eight times in reference to Mr. Osgood's conduct. If I had to characterize these fifty pages, it would be as filth.

REILLY: If I can respond very briefly, your Honor: despite Mr. Schwartz's evoking words like "corruption" and "bribery" and so forth—

SCHWARTZ: Those are not my words.

REILLY: Excuse me. May I continue without your interruption, Mr. Schwartz? In all of the underlying factual material . . . there is nothing that is controverted by way of the facts. Now, either I am right or I'm wrong. All of the facts here are pretty well documented. They are supported by, in some instances, the canceled checks of Mr. Schwartz's own firm.

They have taken the position that they see nothing wrong in taking a fact witness and making him part of the Sullivan & Cromwell litigation team. I say I think that's disgraceful, it's unethical, it tends to corrupt a witness; it is an admission of the weakness of your own case and consequently should be admissible.

Now, neither Mr. Schwartz, Mr. Christ, Mr. Osgood, nor anyone else from that firm will come in and say that my underlying facts are in any respect in error. . . . There are other people, including clients represented in this proceeding by Mr. Schwartz's firm—Nina Zagat and Barbara Johnson—who are accused of fraud, of undue influence, of really criminal behavior. . . . It's unfortunate that counsel representing those two have decided that they would engage in certain tactics which I find unacceptable.

It doesn't strike me as appropriate to answer, "Well, it's not going to cause Milbank or Reilly any harm to seal this." This is not a star chamber; it's a court of law. We're dealing here with a very sensitive and significant issue, the behavior of counsel in one of the most important will contests that's ever been litigated in this court, maybe even in the country. We brought to the Court's attention all of what we view as sordid facts, and they haven't controverted a single one of them; they simply say that this doesn't amount to anything bad. . . .

Essentially the position I feel I am in now is one of deep resentment of having been put here. I've never had to make allegations like this against another lawyer.

SCHWARTZ: We're here, may it please the Court, because Mr. Reilly wants to demean Mr. Osgood. He charges him with attempting to corrupt, to bribe, and to intimidate eight witnesses. . . . I have read—I must say, with disgust—the brief of fifty pages. . . . Your Honor, they do not support any such charge. There is no single piece of evidence which Mr. Reilly offers which would show that Mr. Osgood tried to bribe anybody, that he threatened any witness with bodily or economic harm if he came into the jurisdiction, that he did anything other than try to investigate the facts, hire people to help him. Everything he did, so far as these exhibits are concerned, which is all before your Honor, was proper and innocent. . . .

Let's assume Mr. Malick's testimony for the moment is true. So what? What conceivable inference could a jury draw on the merits of the case, which is the overriding consideration? What conceivable inference could a rational juror draw from the fact that Mr. Osgood misstated the terms of the will to an airline pilot, bearing in mind that the airline pilot is a layman and it's easy for a layman to misunderstand what lawyers say? But so what? How does that assist the jury in rendering a fair and just verdict in this case? . . . It's viewed as bribery that Sullivan & Cromwell retained [John Peach] as a litigation assistant. Now, your Honor, I don't know of any trial lawyer anywhere who doesn't long for assistance from people who know the witnesses, know the background, know how records are kept, knew how the decedent lived, and knew of the relationship between the decedent and his widow. Here was a God-given litigation assistant, who knew who the nurses were, knew where to find them, and knew as much as anyone could know abut how Mr. Johnson lived his life. There cannot be anything wrong, may it please the Court, in retaining him as a litigation assistant at the munificent sum of fifty dollars per hour.

Next, Mr. Osgood is accused of intimidating four witnesses so that they would not come into the jurisdiction and give testimony. There are three nurses—Weisser, Reid, and Bennett—and the airline pilot again. But no single piece of evidence, in all this volume that Mr. Reilly has given to you, amounts to a witness saying, "Mr. Osgood offered me money to testify. He told me that if I came into the jurisdiction, I would have my legs broken or my nose broken," nothing in the nature of unequivocal misconduct. In all the years I have practiced in the courts of this State, your Honor—and I've been in hard battles—I have never encountered or heard of an attack by lawyer against lawyer such as those made here. If your Honor permits that in a public courtroom, I respectfully submit that mistrial is inevitable.

REILLY: I was particularly distressed to hear Mr. Schwartz refer to "Just assume that there was a lie said to Mr. Malick," and then his response was, "So what?" Well, I say, "So plenty." I was appalled to hear Mr. Schwartz say, "No one threatened to break anyone's legs. No one threatened to break anyone's nose." . . . I think it would be really a sorry day for the Surrogate's

Court of New York County if the test on intimidation of witnesses was whether you threatened to break their legs or break their nose or perpetrate some other kind of bodily harm.

It's a much more insidious and subtle way in which pressure is exerted. Giving a poor nurse, who is overwhelmed with hospital bills, payment of $23,000 so she becomes eternally, life-everlastingly grateful, beholden, to a litigant, to me seems to justify an inference that that was an improper way to deal with a fact witness in this case. . . . I think it's a reflection of someone's moral myopia if they don't understand the difference between getting this witness, noticing his deposition, sitting down and asking him, "Mr. Peach, when did you first meet Mr. Johnson?" and following everything through, with the opportunity of cross-examination by other people, on the one hand, and, on the other hand, putting him on the Sullivan & Cromwell payroll and paying him $25,000. I don't think Sullivan & Cromwell has ever done it except in this case.

" . . . a crook and a thief."

*R*eilly's battle with Osgood took place in the privacy of chambers. In the courtroom he now turned his litigation skills toward Nina Zagat. The Shearman & Sterling lawyer and Basia Johnson seemed inextricably bound together by the charges against them. Bland, bespectacled, conservatively dressed, the forty-three-year-old Zagat could easily pass for a suburban matron. Often she and Basia sat giggling together and passing notes like schoolgirls. During her tenure as legal counsel to Basia Johnson, Seward Johnson, the Harbor Branch and Atlantic foundations, and a dozen Johnson-family enterprises, Zagat had a hand in preparing twenty-two wills and codicils for Seward Johnson. In May of 1982, on a page of her diary requisitioned during discovery proceedings, Zagat had made but one enigmatic entry: "Rich." And rich she would be if this will were probated. As an associate, Zagat was not required to turn her fees over to the firm, as a partner would be. Her annual salary of $115,000 would be supplemented by executor and trustee fees potentially worth $30 million.

Zagat was on the stand for nine days. It is axiomatic

that facts are unalterable, but how these facts are viewed makes a court battle. Edward Reilly would try to establish that, although she was lawyer to both the Johnsons, Zagat solely fostered Basia's interests and her own. Under his relentless cross-examination, Nina Zagat's methods and transactions came to seem nefarious. From the outset Zagat was a nervous, evasive witness who spoke in a child's soprano that at times sounded as if it had been cranked down to half-speed. From the moment she took the stand, Surrogate Lambert complained that she had trouble hearing Zagat and reprimanded her, "You have your back turned to the judge and you are facing the jury so that your back is turned also to the lawyers and they are not able to hear you." Zagat's testimony was peppered with "I don't recall." (I counted thirty before losing track.)

REILLY: Are you aware of any reasons for changing the name of the payroll account from J. S. Johnson to B. P. Johnson?

ZAGAT: I don't recall.

REILLY: Did you have any conversation with Mr. Johnson concerning the change in the title of this account?

ZAGAT: I don't recall.

REILLY: You have no recollection of why the title of this account was changed?

ZAGAT: I don't recall.

REILLY: This was not an average month, I assume. Is that correct? [The month was January 1983, when $3.35 million was spent.]

ZAGAT: I really don't recall.

REILLY: Do you recall any other [increases in borrowing] for the month of February 1983?

ZAGAT: I don't recall whether there were or weren't.

Nina Zagat had arranged a $24 million line of credit for Seward Johnson, secured by his seven million shares of J&J stock. On May 3, 1983, he signed a document increasing his line of credit to $25 million. Reilly established that on that same day Zagat's power of attorney, which precluded the sale of his J&J stock, had been replaced by a non-restrictive power of attorney. Zagat testified that she had prepared the new power of attorney because the bank had temporarily misplaced the other document.

REILLY: I direct your attention to the second page of this document [the power of attorney] and particularly what appears to be Mr. Johnson's signature. When you first saw it, did it give you any pause?

ZAGAT: No.

REILLY: Did you have any question about that signature when you saw it?

ZAGAT: No.

REILLY: Were you able to read it?

ZAGAT: Yes, I was there when it was signed.

REILLY: When it was delivered to Citibank, did anyone at Citibank raise any question concerning the signature?

ZAGAT: I don't recall.

REILLY: Isn't that something you would recall?

ZAGAT: Not necessarily.

REILLY: Isn't it a fact that someone at Citibank raised a question as to whether Mr. Johnson was competent?

ZAGAT: No. Not that I recall, no.

REILLY: Do you deny that?

ZAGAT: Yes.

REILLY: Could it have been?

ZAGAT: No, I don't remember that.

REILLY: Didn't someone at Citibank raise a question as to whether there was something wrong with Mr. Johnson?

ZAGAT: I believe people at Citibank knew that Mr. Johnson was sick.

LAMBERT: May I have the answer, please, to the question.

ZAGAT: Not that I recall.

REILLY: Have you read an internal memorandum at Citibank in which a question was raised about the signature that appears on this document?

ZAGAT: Not that I recall.

REILLY: Do you know anyone at Citibank named Joyce Hirsch?

ZAGAT: Yes.

REILLY: Does that refresh your recollection?

ZAGAT: I remember Joyce Hirsch calling me and talking to me about Mr. Johnson's health.

REILLY: Did she talk to you about Mr. Johnson's signature?

ZAGAT: I don't recall that specifically. I remember her saying that she knew that Mr. Johnson wasn't well and that she could see that there was some change in his signature and was there anything that Citibank could do to be of help.

Joyce Hirsch, who appeared as a witness, testified that "before I could even ask Nina, she volunteered that he [Johnson] was mentally competent."

Nobody could miss the fact that Nina Zagat irritated the surrogate, or that Lambert shared Reilly's apparent moral outrage. Zagat's "I don't recall"'s, her slow speech, her evasiveness clearly had an adverse effect. At one point in chambers Lambert said wearily, "All day it's been very slow. The words come out of Mrs. Zagat's mouth as if she didn't go past elementary school." And she interrupted the witness with the following: "Mrs. Zagat, you're an attorney?"

ZAGAT: Yes.

LAMBERT: With a very prestigious firm, from what you've told us, Shearman & Sterling. The least we can do is have you answer specific questions without volunteering.

Through Zagat's testimony it emerged that Shearman & Sterling kept work diaries. Lambert requisitioned these diaries, and by cross-checking it was discovered that 1,508 time cards relating to this action were missing. Zagat had not volunteered any of this information. In chambers Lambert discussed Zagat's demeanor with Christ and Reilly.

LAMBERT: She's not very candid with me. I asked yesterday, "Did you have any diary entries of your appointments, of your visits and meetings and telephone conversations with Mr. Johnson?" She said no. I said, "Well, how did you know when you had to go and have a meeting with him?" She said, "I had it on a piece of paper that I threw away." She never said one word about "Yes, I do have my notes. They would show all of my meetings." You know, that's a little bit of a lack of candor, coming from a lawyer.

You know, I like people to be candid with me. You know me well enough, Donald, to know that I do fine with people when they level with me. But when they're not candid with me, we have problems. And Mrs. Zagat has not been entirely candid, because she knew what I wanted, what I was trying to get, to find out, to pin her down as to the exact date of that meeting. To put it bluntly, he [Mr. Reilly] doesn't believe your client. He has a right not to believe her.

As Reilly attacked, Zagat became more and more agitated. He established that in May of 1981 on the day that Seward Johnson went into the Medical Center at Princeton and was diagnosed as having cancer of the prostate, the cap was removed from trustee and executor fees and Basia was left virtually the entire estate. When Reilly asked Zagat why she had not served as an attesting witness to Seward Johnson's final two wills, Zagat snapped, "Because there are people like you who will turn anything around!" At that, Lambert banged down her coffee mug, excused the jury, and marched the lawyers into chambers. During the recess Zagat and Basia stood in the corridor giggling, obviously elated by Zagat's reply. But in chambers Lambert was giving the lawyers a piece of her mind. "I don't think that is the way she talks to a lawyer, and if anybody talked to you like that, I would land on them like a ton of bricks, and I am landing on her, outside the presence of the jury, like a ton of bricks," she told Christ. "You do have a situation here where suddenly commissions went from a million and a half including attorney's fees and accounting fees to somewhere like twenty-four million, according to the figures I've heard." Reilly, adding fuel to the fire, said that Zagat was getting "an obscene, disgusting form of compensation. She is getting more out of this will as a fiduciary than most people ever get as beneficiaries. I am not so thin-skinned that I can't take insults, but from someone like her I find it very bothersome. She should have thought about what she did over the years with Mr. Johnson and Mrs. Johnson. She should have realized that chickens come home to roost and now they're here." Donald Christ ventured that the procedure was not unusual: "At Shearman & Sterling they're entitled to do exactly what they did, and I think your firm would have done the same thing."

"You speak for your own firm, Mr. Christ, don't speak for mine. We do things a lot differently from your firm, a lot differently in every department."

Marie Lambert jumped in. "I would suggest that you talk to your client, she really owes Mr. Reilly an apology. Let me tell you something, if I had been the attorney, I would have said, 'At least I'm not a crook and a thief.' That's what my answer would have been. He thinks she is a crook and a thief. Am I right? That is what you think about it?" Answered Reilly, "I become more convinced of it every day." Although a moment later Lambert covered herself by saying, "So it is clear for the record, the statement I made is what I conceive Mr. Reilly's impression of this witness is; that is not my opinion," what she'd said would have severe repercussions.

Day after day Reilly pounded at Zagat. When Seward

Johnson signed his final will, Basia Johnson wrote him a
letter stating that, although he had given her discretion to
choose who would receive the $72 million residuary inter-
est in her trust, she would give it to Harbor Branch. After
Johnson's death, no one saw that letter. It turned up over a
year later, thrust randomly amidst 100,000 pages of discovery material submitted to Milbank, Tweed. Zagat insisted that the letter had no legal significance and was "expressing an enormous amount of love" from Basia to her
dying husband.

REILLY: You are saying that this is an expression of an
enormous amount of love?

ZAGAT: That is correct.

REILLY: Is that what I heard you just say?

ZAGAT: That is correct.

REILLY: When she refers in fairly technical language to
provisions of the will and then says, "I hereby agree not
to exercise a limited testamentary power of appointment," you consider that an expression of love?

ZAGAT: It certainly was, I was there.

REILLY: Signed by her and acknowledged by him?

ZAGAT: That's right.

REILLY: And witnessed by two lawyers in your firm and
you are calling this a love note?

ZAGAT: I didn't say it was a love note.

It was established that during the last four months of
Johnson's life he signed four new wills and codicils, two

after a priest had been summoned to administer the Last Rites and one after Shearman & Sterling's Jack Gunther had started to prepare probate papers. During this same period, through her power of attorney, Zagat transferred $5.26 million in cash to Basia's account, and established a $9.5 million trust for Basia, of which Zagat was sole trustee. Reilly presented bill after bill for art purchases during these four months totaling $3.75 million.

REILLY: What is covered in this invoice?

ZAGAT: A painting by Zurbarán.

REILLY: Just one painting?

ZAGAT: Yes.

REILLY: For $550,000?

ZAGAT: A painting called *San Sebastian*.

REILLY: In due course did you pay this statement?

ZAGAT: I don't recall.

REILLY: You have no reason to doubt that you did, do you?

ZAGAT: I don't recall.

In the last month of Seward Johnson's life his New Jersey motor vehicles were transferred to Basia's name.

REILLY: Did you ever exercise the power under this power of attorney to transfer vehicles to Mrs. Johnson's name?

ZAGAT: I believe so.

REILLY: Do you have some doubt about that?

ZAGAT: No, I didn't do it myself, but I have a recollection of there being some documents in connection with this.

REILLY: There's someone else who was authorized as an attorney under this document?

ZAGAT: No, no. I signed some documents, but I never saw the—

REILLY: Then you did do it yourself?

ZAGAT: Vehicle.

REILLY: Then you did do it yourself?

ZAGAT: Yes, I didn't do the . . . All I did was sign some papers in connection with whatever vehicles there were.

REILLY: I wasn't suggesting that you did the typing. When did you transfer title of those motor vehicles to Mrs. Johnson?

ZAGAT: I don't recall.

REILLY: Approximately when?

ZAGAT: After February 9, 1983.

REILLY: How long after?

ZAGAT: I don't recall.

REILLY: How many?

ZAGAT: I don't recall.

REILLY: Was any of them a Rolls-Royce?

ZAGAT: I don't know.

REILLY: A Rolls-Royce limousine?

ZAGAT: I don't recall.

During this portion of the cross-examination, Donald Christ leaned forward and the pencil held in his hands snapped in half. He later acknowledged that he did not know of this transfer.

REILLY: I don't mean to be telling anybody how to litigate, but you have to cross-examine your own client first before you start cross-examining the other side. I don't think they did.

The manner in which Shearman & Sterling's legal fees had been paid was attacked. The bills were sent to Zagat at her Shearman & Sterling office; Zagat, using her power of attorney, wrote checks on Mr. Johnson's account to cover the bills; the checks were then deposited to Shearman & Sterling's account. On May 16, at a time when even the proponents' medical witnesses testified that Seward Johnson was no longer competent, Zagat billed $124,922.26 for legal services and, using her power of attorney, wrote the check to satisfy the bill on the same day.

On her final day on the stand, Zagat's testimony reached its nadir as she refused to answer yes or no to Reilly's question, "Following his [Mr. Johnson's] approval . . . you thereafter drew a check payable to your own firm in the amount of the bill?" After several minutes, Zagat explained her refusal by saying, " 'Your own firm' can mean a lot of different things and if 'your own firm' means that I own the firm, no, I don't." Reilly's face flushed as he replied, "Did you really think that what I was suggesting in my question was that *Nina Zagat* owned Shearman & Sterling?"

Reilly brought out that on May 17, just six days before Seward Johnson's death, Zagat had paid a Sotheby's bill for $2,203,185 with transfers made from Johnson's line of credit. At the time of Johnson's death, the $25 million line of credit Zagat had arranged for him was exhausted, and his checking account was $180,000 overdrawn. He died at four a.m. In the afternoon Basia loaned her deceased husband's account the money to make up the deficit.

At the end of nine days Reilly had called into question the character, motives, and *modus operandi* of Basia's most important direct witness. Said a close observer of the proceedings, "I think Shearman & Sterling should have shouldered some of the blame for what happened here. Clearly, they were expecting a will contest; wouldn't you think that in view of that they would have sent top people to witness the will, insisted that a doctor administer a mental-status test? Of course, if Seward Johnson was senile, then that showed that Shearman & Sterling wasn't keeping close tabs on the situation." In his deposition Shearman & Sterling's Thomas Ford repeatedly testified that particularly in the final years of Seward Johnson's life, information relating to Johnson's wills and estate planning was conveyed to him solely by Zagat. In one deposition exchange Ford was asked with whom, other than with Shearman & Sterling and Sullivan & Cromwell lawyers and his family, he had discussed the question of Mr. Johnson's capability of making a will, and he answered, "I don't recall any specific people, but this is the type of question that comes up at the cocktail type of conversations." When asked on what facts he based his opinion of Johnson's capability, he replied, "What Mrs. Zagat had told me." Perhaps Zagat, as she testified, had been following the suggestions of her superiors at Shearman & Sterling in shoring up for a will contest. In any case, one feels that Thomas Ford, who was in charge of her department, should have come forward to support her and not let her twist in the wind.

REILLY: The best award they could give Tom Ford is Cow-
ard-of-the-Year.

After less than ten minutes of cross-examination, the
frail, brown-suited Jack Gunther, a nineteen-year associate
of Shearman & Sterling who had witnessed Johnson's
April 14 will, was visibly quaking. A spectator observed,
"He's about to crack and cry out, 'I did it. I murdered
Seward Johnson!' " In rapid order, Reilly had Gunther affirm that he had accompanied Zagat to Florida with this
last will and testament, complete with ribbons and seal in
place, and that Seward Johnson had signed the forty-eight-
page will, never having previously seen or discussed it.

Gunther admitted that he had begun to prepare probate papers for the estate of Seward Johnson ten days before Johnson signed his final will and forty-nine days before he died, but said that this procedure "is not unusual."
In chambers during a recess, Lambert commented, "Well,
I think that the preparation of the probate proceeding before he's dead raises certain questions in the minds of any
juror, certainly in my mind, as to why would anybody be
preparing a probate proceeding for somebody at the very
moment he's planning a new will."

The second attesting witness, James Hoch, another
Shearman & Sterling associate, testified that he could not
remember any specific topics discussed with Mr. Johnson
on the day of the will-signing except the weather, and no
specific remarks except "Hello," "Goodbye," and "Thank
you."

During the first weeks of the trial it became increasingly clear that an antagonism was developing between
Marie Lambert and the Sullivan & Cromwell attorneys.
Over the weekend of March 15, with time to reflect, she'd
become upset at the manner in which her authority was

being openly challenged. On Monday, Lambert called the attorneys into chambers and, keeping her remarks general, admonished them for courtroom theatrics, for asking improper leading questions, and for arguing with her in front of the jury.

LAMBERT: I've had a very bad weekend and I've been very upset about this all weekend. I'm not going to allow an impression to be created, either here or in the Appellate Division, that I don't know the law. If any of what happened here had been happening in Federal Court, there would have been people sitting in jail for contempt of court, for arguing with the judge. If we are trying this case for the press, then go try it for the press, if that's what you want to do. But I'm not going to try it for the press; I'm going to try it for the Appellate Division. I'm not putting any gag rules on anybody, but it's obvious to me what's happening in there.

As the third week in March began, Dr. Jonathan Wideroff testified that until May 12, 1983, every time he had seen Seward Johnson, he was of sound mind and memory. Wideroff said that Basia Johnson was an attentive and efficient nurse to her husband and that he'd heard Seward tell her, "I love you." Now Reilly turned his ire on this medical witness. He established that Wideroff and his medical partner had been paid $30,000 in cash and he asked if Wideroff had categorized his frequent stays at Fort Pierce as "baby-sitting a dead man." Wideroff demurred, but said he had used the phrase "baby-sitting." Reilly's question, however, indelibly embedded itself upon the spectators.

* * *

Dr. Fred J. Schilling resembled one of the tribe of portly clubroom gentlemen who people *New Yorker* cartoons. He sat placidly, leaning back in the witness chair, his right leg casually bent at the knee and resting on his left thigh. Three inches of pale skin showed above his sock line. It was Schilling who had signed the affidavit that Seward Johnson was of sound mind and memory on the day he'd signed his last will. Asked if he'd applied a mental-status test, Schilling answered that he'd asked Johnson what he had eaten for breakfast.

Often the doctor tended to pontificate, and his answers drifted into lectures in which he cast himself in the role of expert and ignored Lambert's repeated instructions to be specific. The question of whether to apply "heroic measures" to save Seward Johnson's life elicited the following dialogue.

REILLY: If you had a forty-year-old patient who happened to have cancer, would you let that patient give you any views of his or hers as to heroic measures being used to preserve his or her life?

DR. SCHILLING: Well, we are talking about heroic measures, sir. We are talking now. We are down to the wire.

REILLY: Your Honor, I ask that the witness be directed not to depart any further than he has.

OSGOOD: I would ask that the witness be given an opportunity to respond in the best way he can to the question that has been put to him. He had started an answer and again Mr. Reilly cut him off.

LAMBERT: I think Mr. Reilly is trying to determine whether the patient ever has anything to say, insofar as this doctor is concerned, about whether his life should be prolonged or not, notwithstanding whether we are down to the wire or we are two months away.

REILLY: Correct.

LAMBERT: That is the question.

SCHILLING: And that question cannot be answered that way.

REILLY: Cannot?

SCHILLING: Cannot.

REILLY: Why not?

SCHILLING: Why not?

REILLY: Do you understand the question?

SCHILLING: Yes, I sure do.

REILLY: Then please try to answer it.

SCHILLING: I profess to be a humanitarian.

REILLY: I am sure you are.

SCHILLING: I profess to have feelings for a patient. Never in forty-four years have I seen the individual who is ready to die. We are now talking about whether or not, in a terminal situation, there's no hope, whether we are going to do heroic measures on that patient, knowing full well that we are taking a whip to a tired animal, a horse, a human, and whipping him on.

REILLY: Is that how you characterized Mr. Johnson in April of 1983?

OSGOOD: Objection, your Honor.

SCHILLING: No, no.

REILLY: A tired animal?

LAMBERT: Overruled.

SCHILLING: You are asking a hypothetical question.

REILLY: I am not asking you a hypothetical question.

SCHILLING: You were asking me a hypothetical question.

OSGOOD: Your Honor, Mr. Reilly is arguing with the witness again.

LAMBERT: No, the witness is arguing with Mr. Reilly.

On another occasion, expressing her annoyance at the plodding pace of Schilling's testimony, Marie Lambert took over the examination, while Osgood stood with crossed arms, staring up at her. When Schilling began a long-winded answer and Reilly cut him off, Osgood said, "I ask that this witness have an opportunity to respond in his own words and in his own manner." "That's not what cross-examination is all about," snapped Lambert. "Yes, but that's what a fair trial is all about," Osgood shot back. Lambert did not censure him, but instead launched into a lecture on the proper process of cross-examination.

It was now clear that Sullivan & Cromwell was not going to have the easy time it had predicted. It had set up a "war office" on the sixth floor of the courthouse, and frequently Basia was observed climbing the stairs, accompanied by lawyers, bodyguards, public-relations men, and advisers. One morning the Johnson children's cousin Nicholas Rutgers presented Keith and Elaine Wold with a bright blue tee shirt; the message emblazoned in white read: "MY

LAWYER CAN BEAT UP YOUR LAWYER." Recovering from
the first ten days of the trial, during which every skeleton
had been dragged out of the family closet, the children
now seemed more relaxed; clearly, things were going their
way. On March 7, Mercer County Superior Court Judge
Paul G. Levy dismissed the suit that Basia had brought
against Junior in New Jersey to surcharge him $24 million
for mismanagement of Harbor Branch funds. Levy's decision revolved around the issue of the letter to her husband
signed "Love, Basia," written April 14, 1983, that had
promised the restoration of the Harbor Branch legacy.

JUDGE PAUL G. LEVY'S DECISION: Because of [Basia
    Johnson's] pique at Seward [Jr.] and Harbor Branch,
    and probably for her own benefit as well, [Basia] did not
    disclose this agreement when she and her attorney of-
    fered the will for probate. [Basia's] testimony to the ef-
    fect that the letter was a private matter between herself
    and her husband is simply unacceptable. . . . She
    breached her fiduciary duties in order to promote her
    interests in the New York litigation. Therefore, to what-
    ever ends her claims are made for her benefit, they are
    dismissed as being brought in bad faith with unclean
    hands.

The Johnson children reported that, shortly after the
Levy decision, Alexander Forger had been tendered an un-
official settlement offer by Donald Christ: $20 million to
Harbor Branch, $10 million to each child before taxes, and
legal fees. "That's exactly what you told me you wanted,"
I said to Seward Jr. "Yes, but that was before the New
Jersey case was decided. I haven't slept in a year because of
that case. She could have put my family on the streets."
Joyce Johnson added, "We'd like to see Basia suffer a little

the way we have because of that case. She has such contempt for the Johnsons."

By this time the Johnson children blamed everything that had happened solely on Basia. In the corridor Keith Wold, seeing us talking, cautioned, "Loose Lips Sink Ships," but soon he too joined in.

KEITH: It's not the money—you still can only put your pants on one leg at a time, no matter what you've got. It's a matter of what's right and fair.

ELAINE: Until we compared notes and heard Mr. Reilly's opening statement, we never realized all the things Basia had done.

JENNIFER: It makes me so sad to think what Dad's life was really like.

MARTY: I don't know how I feel, I'm ambivalent. Basia was the one who came to my father's funeral, we were close, but her tactics since this case began—I don't think we'll ever be able to forgive that.

How far this struggle had come from its original intention. The lawyers had opened Pandora's box and demons were flying out. Basia, explaining to a reporter about her relationship with her stepchildren, declared, "No. No. Before, it was beautiful!"

LAMBERT: The problem that you have with this kind of a situation is, as you get into it, you discover more and more things.

On March 20 Alexander Forger ushered the Johnson children and their spouses into Lambert's chambers. Obviously, the surrogate was pushing for a settlement and she told them that she was pretty sure Basia had no taste for continuing the battle. Gretchen, Jimmy's wife, asked how much money they would get. It was figured that if Basia gave each child $11 million, each would net a little over $4 million after taxes. Richards says, "I thought then, 'Only four million?' Look, I rode the D train a lot of years, so I know what money's worth, but in this context that wasn't much." Diana said, "I feel angry to know that Dad was treated like that." She said she didn't want to settle and Jennifer felt the same way.

Lambert said that if they went forward there'd be more attacks in the press, and Richards replied, "We're used to living with that." Lambert said, "You must understand that if you don't settle, your fate will be in the hands of people like a sanitation worker who makes $235 a week, of people who are trying to live on the $12 a day we pay them."

It was then that Joyce Johnson interrupted. "This is a matter of honor. This has ruined our lives. For twenty years we lived a respected life, but these last three years, well, they've been a nightmare." Joyce began to cry.

Surrogate Lambert cautioned, "You'll have to prove fraud."

"We have," interjected Alexander Forger.

"You'll have to prove duress and coercion."

"We're prepared to," said Forger.

When they walked out of chambers, the Richardses told their bodyguard and friend Tony Maffatone what had happened. They were beginning to have doubts—maybe they should settle and move on. But Tony said, "Listen, when you bring a man to his knees, you don't let him up," so they decided to let it ride for a week.

* * *

Just as the children had done, Basia Johnson visited Surrogate Lambert in chambers and the judge rattled her sword by presenting the other side of the argument. She told the widow's lawyers that instead of battling back through twenty-two wills, they might never get beyond this will. If the jury were to decide that there was fraud or undue influence in the bequest to Mrs. Johnson, or through Zagat getting herself appointed executrix, Lambert said she could just knock out all of those provisions and it might be deemed that Johnson died intestate. In that case, only the ante-nuptial agreement giving Basia $10 million would apply.

LAMBERT: That woman walked in here and told me she was being persecuted. She said to me that if she weren't forced to sit here, she could be out doing good for people. She told me in the Solidarity movement "I am the most important to the people of Poland next to the Pope!" Then she corrected herself and said, "No, the Pope is number two." Can you imagine that?

BASIA: I went in there and I looked in her eyes and we understood each other. She is strong, there would have been no settlement without her, but she is typical American and what happened was typical American. I was persecuted right here, not in Poland but in New York. I don't know why she did what she did. I don't know why she acted that way toward me.

"That courtroom was a jungle."

Whatever hopes existed for an imminent settlement evaporated on March 27 with the opening of the children's case and the first surprise witness. The press had been alerted that the children's case would start with a strong witness. They waited expectantly as the slim young woman with the face of a Botticelli madonna mounted the stand.

Izabella Poterewicz had descended on the children like a gift—the answer to Reilly's prayers to St. Jude. She was on no discovery list and her name was missing from the list of servants turned over to Milbank, Tweed. But Izabella had been watching television and had seen Basia depicted as a glamorous Cinderella and the children as wastrels, and she had felt a need to express herself. Izabella had worked as a cleaning woman for Basia Johnson from August of 1982 to March of 1983. She was almost six months pregnant that March when Basia called her lazy and insisted she get down on her hands and knees to scrub a bathtub. The following day Izabella had a miscarriage. She had not been able to conceive since. Izabella said she felt no bitterness toward Basia Johnson, but she did want to

see the truth come out. She went to her subway station and
asked how to get to the courthouse, and when she reached
the Chambers Street exit, Izabella asked a policeman
where the Johnson will contest was taking place. He
pointed to the line of limousines outside the Surrogate's
Court. Izabella went to the fifth floor and, as soon as she
got off the elevator, saw Jennifer Johnson Duke standing
by the phone booth. Izabella approached her, saying she
would like to testify at the trial; a startled Jennifer wrote
Edward Reilly's name and phone number on a piece of
paper and gave it to Izabella, who that afternoon left a
message at Milbank, Tweed. On the morning of March 27
Izabella was due to take the stand at 9:30. Edward Reilly
paced in front of the elevators. The previous day Izabella
and her husband, Mariusz, had told Reilly that they were
afraid of what might happen after Izabella testified, but
that she was determined to do so. At 9:30 Reilly watched
the elevator doors open and shut one more time, dis-
gorging people but not the person he was waiting for. Suddenly he thought, "She's not coming," but then the doors
opened again and there were Izabella and Mariusz—they
had been caught in a Gay Rights protest that had snarled
traffic for blocks.

On the stand Izabella Poterewicz gave her name, but
when she was asked her address, she indicated that she was
afraid to give it and instead wrote it on a piece of paper.
Her English was flawed, but her testimony was devastating. Mrs. Johnson, according to Izabella, yelled at her husband constantly and slammed doors so hard that the plas-
ter fell off the walls.

IZABELLA: Many times I heard her yelling on Mr. John-
    son. . . . Maybe I should tell this way. She was yelling
    almost every day at him and calling him names like

"Stupid Englishman," "Idiot," and I even heard, "You son of a bitch." I remember one day Mr. Johnson was feeling not good. He was in bed that day, and he made some mess in the bed, if I can say it that way, and Mrs. Johnson was yelling on him because of that.

Usually we didn't know why she was yelling. . . . She was always walking and yelling and using her hands and slamming the door. He wasn't saying anything. He was very quiet, he was upset and even two, maybe three times, I saw tears in his eyes, but he never said anything.

REILLY: Who else did she yell at?

IZABELLA: Everybody.

This testimony was only a prelude to the bombshell that was to follow. She described an incident that took place when she was in Seward Jonhson's marble bathroom at Jasna Polana and Basia came in and fired her.

IZABELLA: She stopped me and she start to yell at me. She said I am not good worker, I am lazy, and she said it is not her problem if I plan family, because I was pregnant at the time, and this is not a shelter, she will not help stupid people.

REILLY: Where did this take place?

IZABELLA: In that big bathroom.

REILLY: Did you make any tape recording of Mrs. Johnson's voice at that time?

OSGOOD: Objection, your Honor.

IZABELLA: Yes.

LAMBERT: I will allow the question at this point.

At 12:30 Lambert excused the jury for lunch and called the lawyers to the bench.

LAMBERT: I have specifically asked about guns. I was specifically told that no one who were bodyguards had guns. I find out yesterday through my own security here in the building that there are people who have guns in the outside rooms and that there was somebody in the courtroom who had a gun. I, therefore, was irate about it, but I was irate outside the presence of the jury. If we have people out there with guns and a gunfight ensues—that can happen—I do not want to risk the lives of my personnel and I don't want to risk anybody's life. Now I want to tell you something else: when I have to worry about why a witness refuses to give her address, why a witness should be in fear of giving her address, I have to worry about guns.

OSGOOD: That's phony because these addresses are known.

LAMBERT: You know the witness's address?

OSGOOD: Mr. Reilly knows very well that we have employment files of this witness. We know where her mother lives. We know where she and her husband live, yes, and that was just a ploy. That was a publicity ploy.

REILLY: That is not true at all, your Honor. That request was made by the witness herself, not at my request.

LAMBERT: I know.

Osgood then requested a suppression hearing on the tape, and in chambers Reilly set forth his rationale for admitting it.

REILLY: We think the significance of this tape . . . is not simply in the content of the words used. We don't believe that reading the transcript, for example, can begin to approach the manner in which Mrs. Johnson terrorized Mr. Johnson through her screaming.

The tape, I think, adequately and appropriately conveys the manner in which she terrorized, not just Mr. Johnson, but the witness and everybody else at Jasna Polana and elsewhere. That's the reason we feel it is entirely probative.

We are dealing with a very insidious type of undue influence. How this poor eighty-seven-year-old man, whose body was riddled with cancer, what he had to put up with . . . These outbursts occurred on a daily basis. On many occasions it was Mr. Johnson. On many occasions it was other members of the household staff.

OSGOOD: As I hear Mr. Reilly, the burden of his proffer is this logic: because Mrs. Johnson yelled at A, she therefore yelled at B.

Lambert ruled that the tape could be played solely for the tone of voice Mrs. Johnson used, but not for the content of what she said. Osgood asked for an adjournment to research the legality of the tape. It was refused and the tape was played in chambers, a howling tirade in Polish. Osgood insisted that the marble walls of the immense bathroom magnified the sound, and Alexander Forger responded, being "partially facetious," that perhaps "a site-visit to the large bathroom" might be in order.

In the courtroom Robert Osgood continued to object to the playing of the tape on various grounds: it was made surreptitiously, it had nothing whatsoever to do with Mr. Johnson, the sound level was not accurate. Over and over again he objected until he became red in the face and the veins stood out on his neck. Over and over again Lambert called out, "Overruled." There was a heightened sense of excitement in the courtroom, and then the tape was played on a two-foot-long, silver tape recorder. The terrifying, hysterical sounds lasted six minutes. As the tape played, Basia Johnson remained impassive, the by now familiar smile flickering across her face.

BASIA: That courtroom was a jungle. In that courtroom they fought like in a jungle. I have right on my side. The reason I could sit there day after day and have my dignity is I'm a very religious person. I have reconciled how evil these people are and I only sit there and I know who's right and who's wrong. I have no advisers, I just use my brains. The answer is in your brain, you have to really use your brain. And you have the choice, that's what Jesus Christ meant, you have the choice, you can choose bad or you can choose good. Other people choose bad, they choose it.

LAMBERT: I would love to know who decided how to open up to that jury that she had a Cinderella marriage. Who doesn't scream? I get upset and you can hear me for blocks. I'm much better than I ever was before I got on the bench. Since I'm on the bench, I don't scream, occasionally I do. Before I was on the bench, I would walk into my office, if anything went wrong you should hear me. Everybody used to run for cover. I was not an easy person to try a case with. Forget it. I had a husband that was an angel. Anybody who put up with me for all those years was an angel.

When the howling sound of the tape ceased, there was an absolute stillness in the courtroom. Surrogate Lambert suggested that she find a room in the courthouse roughly the size of the Jasna Polana bathroom and play the tape again for the jury on the pocket-sized Sony on which it had been made. Osgood, desperate to forestall this and perhaps recalling his opponent Alexander Forger's remark, now made an astonishing suggestion: "We would like to take the jury to Jasna Polana so it [the tape] can be heard where the witness says the conversation took place." "No objection!" Reilly called out, and Lambert chimed in, "We will arrange for buses. Somebody arrange for buses Tuesday morning for the jury to be picked up." She turned to the jurors and inquired, "Where would you like to be picked up, at home or here?" The jurors indicated that the courthouse would be the only practical place. "Okay," said Lambert, "on Tuesday morning we will be here at ten and we will all go to Jasna Polana."

In the corridor, reporters surrounded Therese Romer, the Polish translator hired by Milbank, Tweed, who said that Basia had called Izabella "a dumb broad, a monkey, and a word that means a prostitute." From her corner of the corridor Basia Johnson defended herself, saying she had never used any word meaning "prostitute" or "dumb broad." She said she had used a "mild swear word, an expression that was a favorite of my father's, it means something like 'go to hell.' " When I asked her who could have prompted Izabella to make such a tape, she answered, "KGB." Basia told me that she thought the translator was also KGB and said, "They have sent these people to me before, this is the way they operate."

The following day was Good Friday and there was no court, but even though it was a holiday, more lawyers appeared at Lambert's chambers. Susan E. Weiner, of Patter-

son, Belknap, Webb & Tyler, representing WPIX, petitioned Lambert for a copy of the tape and added that the
"counsel for the children have no objection to providing
copies of the tape to WPIX." On Monday NBC sent their
attorneys Devereux Chatillon and Ellen Rosen, of Cahill
Gordon & Reindel, to petition for the tape and for their
news reporter to accompany the jury on the Jasna Polana
tour. Osgood and Christ argued against the release of the
tape and press participation. Izabella had made another
tape in Florida, and Sullivan & Cromwell lawyers raised
the specter of pressing felony charges against her under a
Florida statute. The second tape was withdrawn.

Every day that court was in session Basia Johnson would
meet at lunch with the Sullivan & Cromwell lawyers, co-
defendant Nina Zagat, Arnold Bauman, and various other
people to discuss their progress. These lunches came to be
regarded with dread. After the first week Basia had become increasingly critical of the manner in which her case
was being handled. Basia was in agreement with many
courtroom spectators who felt that Sullivan & Cromwell
was faltering. She saw her character being assaulted in a
way that left her no immediate means to fight back. Everything allegedly wrong with her was placed in full view of
the court, while the scandal concerning the Johnson children was inadmissible. It was a common perception in the
courtroom and in the press that the Johnson children
wanted nothing for themselves and had initiated the action
solely for Harbor Branch. Nina Zagat, Basia's co-defen-
dant, had made a poor showing, Reilly's accusations
against Robert Osgood were further damaging her case,
and her legal counsel appeared to be enraging Judge Lambert, who missed no opportunity to point out what she

deemed to be their incompetent behavior. Everything that could go wrong had.

After the Izabella tape was played, all hell broke loose at a Monday, March 31, lunch at the Broad Street Club. Osgood suggested that settlement negotiations should proceed apace since it was conceivable that their side might lose the case. Christ agreed that a settlement might be in order. Mrs. Johnson expressed her rage at her lawyers, calling Donald Christ a "soft-boiled egg" and, when Osgood momentarily looked away from her, admonishing him, "Stupid, stupid American, don't look away from me. Look me in the eye and write down what I'm saying."

Basia was truly convinced that Izabella and the translator were KGB agents, and that Osgood was unaware of how this organization operated. According to a lawyer who attended this strategy lunch, Basia announced that she wanted someone tougher to cross-examine Izabella, and she accused Osgood of supporting the children, of helping the KGB. Says Basia, "This is absurd nonsense. I told him I wanted an addition to the team. I wanted Mr. Schwartz. I don't know why Osgood quitted." Said an observer, "Let's just say that what her opponent Edward Reilly had been trying to do for three years—get rid of Robert Osgood—Basia Johnson was able to accomplish in one lunch."

Various lawyers were to point to what they considered to be Basia's eccentric behavior. Donald Christ's wife, Iris, had for many years consulted a Pennsylvania astrologer, Joelle Mahoney. While the litigation was in progress, Mahoney did a chart on the case itself. Iris Christ was disappointed when the case was postponed from October 1985 to the following February because Mahoney asserted that the litigation would go much more rapidly and favorably in the fall than later on. Mahoney also highlighted the future date of April 16 as being particularly volatile. "I had indicated that during that twenty-four-hour period there was a configuration that would bring in a lot of fanfare to the trial and a lot of shouting and carrying on in what was a very, very risky situation. There were a couple of other configurations that indicated irrational behavior on all parts and a tremendous amount of pressure on Donald [Christ] at that time." There are those who speculate that Mahoney's prediction was to become a self-fulfilling prophecy.

Iris Christ arranged for Basia Johnson and Nina Zagat to meet Mahoney. The astrologer met with them in a conference room at the Shearman & Sterling offices in New York's Citicorp building at 153 East Fifty-third Street. Mahoney saw them "two or three times," the final meeting taking place a few days before the trial began. Mahoney drew up both clients' charts and found Basia Johnson to be in a particularly strong position as "she was a Pisces and the planet Jupiter, which is the planet of good fortune, was in her sign all year."

During the trial, two lawyers said that Basia Johnson had also consulted a Tarot card reader. The most confusing account of her behavior centers around Roy Cohn, the lawyer who died of AIDS in August of 1986. Basia Johnson's anti-communist sentiments were well known and Cohn had gained notoriety when he'd assisted Senator Joseph McCarthy in his witch hunts against communism in the early 1950s. Several lawyers confirmed that after Izabella Poterewicz testified, Basia Johnson demanded that Roy Cohn represent her, and that a Sullivan & Cromwell lawyer specifically refused her, stating that his firm could not serve as co-counsel with Cohn. Two other lawyers, however, say that when Basia said "Cohn" she used the term in a generic sense, meaning that she wanted a tough (and it is implied) Jewish litigator, and that is also the reason she wanted Marvin Schwartz. Basia herself says that although she admired the way Roy Cohn fought for his clients, she never said any such thing and that in any case she was aware at the time that Cohn was too ill to represent her or anyone else.

BASIA: It was as if I was from Mars! I was so strange to all those people, so strange, even to my own lawyers. Every time I was with them I mystified them because they didn't understand at all. And not just my lawyers, but everyone.

Tuesday was April Fool's Day. Lambert ruled that "the widow has a right to privacy, the Court will not order her to permit the public to be allowed on the premises. The Court, however, in its discretion, will not permit the jury-view to occur unless reasonable access to members of the press is permitted." Lambert also released the tape to the networks. Although the press offered to pool their forces and send only four members on the tour, Christ announced that the trip had been canceled. Lambert then excused the jury for the day. That evening WPIX offered sensational coverage of "the secret tapes." As Basia howled in Polish, the translation, not permitted in the courtroom, scrolled across the TV screen over a courtroom sketch of her glowering face. The dream image had shattered, and the path was cleared for Reilly to put the Johnson marriage dramatically on trial.

New York *Post:* JOHNSON'S WIDOW'S A SCREAM ON TAPE

Newark *Star-Ledger:* JOHNSON WIDOW DEPICTED AS
TYRANT

The New York Times: JOHNSON'S WIFE MISTREATED
HIM, A FORMER MAID ASSERTS IN COURT

BASIA: Of course I screamed on her, she deserved it. I
needed help. My mother had just died. My husband was
so sick, terrible. Why does no one tell this?

Wednesday morning, April 2, at 9:30, the court con-
vened, but Robert Osgood had vanished for good. Donald
Christ cross-examined Izabella routinely.

CHRIST: Isn't it a fact that you attempted to get into an
argument with Mrs. Johnson that day?

IZABELLA: No.

CHRIST: And that you began the conversation?

IZABELLA: No.

CHRIST: She began the conversation?

IZABELLA: She called me. It's on the tape.

Christ never challenged Izabella on her explanation
that she had taped her firing "to secure myself. I didn't
know exactly maybe if I will go to an employment office or
something." Christ seemed dispirited; with Izabella and
the witnesses who followed, his cross-examination often
meandered. He would stand at the lectern, a black loose-
leaf notebook spread out before him, a yellow pencil in his
left hand, reading the typed questions one after another
and then ticking them off with the pencil. The answers,
however, rarely led to another impromptu or penetrating

question as they did with Edward Reilly. Sometimes when Christ read a question that seemed inappropriate, he would catch himself and say, "I withdraw the question."

Christ was laboring under an enormous burden, unsupported in the courtroom, often attacked by the judge, belittled by his client. Basia Johnson had become increasingly critical of him, and to their professional association another element had been added. Donald's wife, the socially impeccable Iris, was the daughter of Consuelo Vanderbilt and Earl E.T. Smith. On the day of the opening speeches, the blonde, trim Iris, in a Lunaraine mink coat, was the most glamorous figure in the courtroom. She had come to lend moral support to her husband and to Basia Johnson, and for the first two weeks of the trial she often sat next to Basia. Then Iris moved away and sat far across the courtroom. Then Iris stopped coming to court altogether.

"Uptown," BY WILLIAM NORWICH, *Daily News,* April 29, 1986: A Vanderbilt is born. Serena McCallum, an eighth generation newcomer to this illustrious lot, was born last Thursday in London.

It was her maternal grandmother, the very beautiful Iris Smith Van Ingen Paine Russell Christ of Locust Valley and Oregon, who recently jolted society when she appeared (unidentified) on the front page of this newspaper, escorting Basha [sic] Johnson on her first day in court. (As you know, the widow of the late millionaire Seward Johnson is waging war with his children over rights to his estate.) Since Iris supposedly loathes press, everyone wondered why she was photographed with a former maid.

Well, here's the answer. Iris' husband, Donald Christ, is Basha's chief counsel. A dutiful wife, Iris decided to befriend the widow. Now, however, I am told that

Basha is complaining loudly to attorney Christ about the progress of the trial. (Rumor has it he may seek a mistrial.) Needless to say, Iris isn't exactly singing Basha's tune these days. You see, when oil and water try to mix, the water would do well not to push the oil around.

BASIA: They call me a maid. They envy what I have, what I have achieved, and would like to take it away from me. Because I have moral character. Do you think Jesus Christ was typical? And they crucified Christ. That's what they did to me. They crucified me in that court-room. Because when you're different, when you stand for something, they destroy you.

SULLIVAN & CROMWELL LAWYER: Poor Donald—Iris was the lady and Basia was the maid and after that he couldn't do anything right. God bless the press!

Christ struggled on for more than three weeks while two other Sullivan & Cromwell litigators, Philip Graham, Jr., and Marvin Schwartz, were being briefed to move in as reinforcements. Christ admitted that he had lost a great deal of his client's confidence. On a May morning he stood outside the courtroom door. He looked bloated, having gained some ten pounds during the course of the case. "How are you doing?" I inquired. Christ swung an imaginary golf club at an imaginary ball and quipped, "I feel like a prisoner on a submarine. I don't know where I'm going!"

". . . you will die, die, die."

A parade of witnesses contin-
ued to bludgeon Basia's reputation, substantiating the contestants' charges. There were moments of high drama and
moments of humor. Anthony Maffatone, a highly decorated Vietnam veteran who was the Richardses' bodyguard
and friend, testified that on a visit to Jasna Polana to survey the security system, he was sitting on the terrace with
the Johnsons when Mr. Johnson asked, "Who are you and
what are you doing here?" "With that, Mrs. Johnson spun
around and she screamed at him, 'You stupid, stupid man,
this is Tony,' and she smacked him in the face [with the
back of her hand] and went into a tirade, screaming at him
that he was a stupid, ga-ga man. When she smacked him in
the face, he grabbed his mouth and there was like a look of
shock on his face. I didn't know what to do, and I just
started fumbling around with my papers."

During cross-examination Christ asked Maffatone,
"Isn't it a fact that you don't like her [Mrs. Johnson]?"
Maffatone replied, "No, I don't." On re-direct examination
Reilly asked him why he disliked her. He answered, "I feel
that she enjoys berating people. My mother and father

were working-class people and when I saw the way she treated her servants, I identified with them, the way she held their jobs in the palm of her hand." And about Seward Johnson he said, "When I see a man humiliated by anyone in front of his guests or friends, it repulses me. I just wanted to be away from her."

Witness after witness testified that Basia Johnson would have prolonged screaming fits during which she called her husband "stupid," "ga-ga," "stupid American." Nurse Judith Abramovitz said that working for Basia was "like being in a psychiatric institution, she raved like a lunatic," and described her tantrums as "unbelievable hour-and-a-half rages." Abramovitz described the incident in which Johnson had sent out for a Crock-Pot in which to make oatmeal. She said that the furious Mrs. Johnson attempted "to come down on him with a cane." Donald Christ elicited the fact that, although Basia "swung at him," she never hit him with the cane, and that if she had wanted to, she could have easily done so.

Mary Howard, a bodyguard who worked for the Johnsons for four weeks in the winter of 1982 while Seward was undergoing cobalt treatments, testified that "We took him to Sloan-Kettering for treatments and then went back to the apartment. I had called for the camper to come to the front entrance. Mrs. Johnson bounded on and told the chauffeur not to put the stairs down for Mr. Johnson. It was a wooden two-step unit to make it easier for him to get in and out of the vehicle, because it was a great height for him. I looked at the chauffeur and he looked crushed, but he did not put the stairs down. I picked him [Seward] up and put him in the camper. The chauffeur helped."

A former security guard testified that Mr. Johnson had asked him for a gun because "he was afraid of his wife Basia and her brother Gregory." The guard purchased a

Luger .357 magnum revolver and a box of ammunition
and gave it to Johnson. It was returned several days later
by Basia, who screamed at the guard, "Don't you ever do
this again, he doesn't know what's good for him, he's like a
child." Another witness, Olindo Carnevale, told an opposite story: he said that Johnson had asked him to remove a
gun from his bedside table and lock it up because he was
afraid his wife might "use it on me." It was after this
testimony that Basia demonstrated a kind of gallows humor. In the corridor she made a formal statement to the
press: "My husband and I were very happily married. We
lived together for twelve years and he was never afraid of
me." Then the moment before she ducked back into the
courtroom, she turned and added impishly, "And he died
of natural causes."

There were other moments of comic relief. A gardener
testified that Basia Johnson had reacted with a tantrum
when she'd discovered that in complying with her demand
for a perfect lawn, he had treated it with wintergreen, a
compound that rubbed off bright green on the guests'
shoes. Mervyn Nelson, the acting coach, forgetting the
name of the Johnson estate, called it "Lollapalooza."
When queried further on places and dates, he said, "I
knew you were going to ask me that and I can never remember, I ought to be put away." But when Christ asked
Nelson if he'd ever won an Oscar for his acting, he was
severely reprimanded by Surrogate Lambert.

One by one, the Johnson children and their spouses
mounted the stand and testified to Basia's rages and profli-
gacies. Keith Wold spoke of the enormous change in lifestyle when Basia married Seward. He described Johnson as
a once simple man who lived his last days in the style of a
potentate. "We used to play a game in the living room
called 'How Many Monets in This Room?'" (There were

four.) His wife, Elaine, testified that she had heard Basia yelling very loudly and using the words that had become all too familiar to everyone: "stupid," "idiot," "ga-ga." Martin Richards testified to Basia's rages, to Seward Johnson's senility. In the corridor Richards talked about how Basia made restaurant reservations not only from the phone in her limousine but also from the telephone in her airplane.

KEITH: This trial started to take on a new meaning for the children, because none of them were aware of the magnitude of the problem. The whole idea of Harbor Branch was still the largest part of this thing, but there was more to it than that.

ELAINE: It made me sick! It made us all ill. When the people got on the stand and said that they also heard her scream and it was 90 percent of the time. We weren't there that much, she did scream when we were there, but when the help got on and all the other people, I realized that Dad was actually victimized. This is something that we didn't realize when we started. So much was coming out. Even Jimmy, Jimmy who never wanted to go into the battle, Jimmy turned. He never knew she was that wicked. He always gave her the benefit of the doubt, which we all did. At that point at the trial we all were very close, all six of us.

DIANA: There were things we had no idea were going on. It was hard to listen to it. It did unite us, though.

April 10, 1986: Two court attendants carried in an enormous blow-up photograph of Jasna Polana. It was placed behind the witness chair and Mary Lea Johnson was called to the stand. After a few minutes of testimony, she was handed a pointer and asked to describe Jasna Polana. Pointing to the top of the photograph, she began, "This is where the help lives and also Basia's family lives up there and—"

Donald Christ interrupted, "I object to this kind of editorializing." Said Marie Lambert, "She can point out if people lived in a particular place." Mary Lea continued, "As you come into the great hall, there are some Flemish tapestries against the back wall. As you go forward, there are, let's see, a Botticelli and a Michelangelo, and two Rembrandts on the wall by the front door. There's a grand staircase that sweeps, it has two arms that go out, and on the landing there was a Brancusi, *Bird in Flight*."

In the living room "on the wall above the couch was a Modigliani and I would say at least four Monets and a Pissarro and several other paintings that are really good-quality paintings, Picasso, Braque, a beautiful Arp piece of sculpture and . . ." Mary Lea went on and on, pointing out her father's bathroom and Basia's dressing room with "a bed that I believe belonged to the Empress Josephine."

I glance over at Basia. A strong light is coming through the tall, narrow windows, and for the first time I see her looking terribly sad. I realize that she might consider this the worst kind of invasion of privacy, having someone point out where every room is, where her bed is, where her bathtub is, where her staircase is, and where the double bed is that she shared with her husband.

At the lunch break Seward Jr. says he feels Reilly has made a mistake by putting the family on. He asks me if I saw Basia's face when Marty was on the stand, and I reply, "No, but I saw it today when Mary Lea was testifying."

"That'll blow any settlement," says Junior. He explains to me that Joyce is desperate to settle. She wants this ordeal ended—there's a tremor in her hand and she hasn't been well. Seward Jr. is fighting the flu. He explains that his accountant has figured that $7.5 to $12 million after taxes right now would equal his trusteeship and executor fees and he's willing to go for the lower figure. "Now that you're willing to settle, do you think she is?" "I think what we said hardened her. Our lawyers say we're making progress with a settlement, but you can never tell. There are about four million lawyers between us and what's actually going on. I don't really know."

Later that afternoon I sit behind Basia, collating my notes. She beckons me to sit next to her. She tells me, "Justice is not being done here. What's happening here is not right. They hated their father and now they turn that hate on me. My lawyers ask them, do you have the facts on this, do you know that? They know nothing. My husband didn't want them around. I am not like that. I said, 'You must see your children,' and I said this could never happen. They know how good I am to their father. They can say I have bad character, but they can't change what was." Basia Johnson is not smiling now. The blue cashmere cape she is wearing makes her eyes look bright green. I ask her if she will settle. She replies, "Never."

As I leave the courthouse, I see Marty Richards. "They're telling us that by tomorrow it may be all finished —settled," he says. "I lost a production because of this thing. No one knew what was going on, and sitting here day after day finding out how bad it really was in that household with Basia is killing the family. We want out." But in the morning Seward Jr. tells me that settlement negotiations have broken down.

LAMBERT: After Izabella testified and the children began with their witnesses, we were talking, but I knew there

could be no settlement until Basia Johnson had a chance
to rehabilitate her reputation. Until her witnesses were
heard, forget it.

FORGER: After that big bombshell we sort of had a quiet
period. It seemed that the trial had gone so badly for the
widow that we would now have to wait a few weeks
until they had a chance at their own testimony to put it
back in balance.

By mid-April the principals and the press were caught
in a symbiotic relationship: the news media created the
images and the Johnsons became players in their own
drama. During the first days of the trial the press and the
participants had resembled hunter and prey. On the second day I observed a sketch artist, wearing froglike magni-
fying goggles, squatting within a few inches of Nina
Zagat's face and sketching away. When Seward Jr. left the
courtroom that same day, I counted seven microphones
and eight tape recorders in front of his face. But after the
initial flurry, after the reporters had written of the scandal,
after the tedious days of medical testimony, the ranks began to thin. Those who were left became the participants'
conduit to public perception.

The barriers have fallen. Reporters occupy seats directly behind Basia Johnson, who arrives daily in a variety
of discreet Madame Grès outfits, her hair freshly coiffed.
During pauses she frequently turns in her seat to explain
her point of view. "That story you wrote," she tells a reporter, "Zurbarán is with a 'Z' not a 'Th.' You spelled it
Thurburan. If you'd like to know how to spell my art, just
ask me."

The Johnson children now face the cameras and reporters with equanimity if not eagerness. Seward Jr. is fre-

quently seen in the corridor giving interviews, explaining his side of the case. Mary Lea, when asked by television reporters why someone with her vast wealth would want more money, smiles confidently into the cameras and answers with disarming candor, "Anyone can use it." Jennifer remarks, "I looked pretty good on TV last night. You know, I'm almost beginning to enjoy it."

In the eyes of the press the Johnson children have become distinct personalities, and Jennifer is a favorite. At forty-six she still resembles Betty Co-ed, a spunky Midwestern cheerleader. On a Friday she laments, "Joe and I are thinking of flying home for the weekend, but it's getting so expensive" (home being Jacksonville). "Of course we could save a lot if we took People's Express. I don't know why we worry about things like this, we're millionaires, you know" (to the tune of $100 million). Diana Firestone is small and wrenlike. She favors hacking jackets, button-down Brooks Brothers shirts, and cotton skirts. She sits on the edge of her chair, a look of determination on her face, but almost never speaks. One day I see she is wearing a copper bracelet and ask if it's for arthritis. She answers, "Yes, yes. Do you need it? Would you like to have it? I have another." Unexpectedly, I feel touched.

Every day a small group of court buffs gathers on the left-hand side of the courtroom. They hit all the hot trials. One of their number I've dubbed "Alabama" because of his thick Southern accent. At the lunch break Diana Firestone stands in front of the large blow-up of Jasna Polana, examining it carefully. Alabama stands next to her. "You like the horses?" he asks.

"Yes."

"I go to the Meadowlands every chance I get, I love them horses. If I had the money, I'd take a little lady like you with me and maybe one day we could stand together

in the winner's circle. Wouldn't that be the cat's meow, to
stand in the winner's circle?"

Diana is nonplussed but polite. "Yes," she repeats.

"Wouldn't that be the kick of a lifetime?" he says. Diana smiles. Alabama is recounting his fantasy to the owner
of Kentucky Derby winner Genuine Risk. Does he know
that Diana has lived that fantasy?

The reporters have learned to steer clear of James
Johnson, who during much of the testimony reads paper-
back books and newspapers. Martin Richards says of
James, "He's the first one to say he wants nothing from
this case. He's so used to rejection that he won't allow
himself to want." Through the many days of medical testimony by experts who never knew Seward Johnson in life,
but describe in minute detail his incontinence, senility, and
the pain of his demise, James continues to read. Mary Lea
articulates what we all sense of this courtroom drama:
"It's like watching a weasel devour a rat, but I'm fascinated by it."

When bumbling handyman Edmund Sulikowski began to
testify, it seemed he was there to provide comic relief.
Even Basia and Nina Zagat could not suppress giggles at
his description of how he'd advised Basia on where to hang
her paintings and she'd given him "the brush-off," telling
him, "Be quiet." Sulikowski described the atmosphere of
Jasna Polana as being like a horror movie, saying people
seemed "unhappy and sad. Something was strange." He
testified that on repeated occasions he had tried to tape-
record Basia's temper tantrums. When everyone else
would run away from the sound of her screaming, he
would run toward it. When Surrogate Lambert asked him
why, he answered, "I'm nosy," and Donald Christ nodded
his head in agreement. Sulikowski described how Basia

had argued with the cook, Ewa Grudzien, screamed at her, and backed her into a corner of the pantry until Ewa collapsed on the floor. Once Sulikowski ran upstairs when he heard Mrs. Johnson screaming, but when he saw her coming down the hall toward him, he panicked and jumped into a closet to hide. "I had no place to go, so I locked myself in and I pulled out the linen and sat on the floor and put my hands over my ears. I was so disgusted."

DONALD CHRIST: Did you have your tape recorder on?

SULIKOWSKI: No. I forget it.

On the dreary, rainy Wednesday morning of April 16, Sulikowski's testimony is drawing to a close. On Tuesday he testified that he'd made a dozen tapes, but today he claims that he has inadvertently erased most of them. One that is intact is played in the courtroom—another Basia tirade in Polish, matching Izabella's tape in its howling intensity. But with repetition the shock value has worn off and several questions come to mind. Sulikowski's tape was made one year after Seward Johnson's death (the question of whether such post-death material should be admitted was soon to be raised); this aside, why did Sulikowski make the tapes and for whom? Also, at Jasna Polana there is a sophisticated security system; how did two servants manage to run around with hidden Sony tape recorders? And another odd coincidence: their tape recorders were identical. Surprisingly, none of these issues was ever explored by Basia Johnson's lawyers.

As the Sulikowski tape plays, a group of people files into the courtroom and finds seats or stands unobtrusively against the interior staircase. As the witness is excused, a crowd surges forward. Some of them shake fists and yell,

"Communist!" "Liar!" "He is spying on our property!" "He is a communist spy!" The voices blend together. For a moment no one reacts, then Lambert shouts, "Be quiet!" As the voices continue, she calls out, "Get the jury out of here! Get them out of here right away!" As soon as the jury is ushered out, Lambert directs the bailiffs to lock the courtroom doors. "Nobody is to leave this room. No one." She bellows at the demonstrators, "You have tried to disrupt my courtroom and cause a riot. This is a serious business. I want names. Anyone who works for Mrs. Johnson." One of the demonstrators, Emilia Fryc, begins to speak, but Lambert shouts, "Be quiet, not one word! This court is not intimidated and this judge is not intimidated, is that clear? Now get in here," she says, pointing to the jury box. Reilly is also on his feet. "There's one," he says. "I know that one works for Mrs. Johnson." Lambert and Reilly are like a couple of wranglers as fifteen Jasna Polana employees are rounded up and herded into the jury box, the gate clanging behind them.

While the demonstrators wait to be interrogated, members of the press and the lawyers are ushered into Lambert's chambers. On the way, I hear Diana Firestone exclaim, "Get me out of this nightmare!" Richards grabs a reporter by the sleeve: "You see now what fear and money can buy." Although Lambert handles the situation fearlessly, she concedes to a reporter that she is "quite shaken. Did you see the size of some of those guys?" Lambert stands just outside her chambers arguing with Harvey Corn about protection. "I want the FBI in here," she says. "I want my jurors protected. I want them picked up in the morning and chaperoned home at night. I want guards at all times." "Take it easy," says Harvey, "just calm down, just calm down right now. Everything will be taken care of. I don't think the jurors need protection. Rethink that

one. It'll just cause them to suspect something's going on."
He puts his hand on her shoulder.

One by one, the demonstrators were questioned. All
were employees of Basia Johnson; thirteen of them were
Polish, two Italian. One of their number, estate manager
John Stroczynski, admitted that he had given the protesters permission to come to court. Lambert sentenced him to
fifteen days in jail (later commuted to one night). Four
other demonstrators were fined $100 to $250. One of the
workers said he didn't have the cash for the fine, but offered his American Express card. Of a leather-jacketed
man with a Don Johnson growth of stubble on his chin,
Lambert asked, "What do you think would happen if you
got up in a Polish court and started yelling?" "Maybe they
have problem?" he ventured. To the six-foot-five Marian
Kapala, Lambert said, "Do you think because you're big
you're going to frighten people?" Kapala replied, "No."
Said Lambert, "That's right, I run this courtroom and I
don't frighten easily." When another demonstrator said
she had stood and shouted "Liar," "because I thought
America was a free country," Lambert's retort was, "And
you know why it's a free country? Because people do what
they're told to do."

Donald Christ sank lower and lower in his chair as the
interrogations continued, interrupted by long waits for in-
terpreters. When Emilia Fryc tried to explain why she
thought Mrs. Johnson was being treated unfairly, Lambert
cut her off: "Don't say a word. Mrs. Johnson has five lawyers here. If you want to testify, tell them and you can
come into court and do it the proper way."

Little by little, a partial story emerged. Several of the
workers had read newspaper accounts of Sulikowski's testimony and how he had "taped his boss." Sulikowski had
been one of their own and they decided to come to court to

face him when he testified. They were chauffeured to the
courthouse in blue Buicks and Oldsmobiles owned by Mrs.
Johnson, and several of the cars were driven by her security men. However, all of them said that Mrs. Johnson had
nothing to do with the protest.

After three hours the press was excused. Donald Christ
used the incident of the riot to move for a mistrial. Reilly
was furious. "I deeply resent Mr. Christ waiting until the
media representatives have been excused before making his
request. It has been abundantly plain to many, many people for many weeks that your case is not going as you have
anticipated, and there has been a concerted effort on the
part of some people to see if there might be a mistrial. I
have no doubt that Barbara Piasecka fully understands
what was done, and the timing of it, the orchestration of it,
and her involvement in it is of greater concern to me than
some lower-ranked employee of hers. Mrs. Johnson has
got to realize that someday the decision of some court is
going to tell her what the final resolution of this dispute is
going to be, and it is not a decision of hers." Reilly said
that during the demonstration Basia had given the V for
Victory, the Polish Solidarity sign, to the protesters.

Marie Lambert seemed frightened of what she perceived to be Basia Johnson's power. "If anything happens
to anybody on this jury, I'll hold the firm of Shearman &
Sterling responsible since Mrs. Zagat is in close association
with this lady day after day and Judge Bauman talks to
her, and if anything happens to anybody on this jury,
that's where the responsibility will be. Somebody has got
to be able to speak to this lady and explain to her that the
court, and I'm sure other groups, will do something about
it if anything happens to anybody on this jury." Arnold
Bauman responded, "I reject that responsibility, that statement is baseless . . . there is not the slightest basis for the

court's imposition on Shearman & Sterling of responsibility for the well-being of the jury."

LAMBERT: She believes that KGB hired Izabella, right? Was I right, then, in being concerned about my jury? I have a responsibility to the jury. Hey, listen, isn't it possible it could be true? Do we know anything really? What sometimes sounds paranoid may not be paranoid. But the KGB's not what I was concerned about. I was concerned about the fact that there are people working for her who are loyal to her. And I was concerned, after the demonstration that occurred, as to what could go on beyond that. It gets to the point where it could be frightening, because, you know, money is power, isn't it?

As a parting shot, Reilly observed, "The fact that Mr. Christ moved for a mistrial removed any doubt in my mind as to the real purpose in getting them [the demonstrators] here." Christ answered, "I totally reject that," and he moved that the transcript of this conversation "not be made available to the press." Lambert refused to seal the transcript.

The events of the day had clearly given the children another advantage. Through Jack Raymond, her public-relations man, Basia Johnson issued a statement that she was "terribly upset" about the demonstration. "The persons involved apparently sought to help me, but it was wrong for them to do this. I regret it deeply." Said Joyce Johnson, "Come on! Basia engineered this, there's no doubt in my mind. I'm sure she decided to do something for herself. A mistrial would give her time to get new lawyers and regroup her forces."

* * *

That evening Edmund Sulikowski's phone rang. It was
Marian Fryc, one of the Jasna Polana employees who had
disrupted the trial. "Eddie, how much are they paying you
for the tapes? How much?" he demanded. Then he began
to threaten Sulikowski and called him "a fucking so-and-
so."

On Thursday morning, April 17, there were two uniformed guards and security barriers at each end of the
corridors. Press identification was required, a log was
signed, tape recorders were confiscated. Mary Civiello, the
Channel Four TV reporter, asked a guard, "Aren't you
going to frisk me?" He declined, but searched her purse.
At noon, in the open courtroom after the jury had been
excused for lunch, Reilly stepped forward to announce
that Sulikowski had received a threat the previous evening
that contained the kind of "profane language we are more
accustomed to hearing from Barbara Piasecka Johnson."
There was a gasp in the courtroom, a feeling that Reilly
had moved in for the kill. Now he enumerated his accusations against Osgood and said, "The fact of the intimidation should be admissible before this jury as evidence of an
admission of the weakness of the proponents' own case."
He asked for an injunction to prevent the proponents from
contacting any witnesses and asked to depose the employees who had taken part in yesterday's demonstration. Donald Christ responded, "I take exception to the remarks of
Mr. Reilly. I think there is an effort being made to create a
sideshow in this case out of what we all agree was a deplor-
able incident. I am personally offended by the suggestion
that an injunction should somehow be levied against Sullivan & Cromwell, Mrs. Johnson, Mrs. Zagat, and other
attorneys involved in this proceeding." Christ added that
he felt the case against Mrs. Johnson so far had been "slan-

derous" and it was natural "for her loyal employees to be as offended as the public at large is by these charges which to me seem to be designed to make this case into a circus rather than a court proceeding."

Christ's speech seemed to incense Surrogate Lambert. "Who made the circus yesterday? Who was responsible for the circus we had yesterday? We're trying this case in an atmosphere with bodyguards where the judge now has to have security outside to search everyone who comes into this place before they come in; that atmosphere is certainly not created by Mr. Reilly or his client."

Lambert exerted efforts to get to the bottom of who had caused the riot by asking that all the protesters be deposed. The lawyers worked till midnight most evenings for several weeks, questioning these employees. By this time tempers were frayed, the lawyers were openly hostile, the last vestiges of civility had been abandoned. Philip Graham, Jr., had been called into the fray on behalf of Sullivan & Cromwell. The first half-hour of John Stroczynski's deposition deteriorated into a quarrel between Paul Shoemaker of Milbank, Tweed and Graham.

GRAHAM: I don't know why you can't have the decency to break that question into two parts.

SHOEMAKER: Don't lecture me about decency.

GRAHAM: You could use a lecture on that, but I hadn't intended to do it.

SHOEMAKER: Don't waste my time with this kind of ridiculous remarks.

In chambers Shoemaker asserted that Stroczynski had been covering up and playing dumb, and he threatened,

"In about five minutes both of these transcripts may go over to Morgenthau's office for an indictment on perjury. I've really had it."

GRAHAM: I suggest that the time has passed when Milbank, Tweed should be appointed a private Attorney General to do that, and if your Honor thinks it should go to Mr. Morgenthau for further investigation, it seems that it is preferable.

LAMBERT: Eventually it will go there. Right now it's going to end up right here, we're going to get answers here.

GRAHAM: If you want to get into these extraneous matters . . .

LAMBERT: It is not extraneous and [Morgenthau's office] has a right to find out whether this is an attempt to create a mistrial in this case.

As the argument raged on, Graham complained that in deposing so many of the demonstrators, "our manpower is stretched very thin," to which Lambert replied, "That's not my fault. I didn't start that riot in there."

GRAHAM: Neither did I, your Honor.

On Friday, April 18, Reilly reported that Sulikowski had received another threat and that another witness, a former Johnson employee, had backed out of testifying because he'd read the newspapers and was frightened. Significantly, Christ answered, "I have taken steps to disseminate the word at Jasna Polana to make sure that this doesn't happen again." Lambert said, "I'll move the court to the witness's house. If you think I'm beyond that, don't think

I'm beyond that." On Monday an exhausted Lambert went home to bed. At midnight her phone rang. "Hello? Hello?" she said, but no one spoke and then she heard a click. The following morning the phone rang again, and a voice so muffled that she could not tell if it were male or female whispered, "If you don't declare a mistrial, you will be killed." When she got to court, she found that Sullivan & Cromwell had filed a formal seventy-nine-page mistrial motion, with the request that it be kept under seal. That night Lambert's phone rang again. A voice said, "Unless you declare a mistrial, you will die, die, die." The last part really frightened her, she said, "because it sounded like it was someone who might not have been completely there, someone who was capable—" but Lambert did not finish the sentence.

Lambert called the captain of security at the Supreme Court and the FBI. She was provided with a bodyguard who escorted her to and from court. She began to have lunch in her office. A tap was put on her home and office phones. Lambert's life had been threatened before, in 1982, when she'd ruled that a $30,000 legacy left by Pulitzer Prize-winning journalist Fred Sparks would be withheld from the PLO because it was a "terrorist organization." At that time Lambert carried a remote-control device that started the motor of her car from a distance, in case there was a bomb wired to the ignition. Now she refused to allow anyone in the elevator with her as she rode to the fifth floor. "If they're going to get me, then they're going to get me," she announced, "but I don't want to take a lot of innocent people with me."

LAMBERT: Aside from the death threats, we also had calls that there were bombs planted, and people sensed without out my knowledge that that—you know, my office protects me—they don't tell me. And, frankly, I don't like to upset my family. I mean, my son heard it from somebody and he went off the wall. I didn't want anybody to know about it during the trial, how bad it was. That could affect the trial. All I was frightened about was that nobody should go near the jurors. You wonder whether anybody on a lower level might approach a juror, either to threaten or anything else, especially where you have jurors who are of modest means and you're talking about tremendous amounts of money."

" . . . so much greed . . . "

*H*arvey Corn termed the mistrial motion "a shot across the bow." It accused Lambert of "misconduct," cited more than a hundred examples of reversible error, and asked that she remove herself as judge. Among the allegations were, "The most damaging thing a trial judge can do in a jury trial is to become an advocate of one side or another, the judge in this case has abandoned her proper role as an impartial arbiter. . . . It has become apparent that the proceedings have become so infected with irreparable error prejudicial to the proponents that any verdict rendered in favor of the objectants will not be sustainable on appeal." The motion stated that it was based "on a pervasive pattern of prejudice running from the opening of the trial to the present" and added, "This court's remarks have doomed this trial."

Seven types of error were cited. The motion claimed Lambert had been hostile in her "cross-examination and criticism of the proponents' witnesses," had "clearly conveyed the impression to the jury that the court regards certain of the proponents' medical witnesses as being incompetent, dishonest or both. The record makes clear that

of all the proponents' witnesses the one held in least regard
by the court is proponent Nina Zagat. The court allowed
the full measure of its contempt for Mrs. Zagat to manifest
itself," and cited the in-chambers conference where Lambert had uttered the words "a crook and a thief," as well as
other criticisms of Zagat.

Examples of unfairness to Sullivan & Cromwell lawyers were enumerated. Lambert "mistakenly attributed a
remark to Mr. Zirinis and proceeded to castigate him in
front of the jury: 'Mr. Zirinis, we have a rule in this court,
we hear from one counsel. If you're going to do that, I'm
going to make you sit in the back.'" When Sullivan &
Cromwell lawyer Theodore Rogers asked her for "the basis for a ruling she castigated him by saying, 'You want me
to do it in front of the jury? I will do it at the end of the
day. Don't let me do it in front of the jury. You know why
I am sustaining the objection.'"

Lambert was accused of "erroneously allowing the jury
to hear inflammatory tape recordings. The playing of these
tapes served no purpose but to appeal to the emotions of
the jury. They were calculated solely to shock and smear.
Their introduction brought these proceedings to a new low
and turned the courtroom into a circus."

Mary Lea observed that by now the case had deteriorated into "a donnybrook of words." Milbank, Tweed filed
a fifty-four-page response and Dewey, Ballantine a twenty-
nine-page one. They were scathing in their criticism of Sullivan & Cromwell. Milbank pointed out that "the proponents' case has suffered somewhat by its fragmented pre-
sentation by no less than six attorneys." (Two more
lawyers would be called into battle before the trial ended.)
"This case has been marred by the calculated disruptions,
carping objections, and other improper conduct of the proponents and their agents. There can be no doubt that the

contemptuous disruption of the trial was orchestrated by at least one of the proponents. Barbara Johnson runs Jasna Polana with an iron hand.

"Of course the proponents said nothing but waited to see how the objectants' case would unfold. Unable to cope with the evidence, proponents unfortunately chose instead to torpedo the judicial process by challenging the integrity of the court." Of Nina Zagat it was said, "She was evasive, argumentative and made self-serving, unresponsive speeches whenever possible." It was noted that Lambert's comments about Zagat "were made in chambers . . . and she was merely expressing what she believed the objectants' view to be." The Dewey, Ballantine memo stated: "The reason for the proponents' motion is apparent. Recognizing the likelihood of an adverse jury verdict, the proponents seek to abort this trial."

Although the mistrial motion had been filed with a request to seal the document, a Sullivan & Cromwell lawyer promptly leaked the story to a well-known reporter. The following Monday, in chambers, Reilly said of the mistrial memorandum, "It was very well under seal! I noticed it in the newspapers." "It was in Liz Smith's column on Sunday," Lambert said to the assembled lawyers. "How did they know that you've asked the judge to recuse herself?" Then Lambert entered the courtroom, denied the motion for mistrial, and officially released all the papers. Members of the press were presented with all the documents, including Sullivan's late-morning entry, an overwrought reply memorandum that stated, "The children have forsaken the low road for the mud. No fair-minded person who has sat through the trial or read the transcript could possibly believe that the court's persistent course of conduct did not impermissibly influence the jury. Can anyone with knowledge of this case look at himself or herself in the mirror and say this trial has been fair?"

In the corridors the orderly battle had deteriorated into guerrilla warfare.

ROBERT DELAHUNTY: This proceeding is enough to make me want to leave this kind of law. It's just plain persecution.

ARNOLD BAUMAN: I've never seen anything like that judge in all my years, it's unbelievable.

REILLY: Mrs. Johnson thought she could engineer a mistrial. Well, it's clear we're not intimidated.

The lawyers now seem more concerned with how they are perceived by the news media than with the case itself. Perhaps they feel the case is over and they are preparing for the appeal, or perhaps their need to defend their own reputations has obliterated the needs of their respective clients.

I leave the courthouse, my tote bulging with motions and replies. The rain is coming down, a waterfall cascades off the green scaffolding that surrounds the courthouse. Seward Jr., Joyce, and Marty Richards come up behind me. "Can we give you a lift?" Marty asks. "I'd love it, but I'd be violating my journalistic integrity," I reply with a grin. "Call it an interview," says Marty, and Seward Jr. playfully pushes me toward the Richardses' limousine. I get into the maroon stretch limousine and sit with my back to the driver, facing the others. There's a bodyguard in the front seat next to the chauffeur. I ask about Mary Lea and Marty says she's sick. The phone rings. As he moves to pick it up, Marty says, "If that's Elaine calling about dinner reservations, don't tell Liz Smith." The previous week

Liz Smith had printed an item that the Johnsons communicate by cellular car phone and Marty had called her to deny that they do. It is Marty's ex-chauffeur calling to say that Sullivan & Cromwell has contacted him. Marty hangs up and says, "What can he say about us? That Mary Lea and I paid him a good salary, that we bought him some good suits, that we were very good to him?" There's discussion about whether, when Marty gets to his office, he should call the chauffeur back and record the conversation. Marty says, "In the past with Victor D'Arc we've gotten used to recording calls. Victor taped our conversations. We taped his conversations. Then we learned how to tape him taping our conversations taping his conversations." Everybody laughs. Joyce says that's the first time she's laughed since the trial began. She has a pain in her shoulder and can't move it. Seward Jr. complains of a backache. Joyce says they've promised their daughter, Clelia, that they'll go to Nantucket this weekend to watch her horse have its foal, but they can see there's little chance of it. "Oh, Seward, I hate to disappoint her," she adds. They talk about the day they'd visited Lambert in chambers and how they could have settled it then and it would be all over. Marty says, "When this started, I wanted to go to Basia. I think we might have been able to work it out, but it's too late for that now. Her tactics are so terrible, and we never knew she treated Seward like that, we would have done something about it. So many terrible things have come out on the stand, it can never be repaired." I remember that Basia too has used the word "never."

Seward and Joyce have another complaint. They say they don't seem to have any part in this case, that Reilly doesn't tell them who the next witness will be, that no one reads the notes they write. Joyce says, "It's so different from the New Jersey trial."

"How?" I ask.

She replies, "That was summer stock, this is Broadway."

On Thursday, April 24, at 12:15, I enter Lambert's chambers to ask for a statement about the mistrial motion. I've hit the right day, Surrogate Lambert is ready to talk. As I sit beside her at her desk, she eats a sliced banana on a paper plate, orange Jell-O from a Polly-O container, and sips coffee with milk from a mug inscribed "Marie." Behind her on a flat table are masses of paper in boxes, in bound volumes stacked four feet high. The overflow, hundreds of pages, is piled under the table. Marie Lambert sees me staring. "It's not just this case. When I'm not doing this, I have to rule on motions, carry on adoption proceedings—there's a lot of other work."

Today she's wearing a black lace top and a red silk skirt. "I have so many clothes, in my lifetime I couldn't wear them all out," she remarks. Lambert looks fatigued, her face is crisscrossed with a mass of lines. She calls out to the outer office, "Harvey, Harvey, have you got that?" Corn enters with an open book. Lambert reads a page and says triumphantly, "That's it, that's right on the nose." Surrogate Lambert has a way of asking rhetorical questions through which one can clearly read her opinions. "Should I be reading the law to them?" she asks. "The Sullivan & Cromwell lawyers complain that I wouldn't let in about the children's wealth. I didn't rule that, I said they would have to lay a foundation for it. They laid no foundation for it. They came in here and told me they didn't know how to lay a foundation for it. And that Sherryl Michaelson, she asked an improper hypothetical question: 'What if someone had presented an affidavit to you, would you have signed it?' Well, what if the moon were made of blue cheese? And their offers of proof—Michaelson brought me this thing that said you couldn't show a body in a coffin. I told her yes, that's true, but you can show a body at the bottom of an elevator shaft.

"They have six lawyers out there now and they've brought in another one and I hear they're bringing in another one, person after person presenting fragments of a case. It's the most inept thing I've ever seen. I don't know about these multimillionaires, they pay all this money and they get these people." Lambert begins to speculate on how much money all those lawyers are making and what it's costing Basia Johnson. She says that Arnold Bauman of Shearman & Sterling "sits in there and holds her hand and his regular rate is $375 an hour or something like that."

Lambert feels that Sullivan & Cromwell has made several basic errors in presenting its case. "I would have said they had a bumpy marriage. The question was whether he had come to terms and accepted it or not. These so-called gentlemen lawyers have no idea of a European woman. I understand families like that. People yell and scream and carry on emotionally, that doesn't mean they aren't good wives. Look at me. I was a good wife. They could have said that was just Basia's way. There's nothing wrong with that if only those lawyers wouldn't have said she never screamed; then I had to let the Izabella tape in as contradictory evidence. After that I had to let in the Sulikowski tape because they said the Izabella tape was an isolated incident." She rolls her eyes toward the ceiling. "Are you sure you wouldn't like some of my coffee?"

"Should they have made Seward Johnson out to be an art expert?" she asks, and explains that when she married her husband, Grady, she was only in her twenties and didn't know anything about art, but that she learned about

Meissen and Dalton and other kinds of china because he was an antiques dealer and now she loves certain of these things but she still doesn't know one painting from another. She gestures to a snow-covered mountain landscape on her wall and says, "I like that, but I don't know what it is. I don't know anything about art. They should have said that he went along and enjoyed and supported her choices."

Lambert is particularly rankled that the mistrial motion has come "when the children have finished presenting their very strong case. Why now? All of this so-called error occurred on March 2. Why not move then? That would have been the honorable thing to do." She tells me that this was the third gesture toward a mistrial. There was one inference early on and a motion by Christ right after Mrs. Johnson's employees "invaded my courtroom. And what was that about? She saw fifteen of her employees and she didn't do anything about it. She didn't tell them to leave. How can they say she had nothing to do with it? Even if she just saw them come in and just asked them to leave, but we know it was much more than that and it's going to come out. Because of all her money, that woman thinks she can control everything. But she can't control my courtroom. My courtroom is my own."

Lambert reviews the children's case. She says that undue influence has been built up through Anthony Maffatone's testimony about Basia's slap in the face to her husband, the attempted hit with the cane; all that was very cleverly placed in the minds of the jury. "There are ways and ways of persuading people. You can't threaten people, you can't take away their dignity." She explains that her husband, Grady, had Alzheimer's disease and when she tried to persuade him to eat, she would say, "If you don't swallow that food, Grady, you'll make me so unhappy and you might choke." As she is telling this story, it occurs to me that everyone I speak to, even the judge, brings a personal experience or bias to this case, because, after all, it is about universal themes: the death of a parent, the fear of old age, the role of a stepmother.

"Harvey!" Lambert bellows at the top of her lungs. Corn appears in the doorway. "Has someone checked on my dentist appointment?" Surrogate Lambert leans back in her chair. "I don't know what good all this money does. You can only drive one car, eat one meal. I've seen that the people in my family are educated, I can only take a month's vacation, that's all I want. In my work I find so much greed dividing families after someone dies—that's the saddest part of what I do."

Lambert asks her final rhetorical questions. "How do you think Basia Johnson will feel if this will is probated and Nina Zagat is in the driver's seat? How will she feel if Zagat is the one to tell her if she can invade the trust or how much money she can get? How is Mrs. Johnson going to like that one?" The questions stay in my head. Unless Seward Johnson's will is totally rewritten, Zagat and Basia will be associated for the rest of their lives.

"You don't argue with the judge."

*T*here is an air of resignation
on May 8 as Basia begins to present her rebuttal case. It
seems an exercise in form without content. Almost thirteen
weeks have passed, and everybody is worn thin. Seward
Jr.'s constant hacking cough punctuates the proceedings.
Elaine Wold is fighting a virulent strain of pneumonia.
During the week Mary Lea is rushed to the hospital with a
kidney-stone attack. Marvin Schwartz and Philip Graham,
Jr., have been brought in as fresh replacement troops for
Basia. The forces of Sullivan & Cromwell have regrouped.
Reilly had opened with his strongest witness, the unflap-
pable Izabella and her devastating tape. Basia's first witness is equally a surprise, Sister Mary Louise Flowers, an
angelic nun in a flowing white habit with a large black
metal cross around her neck. A reporter is heard to remark
that starting with a nun in full regalia is comparable to Bill
Veeck's famous ploy for the St. Louis Browns when he sent
in a midget as a pinch hitter when the bases were loaded
and they walked in a run.

Sister Mary Louise walks back and forth in the corridor, her habit flowing behind her. She stops to press a five-

by-seven-inch white file card into the hand of a reporter. After reading the Xeroxed message, there can be little doubt that the combination of Sister Mary Louise Flowers, Edward Reilly's moral indignation, and Surrogate Lambert's short fuse will make for an interesting day. The Sister's card reads as follows: "Nun 40 years—Geriatric—Psychiatric Nurse Testifies!!! TELLS IT LIKE IT WAS! Expertise = actual care of Geriatric Patients not only in theory. She said, In my professional opinion, MR. JOHNSON, LORD rest his soul, had no signs of cortical dementia nor senility which changes personality. . . . Mr. Johnson always knew his identity, his relationship with his wife and children, his wealth—He was always mentally competent and functional. He was never confused. The testifying nun stated many younger and older patients than Seward Johnson thrive on Tylenol to the last week and a half before death."

Reilly and Schwartz had already crossed swords when the latter had argued against the admissibility of the accusations against Osgood. Soon an argument ensued on whether Sister Mary Louise qualified as a medical expert. At the sidebar, when Schwartz could produce no legal precedent for his position, Reilly said, "If you wanted to learn something about your case, maybe it would do you some good."

SCHWARTZ: I don't appreciate remarks like that. Why don't we try this case and try to be professionals, civil to each other in court? Keep your voice down.

REILLY: Other than broken noses and broken legs, I don't need any lectures from you on anything.

LAMBERT: Let's get some ground rules set right away. We don't shout at the sidebar so that newspaper reporters who are sitting there can hear, and the jury. We try to keep our voices down. That's why I dragged you over here, okay?

SCHWARTZ: May I add, your Honor, that after your Honor left, Mr. Reilly threatened to break my legs and my nose.

REILLY: That is false, your Honor, totally false! Mr. Schwartz's comments on broken noses and broken legs have already been memorialized in the record of this case.

They were off to a bad start. Sister Mary Louise tended to ramble on, and Judge Lambert explained that "I too am a Catholic, I hate to do this, but you must answer the questions." Sister Mary Louise testified about her relationship to Seward Johnson. He had talked to her about "how good-looking the sisters were" and had said, "What is it that makes such young girls not marry?" Sister Mary Louise touched her cross as she went on with her testimony. "I said, 'The same thing that made Mother Theresa: love of God, one, and love of man, not one man but many. You can do for anyone and everyone what they need.' "

Edward Reilly smiled up at Sister Mary Louise. He announced, "I am Edward Reilly," accenting the last name just a touch. He asked her, "During meetings you had with Mr. Johnson, did you at any time try to reassure him or comfort him?"

SISTER MARY LOUISE FLOWERS: I was there for that purpose, sir, yes.

REILLY: You often have occasion to give spiritual aid and comfort to residents at St. Joseph's Home, don't you?

FLOWERS: Yes, sir.

REILLY: And during the time you spent with Mr. Johnson you tried to give him similar aid and comfort?

FLOWERS: When he asked for it.

Reilly stepped back from the lectern and snapped, "Your Honor, I object to any further questions of this witness under Section 4505 of the CPLR *[Civil Practice Law and Rules]*." A four-hour argument ensued over whether Sister Mary Louise was a spiritual adviser, because then such communications with Mr. Johnson were confidential. Even when Reilly was overruled, Sister Mary Louise's testimony did Mrs. Johnson little good because he elicited the admission that her home had received an $850,000 donation from the Johnsons.

The mistrial motion seemed to have little effect on Surrogate Lambert's determination to keep the two new Sullivan & Cromwell lawyers, Graham and Schwartz, in line. During Graham's first day in court, when he voiced an objection, Lambert put her hand out as if pushing back an opponent. "I'll take no speeches. You haven't been here, so you don't know the rules. You don't argue with the judge. You want to try this case, you'll have to learn the rules. And one of the rules is—you don't argue with the judge!" When Marvin Schwartz continued to argue with her, Lambert shouted, "Just say 'object.'" She constantly reprimanded Schwartz for asking leading questions and he reacted like a blunderbuss. Forging ahead, he asked Sister Mary Louise such questions as, "Did he say anything to you about charitable gifts?" "Other than by words, did you ever see her express any affection toward him [Basia toward Seward]?" "Did you ever see, Sister, any sign of physical affection between the two?" "Did you ever hear her call him 'stupid'?" "Did you ever hear her shout at him?" "Did you ever see her hit him?" "Mr. Schwartz, you are leading the witness," the exasperated Lambert repeated, and, turning to the jury, explained, "When you ask a leading question, you are giving the witness the answer."

Although witnesses on both sides had been the recipients of Johnson largess, Reilly alone emphasized the power and profligacy of the Johnson wealth. Michael Loyack, director of development of the Medical Center at Princeton, acknowledged that he had received a $1.8 million donation for CAT-scan equipment from the Johnsons, and that in the future he hoped to get a donation from Mrs. Johnson. Reilly asked sarcastically, "How much do you expect to get—twenty million, thirty million, fifty million?" "I don't know," Loyack responded several times, but finally admitted he would be "happy with $500,000."

REILLY: So you wouldn't want to say anything here today that Mrs. Johnson would disapprove of, would you?

Loyack paused, then answered, "No."

From the marble contractor Maurizio Bufalini, Reilly elicited the admission that he hoped to get a $400,000 contract to furnish the marble in the chapel at Jasna Polana.

REILLY: So you wouldn't want to say anything in court, in front of Mrs. Johnson, that might cause her to award that work to someone else, would you?

Although Bufalini said he could not answer the question with a yes or no, the answer was self-evident.

When Oscar Heil, a marine maintenance man, reported that he had installed a supplementary energy system for Seward Johnson's Florida home at a cost of $200,000 a year, Reilly had him repeat that figure several times until Lambert interjected, "That was the bill for what?"

OSCAR HEIL: Electricity.

LAMBERT: The electricity bill was $200,000 a year?

HEIL: Well, that's an approximate figure.

A major problem with Basia Johnson's witnesses was that most of them had known the Johnsons for only the briefest of times. Sabine Brassart, who ran a cooking school in Sussex, testified that she had visited Basia once and found her wearing a tee shirt with the slogan "SOLIDARNOŚĆ." A nurse testified that she had worked for the Johnsons only one day. The problem was most evident among people of prominence who were called to the stand: Mariapia Fanfani, wife of the president of the Italian Senate; Jerome Wiesner, president emeritus of MIT; James B. Edwards, former governor of South Carolina. I asked Donald Christ why P. James Roosevelt, an Oyster Bay, Long Island, investment counselor, had testified, since his acquaintanceship consisted of one afternoon's interview with Mr. Johnson about sailing, and Christ replied, "It was a snapshot. I thought he was one of our best witnesses."

The celebrity witnesses seemed to rankle Surrogate Lambert, and she was particularly peevish with Mrs. Fanfani, who became more and more nervous on the stand as Lambert continually cautioned her, "Mrs. Fanfani, just listen, please. You cannot volunteer information . . . now are you going to abide by that, otherwise the judge is going to get angry. And I don't want to get angry."

Mariapia Fanfani had visited the Johnsons in Ansedonia, Italy, for a three-day period in July of 1982, the only time she had seen them together. By the time she testified, legal antagonisms were pronounced and she was to find herself helplessly caught in a burst of legal crossfire that took on aspects of a comedy routine.

SCHWARTZ: Mrs. Fanfani, in your visit to the Johnsons in Italy, did you observe them together?

(The interpreter translated.)

MARIA FANFANI: Yes, they was very—

SCHWARTZ: What did you see?

FANFANI: Very nice together, in love, affection.

REILLY: Objection, your Honor.

LAMBERT: Sustained.

SCHWARTZ: Your Honor, that is a matter as to which lay opinion is acceptable.

LAMBERT: "Very nice together"?

SCHWARTZ: Yes. That's what a lay person can observe, seeing a married couple together.

LAMBERT: That's not appropriate testimony. Give me Richardson. [To Mr. Schwartz] Don't make me read it again. [Pause] "But a witness may not testify that two persons appear to have a strong mutual affection for each other. 207 N.Y. 506. Court of Appeals." That's what the Court of Appeals says.

SCHWARTZ: What did you see, when you saw them together, of how they dealt with each other?
(The interpreter translated.)

FANFANI: Normally, as always people—

REILLY: I object.

LAMBERT: Sustained. (To the interpreter) Explain to the witness: what is normal to you may not be what is normal to other people. (The interpreter translated.)

FANFANI: Very affection, with a kind—

REILLY: Same objection, your Honor.

LAMBERT: Sustained. What did you see with your eyes? (To the interpreter) Explain that to her.

FANFANI: Kindness between both. She was kind, very nice. . . . I saw to offer coffee, for instance, kindness, no [demonstrating] so. Kindness.

REILLY: Objection.

FANFANI: And he was thank, thank, nice.

LAMBERT: Sustained. Mrs. Fanfani, kindness is not something that you can see with the eyes.

FANFANI: Smiling?

LAMBERT: Well, that you can see with your eyes, so tell us that. Kindness is not something you can see with your eyes. You cannot tell by looking at me whether I am being kind to my office help or not.

FANFANI: But if I give coffee, kindness, so, and I give—

LAMBERT: No, that's not kindness. What did you see her do when she gave coffee?

FANFANI: Coffee, smiling, with—nicely, I don't know. I don't—

LAMBERT: I will strike the word "nice."
(The interpreter translated.)

FANFANI: Smiling, giving coffee, smiling, just with the arm around the shoulder, so, coffee.

LAMBERT: That's fine.

FANFANI: Sorry?

LAMBERT: We'll get along much better if you just tell us what you saw.

SCHWARTZ: Did you see any displays of physical affection?

REILLY: Objection. Leading.

LAMBERT: Sustained. It's leading.

SCHWARTZ: Your Honor—

LAMBERT: Mr. Schwartz, you're giving the answer to the witness. And if we have a speech to make, let's make it at sidebar, Mr. Schwartz.
(The following proceedings were held at the sidebar:)

LAMBERT: Mr. Schwartz, I am not going to allow you to lead the witness, nor am I going to allow a witness to volunteer information all over the place. This is an American court, and she's well aware of what goes on.

SCHWARTZ: Your Honor, earlier, just a few days ago, I pointed out that Mr. Reilly had asked a similar question and you had overruled our objection. Your Honor, since the jury is not here, I think I should say this: I have been practicing in the courts of this state for thirty-plus years—

LAMBERT: So have I.

SCHWARTZ: —and I have never been pounded upon by a judge before to the extent that I have been here.

Mrs. Fanfani, unaware that she was merely a pawn in the legal war game, left the stand and announced, "I've come to this country of my own free will," and then added that she was thinking about writing President Reagan and sending him a transcript of her portion of the trial to show how inhospitably she'd been treated.

Philip Graham and Marvin Schwartz presented witness after witness to refute the children's case. In the three years it had taken him to prepare for this trial, Edward Reilly seemed to have acquired the ammunition to shoot down most of them. When nurse Judith Smith said that on March 2, 1983, she had prepared a report at the request of Bonnie Weisser, Reilly immediately responded, "Miss Weisser was not employed until March 19th of that year." When a medical expert pointed to the twenty-four frames of a CAT scan and explained that it was the full scan, Reilly pointed out that it was two series of twelve pictures, not one series of twenty-four. Perhaps his single most significant contribution came during the cross-examination of Basia Johnson's medical expert, Dr. Fred Plum. Plum asserted that although nurse Patricia Reid had noted Seward Johnson's confusion during her shift which had ended at noon, it was logical to assume that he had not been confused after lunch when he'd signed his final will and testament. Reilly pointed out that Miss Reid's shift had not ended until three p.m.

* * *

As Graham and Schwartz tried to elicit information that Lambert deemed improper, she censured them again and again. This was never more evident than in the examination of nurse Judith Smith. Smith's medical bills of $23,000 had been paid by Mrs. Johnson. Graham wished to bring this out on his direct examination, but Lambert said, "You aren't going to whitewash your own witness." Graham said, "I really think that's inappropriate." Lambert answered, "You can call it what you want."

Philip Graham, wanting to show that Judith Smith's niece had been killed in the automobile accident in which Smith had had both legs smashed, asked her if there had been a fatality in the accident. Reilly objected. Lambert sustained the objection. But Smith blurted out, "Yes." Lambert, furious, excused the jury and chastised Graham, saying that what the witness had told the jury was absolutely inadmissible. Graham fought back, saying that he felt the jury, in order to understand why Mrs. Johnson "felt an obligation to help," should know that the niece had died. Lambert said, "Mr. Graham, for you to ask about fatalities in order to gain the sympathy of the jury is improper." And Reilly added that if this were charity, Mrs. Johnson could have given the gift anonymously: "You don't do it by paying big sums to potential witnesses."

Reilly's cross-examination of Judith Smith took on Orwellian overtones as Smith testified that the word "confused" in her nurse's notes meant that Johnson was "exhausted," which she said could also mean "fatigued." "Disoriented" did not mean disoriented, it too meant " 'exhausted' . . . I should have used the word 'appeared' for 'assumed.' I found out I was wrong." "When did you find out you were wrong? After you received the $23,000?"

asked Reilly. Under his relentless questioning, Smith sounded ridiculous. After she was excused from the stand, Judith Smith stood staring down at the opaque glass roof of the rotunda below. Then she pressed her forehead against the windowpane and cried.

As Lambert continued to blast Sullivan & Cromwell lawyers, the press began to support the underdog. It was clear that Sullivan & Cromwell was taking a terrible beating at the hands of Lambert and Reilly. This was most evident during the testimony of nurse Luella Johnson (no relative). On the last day of Seward Johnson's life, "I asked him if he was afraid of dying and he looked up at me and said, 'I've tried to be good to everyone that has been good to me.' I said, 'Well, I think the hardest thing in life is to be good to people who aren't good to you. Don't be afraid of dying. When you've been in the ocean sailing and it's gotten rough, wasn't it easier to ride the waves sometimes than fight them?' And he said, 'Yes.' I said, 'Well, dying can be the same. Go with the waves and your Lord will be waiting for you.' "

When the nurse finished her testimony, there was a hush and then Graham requested a recess. Marie Lambert looked over at the witness, who was crying, and snapped, "Mrs. Johnson, did you put anything in your nurse's notes about this conversation?" Luella Johnson answered, "I thought it was personal." Lambert cut her off: "Just answer yes or no." Donald Christ leaned back in his chair and stroked his hair back in a gesture of disbelief. Lambert saw him. "Do you have a comment, Mr. Christ?" He replied, "Only scratching, Your Honor." Lambert instructed the nurse to read every entry in her notes of the eight-hour shift in question. When Nurse Johnson got to an entry in which Seward Johnson cried out in pain, "Oh Jesus, help me," Basia too began to cry.

As witness after witness mounted the stand, although individually they were not strong, with their cumulative testimony another picture of Basia Johnson began to emerge—the attentive nurse, the capable housekeeper, the strong supporter of her dying husband. As day after day one heard of the grueling monotony of taking care of a dying man, sympathies toward Basia strengthened. One day she spun round in her chair and said to a reporter, "I see now you like us," and he replied, "Isn't it amazing now that you're presenting your side of the case how my writing has improved?"

". . . the worst black eye the legal profession will ever have."

The morning of May 12 the trial enters its fourteenth week. The gray days of winter have given way to bright spring, and with the balmy weather there seems to be an awareness that this is an arduous way to spend one's days, that there is a world out there waking to a new season. Only a half-dozen reporters attend the trial on a regular basis. The far left-hand section of the room, once crowded with courtroom buffs, is deserted; they have moved a block away to sit in the courtroom where Claus von Bülow is the defendant in a civil suit brought by his stepchildren. Various Johnson grandchildren who dropped in and out of the sessions and sat attentively, as if attending a Broadway matinee, are also no longer in evidence.

The morning goes well for Basia's side. On the stand James Johnson, subpoenaed by Sullivan & Cromwell, seems bewildered.

CHRIST: Do you have any knowledge as to the value of the assets of your trust at or about the time your father died?

JAMES: Yes.

CHRIST: What was your knowledge in that respect?

JAMES: Sixty million dollars, roughly.

CHRIST: Sixty million dollars?

JAMES: Yes.
(Christ hands James his 1944 trust balance sheet dated June 30, 1983.)

CHRIST: Does reviewing that document change your testimony as to the approximate value of the assets of the trust at or about the date of your father's death?

JAMES: I don't want to retract what I said, but it shows that it is different than what I thought it was.

CHRIST: And what does the document show?

JAMES: If my addition is correct, it is around ninety million.

CHRIST: Isn't it correct that the actual figure is ninety-six million?

JAMES: It is not added up on this document.

CHRIST: Mr. Johnson, when was your father's birthday?

JAMES: It's July . . .

CHRIST: Do you know what day in July?

JAMES: I think it's the 13th. The 12th, I mean. [It was July 14th.]

CHRIST: Did you customarily call your father on his birthday?

JAMES: No.

When James leaves the stand, his sister, Jennifer, and half-sister Diana come up and hug him and Keith Wold reassuringly pats him on the back as if he were a defeated athlete who has tried his best. I return from lunch early to find Basia standing near the window of the empty courtroom, staring out at the small park across the way. Nearby, her head of security, Robert Anderson, practices karate chops at an invisible assailant. "Look at this day," Basia exclaims. "At Jasna Polana, on one side of my front door I have ducks and I leave the grass uncut for them, on the other side there are geese. The ducks were going to leave, but I asked them to stay another day and they did." Basia says that her father was like St. Francis of Assisi and she too has the same talent with animals. "Animals come to me, giraffes in the zoo, chickens sit on my lap, birds perch on my shoulder, and when I scuba-dive, the fish come and kiss me." She speaks of her late husband's favorite dog, the boxer Prince, who died shortly before he did. "Prince didn't know he was a dog, he'd come right up to the table and sit right there and eat with us.

"My husband and I, we were never bored. We always had something to say to each other. He taught me so much. He always wanted young people around. He was interested in everything." She speaks of a sailing trip they took with Jimmy and Gretchen and how afterward her husband had said that his son and his wife were "too old for me." "He always wanted to be around stimulating young people."

Basia grows wistful. "I know my husband. I know his dreams. When I am gone, the dream will be there for others. It won't be wasted. My chapel will be open to the public, there will be an art gallery." I ask her how long she has had this vision. "Ever since a child," she says. I think of Mervyn Nelson saying, ". . . she had this heavenly inspiration. She heard voices, heavenly voices, and they told her that she should go out and make her way in the world and buy up all this artwork. . . ." Arnold Bauman appears at Basia's side and whispers in her ear. She takes his arm and they walk away, out of the courtroom. Basia Johnson had made me forget for this brief interval that she is here to face charges of "fraud, duress and undue influence."

The following morning there was a surprise witness. Ewa Grudzien, who had been the Johnsons' cook and head housekeeper from March of 1982 to January of 1984, had come from Warsaw, Poland, to testify. Handyman Edmund Sulikowski had testified that Mrs. Johnson, during an argument with Grudzien, had repeatedly screamed at her until the cook collapsed on the pantry floor and had to be rushed by ambulance to the Princeton hospital. Ewa Grudzien was sworn in, and Marvin Schwartz, looking elated, asked:

SCHWARTZ: For what purpose, Mrs. Grudzien, did you come from Poland to this country now?

GRUDZIEN (through the interpreter): To help Mrs. Johnson.

SCHWARTZ: On the last day of your employment, was there an incident that led to your no longer working?

GRUDZIEN (through the interpreter): Yes. I got sick. I was born with a heart condition and one day it happened that my heart didn't work properly.

SCHWARTZ: Did you faint?

GRUDZIEN: (The witness and the interpreter converse in Polish.) Yes.

SCHWARTZ: Immediately before you fainted, who was in the room?

GRUDZIEN: (The witness and the interpreter converse in Polish.) There was no one in the pantry. In the kitchen there were three women working.

SCHWARTZ: Was Edmund Sulikowski there?

GRUDZIEN: (The witness and the interpreter converse in Polish.) No.

SCHWARTZ: Was Mrs. Barbara Johnson there?

GRUDZIEN: No.

SCHWARTZ: At any time during that day had you spoken to Mrs. Johnson before you fainted?

GRUDZIEN: (The witness and the interpreter converse in Polish.) Yes.

SCHWARTZ: In what tone of voice did she speak to you?

GRUDZIEN: (The witness and the interpreter converse in Polish.) Quiet.

SCHWARTZ: Did she scream at you?

GRUDZIEN: No.

SCHWARTZ: Assume, please, Mrs. Grudzien, that Mr. Sulikowski has testified to this jury that on the occasion before you fainted, Mrs. Johnson was yelling at you.

LAMBERT: No, no, you don't do it that way. Come on.

REILLY: I object to that.

LAMBERT: You don't do it that way. You give her the testimony. Assume that you have testimony that Mr. Sulikowski was in the kitchen and Mrs. Johnson was yelling at you, identifying you as the cook. And it went from the kitchen to a little room, pantry. And Mrs. Johnson was yelling at her and stamping her foot. By her means Mrs. Grudzien. And finally—

SCHWARTZ: You omitted another screaming, Your Honor.

LAMBERT: And finally she collapsed. And that when you collapsed, Mr. Sulikowski saw half of your face twisting. Like from nerves or something. Is that testimony accurate?

GRUDZIEN: (The witness and the interpreter converse in Polish. Through the interpreter) I didn't see in the kitchen Mr. Sulikowski. Mrs. Johnson did not yell at me, so I cannot state whether it was truthful testimony or not.

LAMBERT: Okay.

For once Edward Reilly seemed stymied. His cross-examination was not strong, but he determined that Ewa had been admitted to the emergency room of the Medical Center at Princeton and had stayed there "several hours." When Ewa was excused, Basia walked up to her and hugged her and they left the courtroom together. That evening Reilly sent a Milbank associate to get the record of Ewa Grudzien's hospitalization. The medical record noted, "Patient complains of burning pain across chest following argument."

Seward Johnson, Jr., too was subpoenaed by Sullivan & Cromwell as a witness. What Junior had been dreading, the moment when he would be asked about his testimony in *Firestone* v. *Merck* where he had said his father was sentient, passed virtually unnoticed. Donald Christ asked if a February 1983 conversation Junior had held with his father in the Boca Raton hospital had been "memorable," "intense," "wonderful." Junior acknowledged that it had been, for these were the very words he had used in his testimony in *Firestone* v. *Merck*. But, inexplicably, Christ never pressed the point that this conversation took place during the very period when, according to the objectants, their father was senile, and he did not ask Junior to confirm that he had testified that his father was "acute," "responsive," "challenging," and "imaginative" at that time. Christ simply moved on to another point and in the morass of legalisms no one seemed to pick up on the discrepancy. The evening news stories commended Seward Jr. for his honesty even though he had candidly explained, "That was my previous testimony, so I can't change it now." The children's side heaved a sigh of relief.

But it was also during Junior's examination that Donald Christ enjoyed his best moment. Junior related how he had made a sculpture of King Lear and had explained to his father, who did not know the story of Lear, that the king "had given over control of his kingdom and in doing so he was kicked out of the kingdom."

Christ asked, "Did you tell your father that King Lear had turned his empire over to his three daughters and that two of them became treacherous and destroyed their father . . . that Regan and Goneril turned on their father after he had given his empire to them?"

Edward Reilly called out, "I object . . ."

Christ shook his head and announced, "No further questions, your Honor." Then he turned his back on the witness and strode away from the lectern.

* * *

On Friday, May 23, Basia Johnson arrived at court dressed
all in black to mark the third anniversary of her husband's
death. As she walked down the long corridor, trailed by
photographers, Seward Jr. popped out of the courtroom
door with Kleenex in his hand. "Get you anniversary
Kleenex here," he called out, handing out tissues to members of the press.

The battle droned on. Medical witness Dr. Fred Plum
was on the stand, endeavoring to refute evidence of Seward
Johnson's senility. Reilly asked, "Is that what you're coming down here for at $800 an hour, to make assumptions?"
Even Diana Firestone was impressed: "He's getting twice
as much as our experts and he's using our charts," she
remarked.

Plum was followed by Dr. Herbert Spiegel, who said
that Basia's screaming at Seward might be "music to his
ears." Reilly made fast work of him by establishing that
Spiegel, who had put in fifty hours at $500 an hour on this
case, specialized in hypnotizing patients to stop smoking.

Basia climbed the stairs to the sixth-floor Sullivan &
Cromwell war office. All that week she was being prepared
to take the stand; Christ worked with her for two days,
Schwartz for two days more. It was then decided that she
would not testify. Several reasons were obvious: she'd undoubtedly be pressed by Edward Reilly to affirm or deny
the Izabella tape and also interrogated on the April 14,
1983, so-called love letter to her husband guaranteeing
Harbor Branch its bequest. In the New Jersey Harbor
Branch case, Basia had asserted that if she wished, it was
within her rights to tear up this letter or forget about it
entirely. In answering the questions of attorney Richard
Altman, Basia's voice seemed laced with anger and on several occasions she appeared to be on the brink of losing

control. "She allowed me to get to her emotionally, and I think that's what hurt her the most," commented Altman. The most powerful reason that both Christ and Schwartz advised Basia against testifying was that they could not predict what she was going to say or how she was going to react. They feared that under Reilly's rigorous cross-examination and Lambert's strictures, Basia might crack and an Izabella-type tantrum might ensue.

By the third anniversary of Seward Johnson's death, after four months in court, all the parties had had enough of courtrooms and legalities and lawyers. Basia Johnson had found that eight lawyers had been unable to prevent her reputation from being soiled. Mary Lea spent the anniversary of her father's death being fed intravenously at New York University Hospital. Elaine Wold's X-rays had been flown in from Boca Raton, and doctors were conferring on whether she too should be hospitalized. Seward Jr. said that that morning his brother, James, had told him, "I want out. As of Monday, I stop paying legal fees." Diana Firestone said, "No matter what happens here, I'm going to my daughter's graduation. I can't miss that."

The previous month, on the recommendation of a friend, Basia had engaged Frederick B. Lacey, a former New Jersey Federal Court judge from the firm of LeBoeuf, Lamb, Leiby & MacRae, to represent her. Although Basia continued to sit between Shearman & Sterling's Arnold Bauman and her alleged co-conspirator, Shearman & Sterling's Nina Zagat, Lacey appeared intermittently. The first time I saw Lacey, an outside lawyer who presumably had no interest in upholding the reputation of Shearman & Sterling or Nina Zagat, I remembered Surrogate Lambert's questions, "How do you think Basia Johnson will feel if this will is probated and Nina Zagat is in the driver's seat?

How will she feel if Zagat is the one to tell her if she can invade the trust or how much money she can get?"

Johnson v. *Johnson* had become a modern-day *Jarndyce* v. *Jarndyce,* a Bleak House of chancery where the lawyers waxed fat while the human toll mounted and the estate was being depleted. Seward Jr. complained bitterly that in the three years he had been represented by Milbank he had never understood that if he lost this will contest he could be removed as an executor and trustee, thereby forfeiting a potential $30 million. Both sides were shocked to learn that, no matter what the jury decided, the legal bonfire could rage on for years to come. When Basia Johnson was told that, win or lose, the litigation could take another five years, "I say to myself, 'No more! I have a life to live, I have a future.'"

Over the Memorial Day weekend Basia tendered a settlement offer of $140 million. Marie Lambert had found a way out. As part of the settlement, Basia's trusts were to be collapsed and over $350 million given to her outright, thereby eliminating the tie to Nina Zagat as well as saving taxes for the life of the trusts and $60 million in trustee and executor fees. The children were tempted to accept this offer, until it was pointed out that the Johnson & Johnson stockholdings in their father's estate had appreciated $40 million since his death. A counter-proposal of $180 million was advanced through Harvey Corn. Basia had said she would never give up more than $150 million. Marvin Schwartz of Sullivan & Cromwell says that it was he who persuaded Mrs. Johnson to do so.

BASIA: They all take the credit. They all want to save their skins. I consider those people very sad, primitive, not seeing further than their own nose. I tell you there would have been no settlement except for Judge Lambert. She is the one who is responsible that there is a settlement.

FORGER: We were told that $150 million was her breakpoint. We were told lots of breakpoints, magic figures. That was okay with us, we'd just as soon go on with the trial, but the clients had a different interest and that's another story.

REILLY: I was opposed to a settlement. We were hopeful that we could establish some very important legal principles. It's not simply winning a case for the benefit of one particular client, we wanted to bring the legal profession up into the twentieth century where it ought to be. I think through what we did, the Appellate Division would have given its seal of approval to the concept of having a finding of undue influence and at the same time a finding of lack of testamentary capacity. Also, we presented a forceful case on the importance of administering a mental status test. Settling the case meant our opportunity was lost. If it went to the jury, we would have won, there was no doubt. I was confident that we'd reach a settlement shortly after the verdict. I'm convinced we would have done even better.

LAMBERT: If ever there had been a summation in this case, it would never have been settled, because the attacks would have been so vicious on both sides. Basia Johnson is a woman who is very, very concerned about her public appearance and her public posture. I just don't think it would have been settled. It would have taken years and years.

The settlement negotiations were to drag on all the following week, with several breakdowns, and during that time everyone began to show his real interests and concerns. Basia's fears were deep-seated. She insisted that the wording of the Harbor Branch settlement be that if the IRS would not permit her to give Harbor Branch $20 million, she would give it $72 million upon her death *or* upon the expiration of her actuarial life, whichever was *later.* Dewey, Ballantine, Bushby, Palmer & Wood, the lawyers for Harbor Branch, referred to this provision as the "don't-murder-me plan," while Basia herself said of it, "Yes, I worked with Terry Christensen [Henry Christensen III] on the wording. I have to protect myself."

When Sullivan & Cromwell offered Harbor Branch a separate settlement, Harbor Branch demanded that the children indemnify it for its $20 million if it was to stay in the battle. During intense negotiations Frederick Lacey announced, "I represent Mrs. Johnson and I alone speak for her." Two lawyers involved said Lacey advised Basia that one of her alternatives was to bring suit against Nina Zagat and Shearman & Sterling for mismanagement of her affairs.

Sullivan & Cromwell and Shearman & Sterling sought additional provisions in the settlement agreement that seemed to benefit not their clients but themselves. They tried to place a gag order on the proceedings. Marvin Schwartz asked for the withdrawal of Milbank documents alleging that Sullivan & Cromwell and Robert Osgood had engaged in acts of "bribing, intimidating, and otherwise improperly influencing" seven potential witnesses. Shearman & Sterling tried to attach to the usual releases between the parties a release of liability for the law firms.

FORGER: That means none of my clients could at any time, for any reason, seek to hold liable for any event any of the lawyers representing the widow for whatever they may have done during the course of the trial or at any other time. I suppose they may have thought our clients would have an independent cause of action against the lawyers for having done something with respect to the disposition of their father's property or having failed to properly prepare his wills. It's highly unusual. I've never seen such.

As late as Friday evening in the surrogate's court where we were writing down a principle of agreement that was going to form the basis of three days of drafting, that's when the Sullivan & Cromwell guys scribbled in the business about the gag rule: we're not going to discuss anything ever, not with anybody. They wanted all the papers submitted on the tampering with witnesses to be destroyed. They tried to kill off any evidence we had filed with respect to what we considered improper conduct. All these papers were to come back out of Sullivan & Cromwell or be destroyed or some such thing.

I went steaming into the judge and said there was absolutely no way that we were ever going to have an agreement on these kinds of conditions. We got hold of Arnold Bauman, not Mr. Lacey, and Bauman said, "I'm in charge here, not Sullivan, and they have no authority to put those kinds of provisions in. They'll come out." So they came out.

When negotiations broke down, it was Lambert who got them back on the track. In one marathon session she stayed with the negotiators for twenty hours. Lambert announced that if this case went to jury, she would break down the charge into thirteen separate categories and if

Basia or Nina was adjudged guilty on even one count, she would put in a court-appointed executor of the will.

Harvey Corn was also instrumental in moving things along. At the offices of Shearman & Sterling he put different groups of negotiators in different rooms and, when the chemistry was not right, changed the players and sent in substitutions and replacements like a major-league manager.

At one meeting in the surrogate's chambers, Alexander Forger stood up and declared that he was leaving. Corn piped up, "Look, my father is a furrier, and when anyone says they're leaving and walks toward the door, we know it's just a question of money." At two a.m., when Forger again announced he was leaving, Corn said that the courthouse had been locked at midnight and he had the only key, so Forger had better just sit back down and talk.

FORGER: What made it a circus during the course of the negotiations is that you had an ever-changing scene of people who were in charge, or who were just learning about the case. The problem of the negotiations was just frightful because I never knew who could speak for her, who her lawyer was, whether it was Arnold Bauman, who seemed to be spending every day with her, or Donald Christ, or other litigators from Sullivan & Cromwell. I tried to negotiate with Christ, and then Bauman entered the scene, and I didn't know who was persona non grata with Basia Johnson at a given moment. The cast just kept changing.

One of the issues that was about to break up the negotiations at the last minute was our insistence that there be protection in case additional assets were ever discovered, because we had no reason to trust anybody. That's when Frederick Lacey launched into a little lecture, I called it an opening statement, about how the widow sought to avoid this constant harassment and litigation. I had to remind him that they had brought litigation in New Jersey and Mrs. Johnson had been found to have "unclean hands" and to have sought to harass the children. I told him that I didn't need to be lectured about this case, I had been in it for a long time. That was part of the difficulty of dealing with folks who showed up for the first time at three in the morning or who had a few days' involvement in the case. The negotiations could have fallen through at any time.

During the frantic week and a half, armies of tax experts popped in and out of chambers and meetings were held day after day at the Shearman & Sterling offices. In the courtroom the case limped along.

On Tuesday, May 27, at ten a.m., after an all-night negotiating session, Lambert sat drinking cup after cup of black coffee while trying to concentrate on the testimony of retired NASA Commander Scott MacLeod. Lambert looked bleary-eyed and incredulous as the wiry MacLeod's testimony began to sound like a scene from *Dr. Strangelove*.

SCOTT MACLEOD: I was very interested in underwater and what he was doing, and he was interested in spacecraft and what we were doing in outer space. It was an inner-outer space discussion. . . . [In 1982] we had quite a long conversation about our next great manned mission, the Mars manned mission. I recall him saying it would probably be something that would bring the world together, since it was more expensive than something the United States could afford.

LAMBERT: Is that what you called it, the Mars manned mission?

MACLEOD: Yes, that's correct.

LAMBERT: That never took place.

MACLEOD: It has not yet. We will go there.

LAMBERT: Huh?

MACLEOD: We will go to Mars.

On Thursday, Joyce MacLeod took the stand. She had known Seward Johnson since 1965 and was undoubtedly the strongest witness for Basia's side. When Joyce MacLeod testified, "Seward and I were very close long before I met my husband or Basia came on the scene, and I always probed him," Reilly objected and Lambert sustained the objection. She called Christ to the bench and asked in her rhetorical style, "Do you want Mr. Reilly to explore the fact that she was his girlfriend? Come on!" Joyce MacLeod then testified that Seward and Basia "were close. They would hold hands, touch, giggle, joke. She would often call him pet names and he would call her pet names and they'd chuck each other under the chin and use baby talk." In 1982, Joyce said, she and Seward were sitting alone on the front lawn at Fort Pierce.

JOYCE MACLEOD: I asked him if he was really happy. And he said, "Yes," and I said, "No, I mean are you really happy with Basia?" And he said that she was the best girl he'd ever known.

With that, Donald Christ rested his case. Basia had not been in the courtroom to hear Joyce MacLeod; she was encamped on the sixth floor, being briefed on the latest settlement negotiations.

On Wednesday night, Iris Christ had called astrologer Joelle Mahoney and told her that the following day the case was to go to the jury but they'd decided instead that they might settle. Joelle answered, "If there's anything you can do to prevent that, let it go right to the jury. I think you'll find Mrs. Johnson will overwhelmingly win." Mahoney explains that "the moon overhead was in the sign of Pisces, Mrs. Johnson's sign, and in astrology that's called a lunar high. It's a day when you are spectacularly fortunate, particularly when the planet Jupiter is in that sign as well. It meant Mrs. Johnson would triumph over her adversaries."

Thursday morning Iris Christ called to relay this news. She reached Nina Zagat at the Shearman & Sterling offices and told her what Joelle had said, but Zagat answered that it was too late, negotiations were under way.

In the courtroom Lambert began to make excuses to the jury as to why closing statements were not taking place. On Thursday night, publicity representatives for both sides telephoned members of the news media to say that tomorrow an agreement will be reached. At the courthouse at nine the following morning, television crews and reporters once again jam the corridors. Seeing a battery of tax experts leaving Surrogate Lambert's chambers, Arnold Bauman remarks that when the Federal government gets its share of this settlement, Seward Johnson "will be spinning three-sixties in his grave." Marilyn Link, chairperson of the Harbor Branch negotiating committee, stares out the window. "If we got rid of all these damn lawyers, we'd be out of here by now," she says petulantly. Edward Reilly stands against the courtroom door looking glum. "I would like to give my summation, I am still prepared to give my

summation," he announces; "I'm not in favor of a settlement." Donald Christ is more philosophical: "I want to do
what the client wants to do. We're just hired hands. The
shame about all this is that the lawyers are the only people
getting paid to stand around and do nothing. But I'm getting ready to sum up. As Yogi Berra says, 'It ain't over till
it's over.'"

By two in the afternoon it becomes clear that negotiations have hit a snag. Reporters mill around the corridors,
afraid to go out to lunch. Someone comes back with a box
of doughnuts and several containers of coffee. The courtroom doors are locked, so we sit on the windowsills and
wait. At three o'clock Seward Jr. comes out of Lambert's
chambers; he looks exhausted. The spotlights are trained
on him, the television cameras begin to grind. "Has a settlement been reached?" Junior grins and makes a quick
horizontal gesture across his mouth as if pulling a zipper.
He heads toward the elevators. The questions keep coming, the lights are shining in his eyes. The elevator door
opens and closes, but Junior does not see it in the glare. He
walks into the closed door, then backs off a few steps,
shakes his head, and stumbles around in a circle like a
punch-drunk fighter.

At four o'clock I see William Warren of Dewey, Ballantine standing in a corner with Marilyn Link. Warren is
holding a credit-card-sized calculator. They whisper, then
Warren punches out numbers on the calculator. Edward
Reilly walks down the corridor holding a briefcase. He
moves distractedly toward the elevator, then halts in the
glare of the television spotlights. A TV reporter walks up
to him and says, "Listen, there's no news to report, so why
don't you give us five minutes of your closing on camera?"
Reilly is not amused. "No comment," he snaps.

At 4:30 Lambert ushers the jury into the courtroom

and excuses them for the weekend. They file out, some of them clutching overnight cases, having expected that they might be sequestered. One male juror holds a toothbrush in his left hand.

On Sunday at noon Donald Christ gets a call to practice his closing—negotiations are falling apart. At 12:15 Harvey Corn calls Surrogate Lambert from the Shearman & Sterling offices and says, "Look, this is just not gonna go." Lambert screams into the phone, "Keep everybody there, I'll be right down."

LAMBERT: I rushed over. Judge Lacey was there, Alexander Forger with the tax people from Milbank, Tweed and all the other tax people. Harvey would go in one room and I was in another room with another group. And that's how I finally got it put together, by Harvey doing some of the language, me doing some of the language, them doing some of the language. There were all kinds of things: if she had assets, the amount of money she would have to hide before you could go after her—you know, those kind of things. Lacey negotiated the Nina Zagat fee. He and Basia negotiated that. They cut her back. I had nothing to do with the Nina Zagat fee. Lacey came in and asked me, would I be willing to collapse the trust. And I said, "Judge Lacey, I suggested collapsing the trust in this case from the very, very beginning. And when I suggested collapsing the trust, I was told that Mrs. Johnson did not wish to collapse the trust."

Sometimes you've gotta sit with laymen and give them a blow-by-blow description. That's very important, that the person understand that you're communicating exactly what it is that's being proposed in a particular

situation. Nobody needed this trial. Nobody needed all
this dirty linen being washed in public.

BASIA: Without her, there would be no settlement. Two,
three months before, she told my lawyers that she could
collapse the trust. But I didn't understand what she said.
They didn't tell me direct. So I didn't understand. Later,
when I understood, I see she make the settlement. I
would like her to know I respect her.

Monday morning, June 2, I return to the courthouse.
Once again reporters are standing in the halls, but this
time the mood is not merry. People have been at it too
long; there is talk about "public waste" and "who cares
anyway?" In chambers there is one last issue, as Forger
insists that if any hidden assets of Basia Johnson are found
that do not appear in the final accounting, they will be
shared with the Johnson children. Marvin Schwartz declares that this is the ultimate insult, but finally Basia's
lawyers acquiesce. There is a make-or-break atmosphere,
the jury is being kept waiting, the hounds of the press are
baying outside the door. At 2:30 Edward Reilly appears in
the corridor. When reporters ask for a statement, he ignores them. Finally, at three o'clock the children exit
chambers, smiles on their faces, and file into the courtroom. At last, making a Marilyn Monroe delayed appearance, Basia Johnson appears in a white dress with black
polka dots and wrist-length white kid gloves. Junior, in
one last quip, says, "She wore them to cover her 'unclean
hands.' " In the courtroom Lambert announces that a settlement has been reached.

When this all began, Seward Jr. had said, "The only
way to get justice would be to rewrite my father's will, but
that, of course, would be impossible." In fact that was

exactly what happened: a battery of legal experts in effect rewrote Seward Johnson's will and designed an agreement that had nothing to do with Johnson's intentions but benefited everybody concerned and, more importantly, got everybody off the hook.

LAMBERT: I really pushed for a settlement. The money should not be used up in legal fees. Let us assume that the jury had come out against her. She would have taken appeals all the way up. That would have used a great deal more money. If the jury had found in her favor, the other side would have appealed all the way up. Now let's assume that the jury found that he was mentally incompetent and this will went out—now we have to try the will right behind it. Let's assume the jury found that he was mentally incompetent and that there was some fraud and undue influence by Nina Zagat. That created other problems. Then you have the additional problem of what portions of the will were induced by Nina Zagat's undue influence and what happened. Let's say the jury found they both had undue influence—what portions were induced by whose undue influence and what happened?

Aside from that, everything that was done in this case is gonna go up on appeal. I was making a speech at the Surrogate's Court Association on the case, and I must have covered about fifteen or twenty items where the points of law were not points that had ever been covered in this kind of case. They offered evidence to show what the children's interest would have been if they had never spent any of the money. My gut told me it should go out of evidence, but there's really no law on that. I said that couldn't go in. Now, I'm not sure that that's absolutely right. Everything that was being brought on questions of evidence—are the tapes really admissible? I don't know. They are in criminal cases, but we don't have a civil case on it. If you don't have testamentary capacity, can you have undue influence? Assume that you have diminished testamentary capacity, is it easier to influence someone with diminished testamentary capacity than it is to influence one who is perfectly capable and knows exactly what they're doing? None of the rulings that I made have clear precedents in the law. A great many of them were rulings where, whichever way I went, I could be reversed. And if that happens, you are dealing with literally millions of dollars in appeals.

By the end of the trial there were to be so many convoluted legal issues and self-created legal constructions, the law itself was to be so tortured, that the profession might have choked on this indigestible glob. Money and lawyers had spun off into incomprehensibility. Two hundred and ten lawyers had a hand in the litigation. Thirty-one lawyers were involved in the final settlement negotiations alone. This case proved a stunning example of the legal profession as an out-of-control juggernaut, rolling forward, fueled by a seemingly inexhaustible supply of money. The final settlement:

• Each child received $6.2 million after taxes, with an extra $8 million to Seward Jr. to make up for his lost executor and trusteeship fees.
• Harbor Branch received $20 million, four times the $5 million value that IRS tables indicate would equal $72 million in thirty years (Basia's actuarial life expectancy).
• Basia Johnson's marital trusts are being collapsed, severing her from Nina Zagat's control, and—the big bonus—instead of income only, she'll receive outright in

excess of $350 million. All charges of fraud, duress, and undue influence were withdrawn.

• Shearman & Sterling's Nina Zagat was granted $1.8 million before taxes, instead of the $30 million she would have received based on her actuarial life expectancy. All charges of fraud, duress, and undue influence were withdrawn.

• Surrogate Marie Lambert's trial record would not come under review by the Appellate Division.

• The IRS would receive approximately $86 million in taxes.

• The lawyers' fees were estimated at $24 million.

DEBRA CALIFIA, JUROR: I suspected the children were going to get money, but I didn't see how they were going to get it—having not been in the wills. I did feel a little cynical about it. I think the court was used wrongly by these rich people for their own ends.

JEFFREY SCHWAB, JUROR: Next time spare us the seventeen weeks, that's taxpayer money so they could play out their little game.

The Johnson will contest was, according to one of Basia Johnson's lawyers, "the worst black eye the legal profession will ever have." Said another lawyer, "No one is proud of this case. I do think certain methods and practices on the part of certain lawyers involved got out of hand, but then we had all that money—*carte blanche*—isn't that exactly what Dr. Faustus was offered?" Said Donald Christ, "I've said from the beginning it's cases like this and the big fees involved that give the legal profession a bad name." Said Alexander Forger, "I'm sort of a bar nut, and one who has a concern for not only the actuality but the appearance, because we as a profession aren't number one in the hearts and the minds of the public. When events arise as seem to have occurred in this case, it tends to support the unfavorable view that many have of the profession. The role played by Nina Zagat would reflect poorly on the profession. What does the profession do with that? When you're in law firms, you have to make certain you have rules and standards that are well articulated. I can understand how it looks like we're all one big fraternity and that was posturing and it's all over now, and the big payoff, and everybody goes back to doing what they were doing before. The profession didn't come out of this very well."

Said someone connected with the Surrogate's Court who observed the proceedings on a day-to-day basis, "Maybe Surrogate Lambert should be criticized, but maybe she had more than enough reason to respond the way she did. I think it should stop here. If there are any post-mortems, God knows what will happen to the profession. Let's just paraphrase an old saying, 'Absolute money corrupts absolutely.' "

". . . *a great victory* . . ."

*T*he final round was for the news media. Jamming into elevators and clanking down the stairs, the camera crews and reporters reassembled in the rotunda for press conferences. Basia Johnson tells the press, "I feel wonderful and now I am free to do what I want to. I like to carry on our plans, our dreams, my late husband and mine." Why had she settled when she had vowed not to? a reporter asked. "Peace is better, intelligent people always change their mind, I changed my mind. I wanted to take the stand, the attorneys changed that." After a few minutes of posing for pictures, Basia is ushered out of the courthouse by six bodyguards.

A second press conference, held by the children, starts with Alexander Forger reading a formal statement based on what Edward Reilly had hoped to say to the jury: "We believe that by virtue of this will contest attorneys will be more careful before drafting wills, trusts, and other important documents for their clients, particularly the elderly, and those that are senile, ill and infirm." This point, no matter how valid, is a far cry from the Johnson children's original intention. As the reporters fire questions, Seward

Jr. as usual becomes the spokesman. "Who are the winners and who are the losers in this contest?" Junior replies, "I feel there's no question that Nina Zagat is a loser, that Basia, who said she would never settle or give us a penny, has settled quite a few pennies. And why didn't she testify? I think she was afraid. I think Ed Reilly had a few things up his sleeve they never dreamed were going to happen."

"Will you ever be friendly with her again, will she ever be close to you again?"

"I feel that if someone pulls the things that have been evidenced in this trial against one's aging father—We suspected a lot of stuff, we knew some of it, but during this trial we found out that all of it was there." Junior seems to be groping, as if to say something more.

"But what did you prove?" a reporter yells.

Martin Richards steps in front of Seward Jr. and takes the microphone in his hand. "First of all, I'd like to say my wife is ill, she's not here, so I'd like to speak for her. I want to tell you that Basia Johnson found out one thing. She always said the Johnsons were weak. She found out that they were strong. And that's terrific!" When reporters asked what the other children felt, James Johnson walked to the microphone and said, "My sentiments are expressed in the statement of Alex Forger," after which he just stood there staring at the floor. Jennifer, noting his distress, came up beside him and said, "I'm really glad it's over. The last week has been tense and everybody has worked so hard and I am so happy." Finally, Diana Firestone stepped to the microphone and in a voice just above a whisper said, "We think this is a great victory and we're very happy it has come to such a good conclusion. I found out things we never knew were true and it's a great feeling to bring that all out."

* * *

When the rotunda cleared, the Johnson children took the
judge, the jury, and several reporters out for a drink. The
group headed for the Odeon, but when the *maître d'* indicated he could not accommodate so many people, Edward
Reilly removed from his pocket the Zagat guide and
looked for another restaurant. Over drinks and salami at
Le Zinc, jury and contestants and judge and reporters
asked each other the questions they had wanted to ask for
four months.

"Did they try to get to any of you or to threaten any of
you?" Lambert asked of several jurors. "Did you know my
life was threatened?

"What happened when we were forced out of the
courtroom, when those people protested?"

"I have a question," said another juror, the one we'd
dubbed "the sleeper." "What was the relationship between
Harbor Branch and the children of Seward Johnson anyway?"

On Thursday Mary Lea returned from the hospital. That
same morning selected members of the news media were
invited to Jasna Polana. Basia Johnson was about to create
the image that she was a winner. The victor was the person
who declared herself victorious. Image superseded reality.

It is a glorious June day, and, as in a scene in a Fellini
movie, the characters are transformed, seen in different
costumes, in a different setting. Faces one saw every day in
the courtroom one now sees in the bright sunshine. Basia
Johnson receives the press like Jacqueline Kennedy con-
ducting a tour of the White House. As we approach the
mansion, she stands at the front door murmuring over and
over again, "Welcome home. Welcome home." Once the
group has assembled, Basia makes a sweeping gesture with

her right hand and says, "I want you to see not the quantity of my money but the quality of my money." In the living room she points out, "You are standing on the king's carpet." (The king being Louis XIV.) She shows us her Rembrandts, Castigliones, Renaissance bronzes, the Adam Weisweiler secretaire for $1.5 million. Reporters ask, "How do you spell that painting? What do you call that chest? Did she say something about a secretary?" Hal Davis from the New York *Post* takes a handkerchief out of his pocket and wipes his forehead. "I'm really rusty on this furniture journalism," he announces. We move to the top of the stairs and wait while Basia Johnson disappears into a bedroom and emerges carrying several framed color photographs of her late husband. We wait again while she and security chief Robert Anderson go to fetch her $4.8 million Raphael chalk sketch, which she tells us "must be kept in the dark." A reporter asks Jack Raymond, "Does the Raphael hang in the bedroom?" He answers, "I don't know where it is now, but at one time it hung there because Mr. Johnson loved it so much. He used to like to look at it from his bed." "Impossible—that Raphael was purchased a year after Seward Johnson's death," I hear myself saying with the intonations of an Ed Reilly.

Then Basia Johnson holds a press conference in her Italian garden; the video cameras and the still photographers go to work. "Wave, wave, Mrs. Johnson," they say, "okay, hold that, that's great." Basia suggests some camera angles—"I'll stand here, it's beautiful," she announces.

The questions begin. "Why did you have us here today?"

"I thought that you supported me always in the courtroom. I saw your friendship for me and that's why I asked you here to celebrate my freedom. I decided to make an end to this nonsense that was going on in the courtroom."

"How do you think Judge Lambert handled this case?"

Marvin Schwartz cuts in: "I really don't think she should answer that." But Basia Johnson does answer. "She represents American justice," she says. Schwartz steps to Basia's side and declares, "I really don't think we'll go into this."

Mary Civiello of Channel Four News is not intimidated. "Why? she's a free person, she should be able to answer. All the time throughout the trial, people have been telling you, 'Don't talk, don't talk, just smile, smile.' So as a result we see you floating around and smiling all the time. You must have a little anger about what went on in the courtroom." Tim O'Brien of the Newark *Star-Ledger* asks, "Mrs. Johnson, do you agree with your attorneys that the judge irreparably injured this case?"

BASIA: Listen, I am in this country, I'm the most happy in this country and I take as it is.

SCHWARTZ: Her position has been stated. Mrs. Johnson accused the judge of gross misconduct which required a new trial in the interest of justice and stated on the record in plain English, black and white, that the judge had been unfair, and I really don't think Mrs. Johnson should be asked to characterize in lay terms the arguments which we made on her behalf.

MARY CIVIELLO: How would you characterize them?

SCHWARTZ: What we said in the papers which are on file, that her conduct was biased, hostile, unfair, and unjust and required a new trial before a different judge. That's on the record in the court proceedings. I don't know how to put it any stronger.

CIVIELLO: What is your reaction to the fact that she went to a victory party and drank with the children and the jurors right after the settlement was reached? Do you feel that was proper?

SCHWARTZ: I am shocked. Shocked.

CIVIELLO: But you're inviting us here.

SCHWARTZ: This is not the judge and it's not the jury.

MICHAEL AARON, New Jersey Network News: Mrs. Johnson, a lot of people think an estate like this is too much money, it's a vulgar display of wealth, people do feel that way. What would you say to people who think that one person should not have all of this?

BASIA: When you came here, did you see the vulgar things?

O'BRIEN: No, we saw beautiful things.

BASIA: . . . I know that I have gorgeous masterpieces and the best-quality paintings and objects of art.

HAL DAVIS, New York *Post:* And what do you want to do with that?

BASIA: Well, I like to share this beauty with others, with the public.

ELLEN POLLACK, *American Lawyer:* Mrs. Johnson, when you sat through the trial and you heard what the judge was doing, did that have some bearing on your decision to settle?

SCHWARTZ: Once again, I don't think . . .

CIVIELLO: Come on, let her answer a question.

SCHWARTZ: No, Mrs. Johnson's position has been . . .

BASIA: I learned a lot. I learned that I cannot trust many people and I met also the most wonderful people. The most prominent Americans, Italians, French, came here and testified on my behalf.

JEANNE KING, Reuters: What do you think that your husband would have felt about the way this all ended?

BASIA: I think he would feel the same way as I did. Which is freedom, peace, and the future is the most important, and the life is the most important.

IAN SHEARN, Trenton *Times:* What are your feelings about his children now?

BASIA: Well, they have their problems, let them be.

O'BRIEN: What are your goals now for the remainder of your life?

BASIA: I'd like to continue my husband and my dreams, which were to be charitable, to help less fortunate people, to share great achievement as collecting beautiful art and share with the public. We were fortunate to own the money, we put the money in the greater meaning.

JACK RAYMOND: Two more minutes, please.

KATHLEEN BIRD, Associated Press: How did you spend your yesterday, your first day?

BASIA: I hate telephones, but I had to answer so many telephones from all over the world, my friends were calling me and congratulating me.

BIRD: You feel you've won?

BASIA: Oh, they know that I like to be free, and I was not free.

CIVIELLO: You could have been freed much earlier, why did you choose not to?

RAYMOND: I think that's outside the ground rules here.

BASIA: Money is to spend for better things and you can share your money with others and that's what my husband and I were doing. We create Harbor Branch foundation, which was created when I appeared in his life, not before.

POLLACK: It is important to you what the public thinks about you?

BASIA: I have to live with myself and I know who I am. I could see that I have great friends and they support me during the trial. . . . I know that God has favored me so many times, I am very fortunate and I know that I like to help other people less fortunate and that's what I did.

KING: Do you think you'll marry again?

BASIA: I didn't give any thoughts about that.

From the back of the group of reporters, Tim O'Brien bellows out, "Marry me! Marry me!"

We repair to a lunch by the tennis court and eat open canapés of salmon with dill, ham and cucumber, and an assortment of delicate cookies and drink iced tea and orange juice and white wine, as at a ladies' tea party. We sit in front of the tennis court, surrounded by a heavy wire-mesh fence. On the lawn to the right is an enormous white tent. I'm told that Basia's nephew is going to be married here. I ask Mrs. Johnson about it. "Yes, yes," she says, "I will introduce you," and with that takes me by the hand and leads me over to a very pretty Chinese girl and a young man. Both are dressed in white uniforms; the young girl has just poured my iced tea.

Frederick Lacey and several other lawyers—Marvin Schwartz, Robert Delahunty, and Nina Zagat—chat with members of the press; no Robert Osgood, no Donald Christ. As we stroll toward the chapel to be constructed over the Johnson nuclear-bomb shelter, Delahunty becomes impassioned. He tells me, "There are people who like to attack the American upper classes and they would tear Jasna Polana down, stone by stone." He says he has ceased to believe in American justice because of Surrogate Lambert and that he is leaving Sullivan & Cromwell to work in the District Attorney's office. Delahunty then turns to Zagat and says, "And then there are people like you, Nina, who try to defend the American system." "Thank you," murmurs Zagat.

As the afternoon draws to a close, Basia Johnson stands by the massive wrought-iron gates of her estate and tells us, "Most people can't have their dreams. I have made my dreams come true." She thrusts her arms high above her head and with the fingers of both hands makes the V-for-Victory sign. The photographers snap away. The following day the New York *Post* ran this photograph under the headline, "WALKING ON HEIR."

BASIA: Whatever happened to me was the most typical. The lawyers were the most typical and the judge was the most typical. She was typical American. And this is America. Don't try to cover up. A person like I am from

Europe who came recently, they can see very clearly. You cannot see that, you see things that don't exist, you think Americans are good, you think that evil doesn't exist. The lawyers, how they represented the clients, that was terribly typical. What happened in that courtroom was the most typical for America. I'm much better being in control of my own destiny. Now the windows are all open. That's why too I choose new lawyers. I have to get on with my life, to find good people.

LAMBERT: Look at the promises that were made to all those people who came in to testify, and I'm wondering how many people of those whom she didn't like their testimony are still working for her. Some of them didn't do so well. I wonder if she's kept her commitments to the guy from the hospital, to the nun, the marble contractor, to various other people. I just wonder how many of those commitments were kept, and how many will be kept. Listen, what does she have to be angry about? I'm a typical American? She realized the American dream.

For Seward Jr., his unpublicized victory was the real one. This multimillion-dollar settlement represents a restoration of family honor, a confirmation of his bloodline, and an affirmation of his self-worth. The litigation that consumed his life for three years had finally ended. Down came the photograph of Donald Christ which Seward Jr. had humorously set up as the target of his karate sessions. His brilliant and supportive wife, Joyce, returned to her typewriter to finish her novel. His children, John, twenty, and Clelia, seventeen, resumed their lives without a daily dose of publicity.

He was now in charge of Harbor Branch with its $160 million endowment (counting the $20 million received

from Basia Johnson) and had ambitious plans for the fifty
scientists who were exploring our oceanographic resources. SeaPharm, a company that was his idea, was
working in conjunction with Harbor Branch to find sub-
stances from the sea that could be helpful in fighting a
variety of diseases. In the two months after the trial's end,
SeaPharm had been given $3 million to build a plant in
Spain, the Estée Lauder company was experimenting with
one of SeaPharm's enzyme discoveries to stabilize its products, and another enzyme had been developed that, according to Junior, converted "chicken fat to chicken
meat." Said Junior, "It would be a tremendous satisfaction
if I could build a drug company that might be very potent
in the future, because I was forced out of Johnson & Johnson."

DIANA: At the end I was ambivalent, but I was happy. I
certainly could see Ed Reilly's point of continuing, but
in another way there was a lot of unknown aspects to
the thing of getting a jury verdict. At the end we had a
much clearer picture, certainly of the last three months
of the year that he lived.

BERT FIRESTONE: I would have liked for it to go to the
jury and I think we'd have won.

DIANA: That's right, but I was happy to be . . . to walk
away from it. I was happy to be home, to have it behind
us.

ELAINE: We've had lots of rejoicing and wonderful times
since, we have so much to be grateful for. It's just wonderful to have the trial over with, and we can all look at
ourselves in the mirror and we can tell our grandchildren that we did what we had to do. I'm very glad the

trial is over, it would have meant dragging on and we might not . . . Anyway, we're smiling from the inside out.

JAMES: I have no other comments.

LAMBERT: It's ironic, but Basia was the big winner. She got money outright. She was better off than if there'd been no contest.

FORGER: If you mean Basia won in that she didn't go to jail, that's right. She gave up $170 million, I'd call that defeat.

NINA ZAGAT: Seward Johnson wanted two things: his money in trust for his widow, and to pay as little tax as possible. What happened speaks for itself.

MARY LEA: July 8, 1986: Maybe I should call Basia, she must be very lonesome.

MARTY: Are you crazy, Mary Lea?

After the trial Mary Lea concentrated on a musical production of *Madame Rosa* to be presented in conjunction with Harold Prince, and Marty on a film version of *Chicago* to be directed by Bob Fosse. When an article appeared in *Vanity Fair* in which Mary Lea told of her father's incestuous relationship with her, she began to receive letters from people all over the country, commending her on her courage. There were also those who confused the victim with the perpetrator of the crime and said that she should never have revealed this abuse. Dr. Henry Giarretto of Parents United declared, "When someone like Mary Lea Johnson comes forward with courage and truth, she helps save people throughout the nation."

In October, Mary Lea and Marty went to Paris for a

vacation. As they were checking in at the Ritz Hotel, there was Basia Johnson standing in the lobby. Basia saw them and dashed behind a pillar. The Richardses' bodyguard, Anthony Maffatone, stepped forward to confront Basia's head of security, Robert Anderson. The two men stood three feet apart, staring at each other. Would the lobby of the Ritz become the scene of a millionaires' *High Noon?* Finally, Maffatone spoke. "Let's not make a thing of this," he said, "just tell us when you're leaving." Basia Johnson checked out the following morning.

By December of 1986, Basia had "made a clean slate of my lawyers," dismissing both Shearman & Sterling and Sullivan & Cromwell and replacing them with Frederick Lacey of LeBoeuf, Lamb, Leiby & MacRae. Basia said that Lacey was "helping [me] to learn about the trial . . . things that I was not aware." Shearman & Sterling, where Nina Zagat was still employed, was owed over $1 million in legal fees, and Basia was refusing to pay Sullivan & Cromwell an outstanding balance of $5 million on a $10-million bill. Donald Christ appealed to Lambert, who has the power to force payment. In his application Christ listed $500,000 in disbursements and claimed seventeen partners and eighty-seven associates had labored for 45,000 hours on the will contest.

By this time, most of the lawyers concerned with the estate of Seward Johnson had turned to other matters. Donald Christ is involved in negotiations on an out-of-court settlement in a corporate suit. Robert Osgood has been promoted to managing partner of Sullivan & Cromwell's litigation department, a group of eighty lawyers. Alexander Forger, chairman of his firm, is involved in opening a Los Angeles office and has attracted several new multimillion-dollar clients in that area. And Edward Reilly's new assignment is another will contest. The children of the deceased are contesting their father's will, in which he left virtually his entire estate in a marital trust for their stepmother. This time Reilly is representing the widow.

Photo Credits